DATE DUE

JUN 0 5 2006			

THOMAS CRANMER IN 1546
From the painting in the National Portrait Gallery by G. Fliccius

CRANMER

BY

HILAIRE BELLOC

With Photogravure Frontispiece

CASSELL AND COMPANY LTD
London, Toronto, Melbourne and Sydney

FIRST PUBLISHED - 1931

Printed in Great Britain

TO MY SON PETER

This is not a life of Cranmer; it is but a study of his character and motives, with exposition of, and emphasis upon, his literary genius and its legacy to the Church of England. For the most of the facts related I have based myself on the scholarship of Professor Pollard, as must everyone since the publication of his monograph, which treats of Cranmer as a "Hero of the Reformation." I have alluded in brief notes to such few errors as appear in that work and call for correction.

H. Belloc.

Kings Land,

The Feast of the Assumption, 1931.

CONTENTS

I

THE BEGINNING

CRANMER

IN a flat hollow of dull country, proper to the English Midlands, on the small stream of the Smite, stood throughout the Middle Ages and at their close a little group of houses, more important perhaps in the earlier centuries than in the later. The hamlet was called " Aslacton." The modern descendants of these buildings, further dwindled in numbers, pass under a slight change of name and are called " Aslocton." The place never had been nor was to be of any moment save for one birth.

Here, on the second of July in the year 1489, was born to the gentleman who was lord of the few villagers and head of no very wealthy family, a second son, one of many children (seven at least) and christened Thomas in the little chapel of the Trinity.

Neither in the family nor in the landscape nor even in fortune was there anything distinguished about that birth. It opened the life of a man who continued, in spite of talent long unrecognized, obscure till his fortieth year ; and all that anyone could have seen in the surroundings of that opening life—the small Manor House, the narrow income, the few fields—would have matched well with such obscurity. But a Fate was watching, whereby the child—grown to a man already middle-aged—was to be thrust suddenly, in spite of himself, on to the full stage of public affairs. He was to be given a chief part in one of the great dramas of Europe, reluctantly to play under the glare thereof, and to stand out ever memorable in the story of England for a group

3

of four mighty things : For genius unknown perhaps to himself, certainly unknown to others, in the use of the English language ; for finding himself the symbol of that complete transformation of the English mind, whereby it passed from Catholic to Protestant ; for a fierce publicity by which there sounded about his form—conspicuous before all Christendom—the clamour of the supreme religious battle ; and, at the end, for a fearful death by fire.

The family, as I have said, were gentry, but gentry of no important kind. There were Cranmers in Lincolnshire close by in the height of the Middle Ages ; they may already have had arms as they later had, three Cranes, drawn from the nature of their name—the Marsh of Cranes. They raised themselves by a marriage with the heiress of that family which had been lords of Aslacton until those days when the Lancastrian usurpation had begun the great troubles of England but had also given the nation its memories of Agincourt and of the attempt at uniting the French and English thrones. For it was in those years that Edmund Cranmer, marrying the girl in whom the feudal rights and family of Aslacton ended, gave a new name to the squires of the petty place. His son succeeded him, and his son's son—by name Thomas Cranmer. This Thomas Cranmer lived through the closing last century of the old mediæval time ; he lived when the first printing press was being set up in England ; he saw the fall of the Plantagenets ; and he survived to hear of the discovery of the New World. This was the father of that famous child called, like himself, " Thomas Cranmer," who was born on that July day of 1489.

The baby grew up to boyhood in the modest house, no more than the chief house of the village, having about him the country life of the time ; seeing from day to day his father's friends—as might be the Abbot from the great Abbey of Welbeck, a long day's ride away through Sherwood Forest—for the Abbey held the tithes of the little parishes round; or the Rector of Whatton, the somewhat larger village close at hand. The great open fields of the time with their ploughing and harvesting in common were the daily experience of his eyes, and from time to time he would be taken to markets and fairs. He might see the walls of Nottingham and the great castle in its midst, ten miles from his home to the west, or Newark somewhat closer at hand to the north, or to the east Grantham. The considerable travel of the time had no occasion to pass through Aslacton. The Fosse Way, which was still in general use from the south to the north, left the hamlet a mile or two on one side, and even the road from Nottingham to Grantham left it a little to the north, serving Whatton.

So little distinction was there about those first years that we do not even know who gave Thomas Cranmer his rudiments of Latin while he was yet a child; he may have gone to one of those grammar schools which flourished everywhere throughout England and of which there were not a few close in touch with his home; he may have been put under some chantry priest. What we do know about that first teaching is that he himself ascribed to its methods that constant hesitancy or timidity of his which in great trial turned into rank cowardice; which he ever deplored throughout his strange life yet did not shake off—save in one exasperated moment of defiance, goaded by calumny. It is likely enough that this blaming of his schoolmaster was but an excuse—men love to make others responsible for their failings—but at any rate this schoolmaster, whoever he was, must have been a bully and perhaps cruel, for the memory of him to haunt the life of the man whom he had oppressed in childhood.

Yet in all things of the countryside the boy grew up robust enough. His father saw to it that he should shoot, though he was short-sighted; and what was remarked of him from the beginning and was a pride of his almost into old age was his mastery of riding. He feared no mount. Perhaps he could break in, he could certainly control, the roughest; and his insufficient presence (he did not grow to be a tall man, but was rather noted for mediocrity of stature) was at its best in the saddle: he always made something of a figure there.

It would have been well for little Thomas Cranmer if he had lived on as all seemed made for him to live, in the dull countryside of the Midlands, the parson of some village, perhaps—saying his weekly Mass and administering the sacraments in perfunctory fashion to the villagers of a plough-land parish; or as a humble cleric-lawyer in a market town of his native Trent country or of the Fens. He was all made and moulded for that. Better still for him to have been born the elder son and to have lived on, as his brother did, the small squire of the small place, for that was what suited him: riding, and the chase—no alarms—no eminence —dogs, and shooting with the cross-bow and the long.

*   *   *   *   *   *

In the summer during which the baby Thomas Cranmer came to be two years old there was born in the great Palace of Greenwich by the broad clear tidal Thames another child, on the 28th of June, 1491; he also was a second son, but the son of a King. They baptized him Henry. That child was to grow into the man that should occasion, long years after, all Thomas Cranmer's belated eminence and effect huge catastrophe. For he became King Henry VIII of England.

Greenwich after that birth was full of rejoicing. The doubtful new usurping dynasty which the father, Henry Tudor, had founded needed provision of heirs; there was only one other son, and there had been an interval of nearly five years since his birth; it was not six years since the last Plantagenet King of the right Blood Royal of England had fallen on the field of Bosworth, and this secretive sharp-faced delicate man—grandson of an adventurer and servant in the Palace—had chanced upon the throne, when his little army of Frenchmen following him for pay had received the treasonable aid of the Stanleys even as the battle was joined.

It was not the baby's mother in that Palace of Greenwich—herself a true Plantagenet from whom he could claim the Royal blood of England—it was rather the dwarfish, pious and much-beloved grandmother who played the chief part in the nurture and conduct of the new child Henry. She was Margaret, Countess of Richmond, mother of the new usurping King, whom she had borne when almost a child herself—not fifteen years of age. Her counsel, her character, coloured the Court; for she also was Plantagenet, though of the bastard line of Beaufort.

See through eyes of English kingship how the new kingship stood there in the Palace of Greenwich in this year 1491. The great river ran through meadows which were marshy upon the farther side, and ran up to hills, marked with clumps of wood, upon the nearer. Twice daily, on the flood, the ships and barges passed up to the town which showed to the north and east, only three miles away round the bend of the river, clustering with spires. There nearest, and clearly seen in the summer air of those times, were the white turrets of the Tower and the eastern wall of the City with its bastions. There, shooting up into the sky, was the cross of St. Paul's on its slender steeple, the highest in Europe, and on the hither side the broader mass of St. Dunstan's; and one would just catch above the few buildings of Southwark and the roofs of the great nunnery at Bermondsey the houses with gaps between them upon the long Bridge of London and the Church of Southwark at its end. Below it was a crowd of masts in the Pool, and perhaps from the highest of the Palace windows, across the flats far off, the distant lump of Westminster Abbey could be distinguished; and on the opposing shore, smaller but still to be perceived, the new brick towers of Lambeth where the Archbishop of Canterbury had his town house. Him also, John Morton by name, the King had raised, for his great fidelity to the usurping cause and his zeal in heaping up the Royal treasure: the first of those Tudor priestly servants of whom Cranmer was to be one.

That Kingship of England which the son of the Countess Margaret had seized—Henry, the VIIth of the name—was great in its way, though it was not equal to the chief Princedoms of the West. It ruled only to the Scottish Border, with some hold over the eastern ports of Ireland and a claim to lordship over the rest; but the long civil wars in England had almost let Ireland go.

Overseas England held Calais, and thereby the Straits; its trade was with the Channel ports and still more with the Netherlands—the great market over the North Sea. But all the revenues of its King combined were not so great as that of the Seigneury of Venice. The arable land of his realm—at a time when nine-tenths of life was on the fields—counted not one quarter, perhaps little more than one-fifth, of what the King of France and his feudatories governed, much less than the Empire, less than the newly consolidated monarchy of Spain. But it was prosperous, and strict administration had given considerable money-power to its ruler. It counted perhaps four million souls, but we must not conclude that, with less than one-tenth of the people which the same area holds to-day, you would at that time have had an impression of an empty land. The villages and little market towns which were the whole life of England then were busy, the husbandmen in them numbered more than they do now, and the

8

come and go was continual on roads as yet unspoiled—
for they were well kept up, and so remained until the
fall of the monarchy and all the other effects of the coming
religious troubles, of which no man yet dreamed,
began to leave them to decay. The English building
was famous everywhere throughout Europe—the parish
churches of that wealthy time remain to us for evidence,
while the larger collegiate shrines, the splendid greater
monasteries, the Cathedrals, had taken on everywhere
the last beauty of the Middle Ages.

It was an England still part of one Christendom—
feeling itself but a province of the general Christian
life—yet already national, even to the details of its
superb architecture, which, in the earlier days of the
Gothic had been much the same throughout the West,
but was now in each country of a type peculiar to the
district and here, in England, most distinct. The
painted windows in the private houses, as in the public
halls and churches, were at their most glorious ; Italian
sculptors had come to ornament palace and tomb
with the life of the Renaissance, and portraiture was
of long standing, so that we can know the features of
the greater men and women of the day as we can hardly
know those of an earlier time unless from tombs.

In such an England grew up that second son of the
King, moved from one palace to another, principally
in Greenwich, his birth-place, but also in Windsor and
St. Stephen's, Westminster ; and all seemed secure—
especially the Church, with its immense wealth, with
law courts of its own and hosts of officials, the greater
ones most sumptuously endowed, and everywhere its
presence in stone dominating men's eyes.

*   *   *   *   *   *

On what a world did these two boys look in their
childhood : what England did they know ? The one,
the Prince, growing up in the Court, and for half his

time acquainted with the life of the town, had a very different environment to form him from that which the other destined child in the lowliness of his small country home could find. But the little Prince also grew on into his teens with much knowledge of the countrysides, and the England in which they were each to play so great a part was then an England of the fields.

There was but one great city, London, a mile square and with a hundred thousand or more of people. With London no other centre could compare. The next main ports were nothing to London. The inland towns, some of which had been large in the past, had decayed; Norwich, for instance, once half the size of London, was shrunk within its ancient walls, showing great empty spaces.

For the high life of the late Middle Ages had been snapped a century and a half before by the catastrophe of the Black Death. The England of the Conquest and the England of the true Middle Ages may have had six million or more, if Wales had been counted in. The England of these days, upon the eve of the Reformation, had but two-thirds that number. Yet it was prosperous, nor certainly did it give an effect of being ill-populated, for there was active movement and the people were well distributed. Most men owned. Those countrysides of England upon the eve of the great change, the England of the Middle Ages, were then as they are to-day wherever they are still unspoiled, grouped into those English villages the like of which for beauty and for peace and for the harmony of human habitation with the soil and the trees are not to be matched in the world. The market towns were little more than overgrown villages; the walled towns were distinct, and being things of which we have lost the memory, they are things which we must vividly envisage to see the world in which those children moved.

Irregularly scattered up and down the face of the country, those towns which had been fortified stood clean and cut off from the fields around. Their wooden-framed or small brick houses were commonly crowded together, their streets narrow ; their walls in a continuous ring, entered by few and guarded gates.

Each town had strong individuality and personal life, its officers ruling it, and each possessed customs and privileges of its own.

The walled town was one chief mark of the English landscape which then characterized it most strongly, and which we have to-day most completely lost. The men dwelling within these walled towns were not what we call to-day urban in type ; the places were too small for that and the admixture with the neighbouring fields too close. They were a part of the England of the husbandman, though they boasted elaborate crafts and trading and working traditions of their own.

Besides the towns, one other feature, of which we have kept in many places the ruins, in some almost preserved the original structure—I mean the stone castles—marked the landscape ; from the smaller fortified houses to the great military keeps, they still stood everywhere, at distances of a few miles one from the other, guarding the fords, the crossings of main ways, bridges, crowning small isolated heights, sometimes artificial, and their elaborate structure intact, for artillery had not yet the power, or was only just beginning to find the power, to master them. Also, each walled town would, as a rule, have its castle within the circuit of its fortifications.

The human society of these boyhoods had inherited from a tradition of many hundreds of years, a tradition going right back to the Christian origins of Europe, a certain ideal of security and status which in the interval between us and them disappeared almost as thoroughly as the walled towns.

Life from the very far-off date when the old Roman Empire had gradually been transformed and fallen into the conditions of the Dark Ages, was arranged for Christian men under the concept that each should have his place and each be sure of his livelihood, each with his duties and each with a free mind so long as those duties were accomplished.

The typical arrangement, that under which the great mass of men lived, was the arrangement of the village, for which the general name was the Manor.

The dues which the villagers paid in money or in kind or in labour to the lord of the manor, as also the rights which that lord had (in common with the villagers and in proportions which varied with each place) in the woodlands and in the fisheries and the rest, the fines that could be levied in the little manorial court which governed the village, the rents received from freehold land, all such annual payments lumped together, made up what was called " the worth of the manor." Every such manor had its " worth," and the manors belonging to the clerical body were a tempting booty on which the rich laymen already looked covetously.

There was no regular revenue from taxes. The expenses of the State were met from the king's own revenues. The public fortune whereby the king was maintained and with which he supported the affairs of State came from payments in the courts, dues from vassals, and from a mass of manorial and town incomes of which the king was lord, and from great spaces, often wooded, sometimes of bare mountain-land, part of them, however, cultivated, which stood outside the manorial system and were called " forests." Certain very great men not only held many manors themselves, but were also the overlords of small one-manor lords. Such were the heads of families like the Howards, the Nevilles, the Greys, and at most a hundred others, in declining scale.

Side by side with the lay fortunes each known and

secured and its function appropriated to it, were the various endowments of the Church; each bishopric and all its official body, the clergy of its cathedral, its chancellor, its various offices, lived on manorial endowments, and on house rents paid from within the boroughs and on profits of ecclesiastical courts, for the Church in those days stood side by side with the State, having its own courts, which tried for spiritual offences and which dealt with a mass of things now the business of the ordinary courts: in particular the Church courts dealt with wills.

The greater and lesser religious houses were strewn over the land even more thickly than the castles. There were hundreds of them first and last: the most magnificent of them as great or greater than the households of the nobles. The revenue of these also came from manorial and burgage rights. They also were lords of manors and owners often of livings as well. The village churches were served by a secular priesthood also dependent upon endowment and with their ecclesiastical superiors the bishops. With the monasteries large and small, the total amount of surplus manorial wealth paid to churchmen was a very large fraction of the total manorial wealth of the country—some said it was as much as one-third: it was certainly at least one-fifth. There were princely revenues paid to the greater clerics, and all within the ecclesiastical body, as without, was ordered for security, each place having its income and its function attached to it.

Just as the village was organized to be self-supporting, and every unit in it secured in revenue as in function, so the other activities in trade and in craftsmanship were organized for security: banded together in guilds wherein the quality of workmanship and prevention of oppression of the lesser by the greater or the absorption of the small man's goods by the richer, was carefully watched.

There were exceptions to this scheme of order, of course, as there are to the dominating character of any society. Even in our own modern society of competition, insecurity and chaos, there are exceptional islands of security, endowment and peace—the university endowments, for instance. So in that last society of the Middle Ages there were exceptions. There was the beginning of a proletariat, that is, of men without any place or any security. But they were nothing compared to the rest of the community and were numerous only perhaps in London, into which drifted the dregs of England. There was some speculation and some competition in the merchant world. Men grew rich, or were impoverished, by ventures therein ; but most men, even among the greater and lesser plyers of a trade, had something of security, as had the mass of their fellows in the more stable occupations. The lawyers had a freer competition and therefore more ups and downs of fortune, but among them also were the great secure positions as there are to-day, and they also formed a guild for mutual protection which has survived to our own time and is to-day the strongest association by far in the English state.

Such was the framework in which society lay, the mechanical form of it. Politically it was, as I have said, a kingship. There was already a sense of nationhood which had been growing for two or three hundred years ; and during nearly the last hundred there had been a community of tongue. For the wealthy governing people had gradually ceased to speak French, and, quite a lifetime before Cranmer was born, were speaking the language of their inferiors. But this idea of nationhood was all mixed up in men's minds with the crown, or rather with the living and real personality of the prince, the monarch. He was " the natural lord " whom men must in duty and by custom obey, of whose authority there could be no question, of whom the judges were merely delegates, who had power of life and death, who made every appointment and decided peace and war.

He controlled all, for he was immensely wealthier than his wealthiest subject and stronger than the strongest. This government by a king was aided and supported by the greater squires, the very rich lords possessed of many manors, who formed a sort of Great Council under him to be consulted in grave moments and with him to make laws. These were the peers ; but they were peers only because he summoned them. Having been summoned, however, it was already a right that a man's descendants should be summoned after him and peerage was hereditary. When, under the stress of exceptional expenditure—which was nearly always the exceptional strain of war—the government needed more money than could be found from the king's personal revenues, he summoned a General Great Council, which had been called for the last two hundred years and more (the device had arisen three hundred years before) the full Parliament, with not only himself and his peers, but also a body of men sent from the shires and from the towns, forming what we call to-day the Commons. They were in practice manorial lords, great and small, with now and then a burgess among them, and a small sprinkling of lawyers. There was, of course, nothing of the populace about them. It lay with these to confer and decide what the manorial lords and the merchants, and perhaps other men as well in times of great necessity, could provide as an exceptional aid for the government in its necessity.

But this bodily framework of the State was informed by a general spiritual condition common to all Europe the understanding of which is the understanding of the time.

For far the most important feature in that society was its religion. By the religion of a society is its whole character determined, and it was Cranmer's attitude to religion which determines all his place in history.

Now on that point of religion at the end of the Middle Ages, the moment when all was changing under the spirit of the Renaissance and the great discoveries, especially in the matter of the religion of England in that day, it is most difficult to be just. Not only has passion warped judgment, not only has the later history of the country overlain that past, so that we see it distorted through belts of changing mood which succeed each other during three generations, while England was being transformed, but the complete unfamiliarity of modern men with the mind of the late fifteenth and early sixteenth centuries makes the task of description almost impossible.

All manner of errors flourish in this connection. There are those who imagine an England just before the Reformation strictly disciplined in Catholicism and at the same time enthusiastic for its doctrines and practice. They think of it as they might think to-day of Poland or of Ireland. But the England of 1500 was not so. There are others who make a still grosser error, thinking of English religion at that date as something alien to England : something imposed : something from which the Englishman was struggling to be free.

There are those who confuse the effort at reform with the effort at destruction, and there are those, very numerous they are, who mistake the enthusiasm of a few in any period for the general spirit of society.

England upon the eve of the Reformation was a completely Catholic country, less moved by the stirrings of doubt or of indignation against the structure of the universal European religion than was perhaps any other province of Christendom. Also the corruption of the Church, which had everywhere proceeded far, was less pronounced here than perhaps in any other place. But the mass of the people were lethargic in religion. Their strongly conservative instinct would certainly react against any sudden or pronounced change. But the very fact that they took the Church for granted, that its Faith was the air they breathed, would make them see in a new church experiment or a new church policy nothing very perilous, unless it were in too startling a contrast with their habit.

The clerical body as a whole—then very large, rich and powerful—was official in temper. The chief Bishops were statesmen and bureaucrats, ambassadors, ministers, used by the Tudor monarchy. But in *one* field which will closely concern us throughout this book, the clerical body was ready, in part, for spiritual adventures. That field was the universities.

A small country, such as England then was, counted but two universities, Oxford and Cambridge. Their numbers had dwindled, their old activities of the Middle Ages had died down, but it was within their body that all the leaders of the priesthood were formed.

It is from the small clerical colleges of those two corporations that the Bishops were drawn; the cliques of men who advanced and who combated religious change grew to know each other in the narrow companionship of those few scores who studied and taught —slackly enough—within the old foundations.

We must not conceive anything like the modern university life. Small corporate bodies living poorly —often at the rate of no more than 30s. or £2 a week —occupied as much in the offices of religion as in those of study, following for the most part an ancient routine which was very lifeless and which concerned but a few, it was still the universities who gave the rare degrees whereby a man might claim to practise law or to profess theology. There would be years in which not half a dozen Doctorates of Divinity were granted—once only two !—but such as could call themselves Doctor would have had to obtain the title at Oxford or Cambridge. And to be Doctor of Divinity was to have authority in religious debate. It was from the small body of men so hall-marked that all the leadership in favour of the religious revolution and most of the defence against it must come.

There was no feeling of social rank about the universities in those days. They were, as the Scottish universities are to-day, recruited mainly from the mass of the people. Many scholars got their living and teaching as a free gift; for no one was the higher education a notable expense. Many came from quite the poorest ranks, most from the lower middle classes; a sprinkling from the rather wealthier part of society, the lords of manors. These were usually the " cadets," the younger sons who had their way to make, and especially, of course, those who were destined for the Church.

Of such was Cranmer, when, as a boy of fourteen, in the year 1503, his father being already dead, his mother got him upon one of the endowments of Cambridge. There he was to be prepared for the priesthood and to live in a small way upon the endowments of religion: an unimportant petty routine with, one may be fairly sure, nothing of a *vocation* about it. Cranmer was not passed as a lad through the open doors which led to priesthood because he was suited to be a priest. Rather was he sent off to find a means of livelihood and to procure relief to the small estate of his elder brother. There, at Cambridge, would he proceed in his regular course; he would take his degree of Master of Arts, after his Bachelorship; then he would be elected to one of the modest little foundations. He would be ordained Priest. He would be given his Doctorate of Divinity. He would teach his small class-room, examine, perhaps write a thesis or two. He would draw his two or three pints of ale a day, his bread and cheese and eggs; say his Masses; vote on the humble affairs of the little community, and live and die unknown save to a few companions.

II

CAMBRIDGE

THERE stood on the Eastern edge of the town of Cambridge, just beyond the King's Ditch, as it was called (a runnel of water, the Long Rithe, which drained that flooded land and led from a mill above), a little place already known in this year, 1503, as "Jesus" College, after the name of the street which it faces, "Jesus Lane."

It had for centuries been a nunnery, starting we know not how, but in the very depths of the Middle Ages, and already existing, as a humble community of cloistered women, just after the Conquest. Perhaps it was older still. Its lay buildings, part of them still showing the old wall of hardened mud and timber, stood upon the edge of that great meadow outside the town called the Green Croft, adjoining to and perhaps originally a part of the great meadow which the citizens of the small mediæval borough, the descendants of a Roman or pre-Roman settlement, enjoyed in common. The house had been built upon a patch of gravel which gave a firm foundation : for the big common meadow outside was artificially flooded by the banking up of the river Cam during the winter months of the year, in order to provide good pasturage in the summer.

The rule of that nunnery had been Benedictine ; it had flourished in its simplicity while still the Middle Ages flourished in *their* simplicity and strength, and before the great catastrophe of the Black Death and the gradual hardening and imperilment of that high civilization. For more than three hundred years its charters had been preserved.

As the Middle Ages decayed in body as they had

already decayed in mind, as the outward, material part of them failed, this little thing began to fade with them. At last its small endowment of less than £2,000 a year in modern money, made up largely of rents from the tenements near by, could not be properly collected. The house had lost its discipline; and at last, in the days when Cranmer was a little boy playing round the manor house of Aslacton, only two nuns remained, and one was gadding about and of bad repute. The rents were not collected. Nine houses of the little property were empty and without tenants, the place was ruinous —such was in many another example the death of the Middle Ages.*

There was in those days a very active man, one of those clerical bureaucrats whom the new Tudor dynasty was using so successfully, by name John Alcock. He was Bishop of Ely at that time when Cranmer was growing up into boyhood at Aslacton. This man Alcock had been an endowed clergyman of London, used by the Government in various capacities, because while the Wars of the Roses were yet raging his talents had been given to the Lancastrian side. When the Tudor usurper (later crowned as King Henry VII) was still prowling about seeking an entry into England (having a strong party to favour him should he land), Alcock, as a young energetic man, had worked, probably secretly, upon his side. He was a Yorkshireman of Beverley, who had taken his Doctorate in Canon Law in the university of Cambridge in the year 1470, during the heat of those struggles between the branches of

---

* In connection with this ruined old convent, Professor Pollard, whose monograph on Cranmer is by far the most scholarly work on the life and time, is misleading. His very strong religious feeling has led him into a piece of false history. He tells us that the house "had been dissolved on account of the gross immorality prevailing among its inmates." The sentence gives the impression that there was a whole community—a community of consecrated women—given up to peculiarly vile forms of sexual licence; nothing else can be gathered from the word "gross" and the word "inmates."

the Plantagenets which were called the Wars of the Roses. He had been made Bishop of Worcester in 1476, and when the battle of Bosworth put the strange Tudor claimant upon the English throne in 1485 and ended the great tradition of the old Plantagenet blood, he was at once marked for promotion. He was given the rich bishopric of Ely a year after that.

All of this is to be noted, for Alcock was the man who made Jesus College out of the all-but-dead nunnery, and it means that the little place was filled with a tradition of the new Tudor claim and of devotion to the new upstart Tudor kings.

So, the old convent having gone to pieces, John Alcock got leave from the King, with whom he was such a favourite, to make something out of it. Nuns were there no longer; the property was falling into ruin. Ten years after his getting Ely, eleven years after Bosworth Field had been won, and the furtive, crafty, determined man who had made himself king was master of the State, in the year when little Thomas Cranmer was seven years old, in the year 1496, Alcock took over the broken and derelict foundation and determined to make of it a place of instruction which should remember him when he should be dead.

As the old nunnery had been small enough originally, and had lately shrunken to nothing, so this new foundation was small enough, even among the small foundations of those days. Alcock's plan was for no more than six fellows, with a master, and these were to look after a sort of little school wherein there were to be only six boys on the endowment. But to make a foundation of this sort was like planting a tree. Further endowment would come if it justified itself.

The ramshackle estate was taken over and properly administered. It seems to have begun to give something like its old return, and on the modest £2,000 a year or less, the place was supported: a mere school, with a schoolmaster at £200 a year (but given laundry, and shaving, and food and drink and all that was needed for his chapel), an usher coming in to help at a quarter that amount, six members of the community under the Master, and such few students as might care to pay money for their keep and learn in the University at hand.

The old nunnery had had a parish church attached to it, in the grounds of which was held a public fair. Alcock began to build, took over a portion of the nave of the church, making rooms of it for his new community, and in general furnished the buildings towards the service he had designed for them : a modest place of education, principally for half a dozen young boys hardly yet in their teens on the boundary of the town— the site had just been included within the boundaries of the municipality. He had begun to build among other things the gate tower, and just afterwards came that lovely portal, one of the final triumphs of mediæval art, which we may still admire.

Thither by that portal in 1503 came in the boy Thomas Cranmer at fourteen years of age.* He was to be thenceforward a " Gesuanus," for that was the nickname given to those belonging to the little place.

He was no longer of an age to be among the little boys of the school. There was probably no regular place for undergraduates on the small foundation. What situation he held we do not know ; it is possible that his widowed mother paid some trifle for his lodging and perhaps for his tuition, but, at any rate, there he must have grown up during the next seven or eight years, until he was twenty-two years of age : a very slow and belated process. There did he get his grammar, the better part of his Latin, his opportunity for reading ; and to that Corporation he continued all his life in spirit to belong, attached to it in affection until he died.

* There is no documentary evidence, but it is a certain presumption, for he appears as a member of the foundation on taking his degree.

The little university and town were filled in that day by the presence of John Fisher, also a Yorkshireman like Alcock, and now in his thirty-fourth or thirty-fifth year, and also from Beverley, the son of a mercer there —and between Beverley and Cambridge there was a further connection, for the school that had taught Fisher his Latin in Beverley belonged to the collegiate church there, the Provost of which was Rotherham, Chancellor of Cambridge. Fisher's wealthy father was dead some five years past when, as a young man of eighteen, he entered the college of Michelhouse, with Melton, who was later the Master, to teach him ; and in the year when Cranmer was born, Fisher, just of age, had got his Mastership of Arts. Three years later he was the Chief Proctor—spokesman for the University in external affairs ; three years later again he was Master of Michelhouse, the wealthiest of the small foundations of those days ; and now this lad from Aslacton, shy and new, heard the name of Fisher upon every side ; for Fisher had been Vice-Chancellor already two years, and it was under him that something began to stir in the life of the restricted half-dead place— long torpid like so much in England at the end of the Middle Ages. Thus late, the spirit of Italy and the Renaissance was beginning to send some slight influence into England, and that new air it was which was now breathed by the lad Thomas Cranmer.

The King's mother, the Countess of Richmond, whom people called " the Lady Margaret " and who had made Fisher her confessor in 1497, founded in that same year in which the boy came to the place her new Professorship of Divinity, giving payment for it of £300 a year, and Fisher was the first to be chosen for the task of reading early in the morning, in the hour from 7 to 8 o'clock, from the works of Divinity. It was Fisher who awoke his patroness to the duty of founding preacher-ships as well, for in that tangled struggle against sundry

disruptive enthusiasts the official Church—taking the
wrong defensive—had thought it better to discoun-
tenance preaching altogether, since her experience of it
was that by preaching was rebellion fostered. In that
same year the Pope (it was the Borgia pope, Alexander
VI) sent his Bull appointing twelve preachers for the
island, and apart from the new professorship and the
new preachers it was in this broadening time of Fisher's
hold over Cambridge that new foundations began and
that buildings—interrupted by the long civil wars—
were completed, notably the glorious structure of
King's. Very large amidst the low roofs stood those
unfinished walls of King's College Chapel when young
Cranmer was walking those streets ; and there it was,
when he was already seventeen years old, that he saw
three years after his entry the elderly King, now already
ailing, come in with his little alert old mother upon a
pilgrimage to Our Lady of Walsingham. It was under
the temporary roof of the choir in that unfinished place
that the King and the Countess of Richmond heard
Mass, and it may be that with them had come the great
Erasmus—or rather the Erasmus who *was* to be so great :
with a greatness which he knew to be his due, yet in that
day was half denied him. And Fisher, who had resigned
from Michelhouse and was now the President of his
patroness's new college, Queens', received him there
later.

Few pupils came to Erasmus and little money. The
unimpressive figure, the colourless flaxen Batavian hair,
the pale blue eyes, made but a sorry presence.

It was just in those years when young Cranmer was
finishing the first part of his course, the years from
1509 or 1510 to 1514, that the great scholar had come
back from Italy, more fully possessed of Greek than
ever, to see whether England would not give him the
living which the Continent denied. They gave him the
Professorship that Fisher had held, the Lady Margaret

lectureship, and he delivered his first address when Cranmer was in his twenty-second year. Yet of such a mind, such learning and such wit present amongst them, the still cramped place took little heed; they lodged him high up in his tower at Queens', but he learnt no English. He disliked the fogs of the Fens. He disliked the local ale.

He was not poor, save in his own estimation, for he rightly thought himself worthy of great rewards. Wareham, the Archbishop, had given him the living of Adlington in Kent, and what with his Professorship and an added income from Warham's own purse and something from Mountjoy and £100 a year more from Fisher himself, Erasmus—isolated in the top room of the tower at Queens', writing away at his "New Instrument" which was to have such prodigious effect—may have had from £1,000 to £1,500 a year. He thought it not enough and left England disappointed. Yet here in England and at Cambridge had he completed that weapon wherewith others not to his liking were to attack the very foundations of the Faith. Here, in that tower room of Queens' College, had he laid the train of powder whose explosion was to dismember Europe. For this "New Instrument" of his was an appeal to the Greek Text of Scripture, the beginning of modern criticism, the beginning of that annotation of the New Testament upon which both the reformers and the rebels against religion were to build.

But all this as yet was for Cranmer nothing, or at least nothing that we know of. He had learnt his old-fashioned scholastic. It had left him unsatisfied, and he found the teaching lax and the teacher disingenuous —pretending to knowledge which he had not. He was in his twenty-third year when he was chosen one of the few Fellows under that humble roof; the original half a dozen had grown at one moment to ten; they were soon to be reduced to eight. He lived on his commons

at the rate of what we should call 30s. a week.
On such a scale, in numbers and income, was the
Cambridge of that time. He heard his weekly Mass of
the Holy Name of Jesus, the particular service of his
foundation ; he passed Bachelor of Arts thus late ; he
did not present himself for Orders, so he had made no
vows of celibacy. He read, still dissatisfied.

So had passed those seven years from boyhood to
manhood in which a man's character is formed, and we
know from what that character became the kind of
stamp which had been put upon it.

These decisive years of the teens, when a boy grows
into a man and when attraction and repulsion are
impressed upon him for ever, were passed under the
old, now dreary and lifeless, routine of a scholasticism
grown petrified and fossil. The highest philosophy
man has known, the glory of the true Middle Ages, had
so been allowed to mummify and fail. All repeated its
formulæ. None were nourished.

Yet the discipline had value. It made scholars, and
Cranmer among others. His languages were learned
thoroughly, certainly Latin, probably already Greek ;
but his intelligence was not appealed to, and those
faculties in him which have justly rendered famous his
later work, his mastery over words, were offended by
the dullness of his teachers, but his hesitating caution
and reserve only confessed this much later in life. He
received what he had to receive, noting that it was
insufficient. Yet was he perhaps ungrateful in his
impatient later scorn of those years, for at any rate they
taught him *Form*, without which no man in any art can
reach enduring fame.

For Cranmer in those years was—unknown to himself
—growing to be that artist whose pen touched with
magic, years after, the prayers of the new establishment :
of an English liturgy which no man in those earlier years
could have dreamt of. There was never a writing

man yet in prose or verse whose talent did not come to him before his twentieth year, and though Cranmer knew it not, though no man praised him for it throughout all his life, such talent was given him in the writing of English that he made permanent what, but for his prose, could not have lived : the Anglican Liturgy.

See him, then, a youth bent over the desk with peering, short-sighted eyes close to his paper and with slow pen forming himself to that which, after thirty years, was to reach so great a height. See him carefully chiselling the phrase.

For the genius of Cranmer in this supreme art of his —the fashioning of rhythmic English prose—was not of that spontaneous kind which produces great sentences or pages in flashes, as it were, unplanned, surging up of themselves in the midst of lesser matter ; he was not among prose writers what such men as Shakespeare or Ronsard are among the poets—voluminous, uneven, and without conscious effort compelled to produce splendours in a process of which they are themselves not aware. He was, on the contrary, a jeweller in prose, a man who sat down deliberately to write in a particular way when there was need or opportunity for it, but who, on general occasions, would write as might any other man. We have a great mass of what he did, in long letters to Boleyn, to the King and to Cromwell, careful arguments transcribed at length in his disputations, as in the famous one with Gardiner on the Real Presence ; it is always scholar's work, careful and lucid. But when he sits down to produce a special effect all changes. He begins to carve with skill and in the hardest material. He is absorbed in a particular task, creative, highly conscious, and to his sense of beauty vastly satisfactory.

Cranmer being of such a kind in his work, that work reached heights which none other reached—not even Tyndale, whose great sweeps of rhythm underlie what was, a century after his death, to become the standard English Bible. But, unlike Tyndale—the other and older great master of prose in that generation which fixed the English tongue—Cranmer's work was deliberately limited, as its very nature demanded. It was set in small frames, as it were, and put apart from all the rest he did. Left to himself, I think he would have spent all his energies upon that one occupation in which he must have known himself to be a master, although contemporaries but vaguely appreciated his unique powers in that one field. For he was not a man to give an impression of power. Indeed, he did not impress at all. He shrank, withdrew, was suave and unguent—also by nature mild in his external manner. His presence did not suggest genius of any kind. When he was forced into public life there fell upon him that penalty of public life, the fixing on a man of a label which has little to do with his real self. He passed for a courtier or a protestant hero : he was no more than a poet. But the effect of a poet is enduring.

He was not of those to whom a fountain of creation fills and who declaim, as it were, great matter. His art was of the kind which must work very slowly and in secret, isolated ; his sentences when he desired to produce his effect must be perfected in detail, polished, lingered over, rearranged, until they had become so that one could feel them with the finger-nail and find no roughness. But when he was composing a letter, a proclamation—anything which had to be done for workaday business and where there was no time or occasion for lengthy toil—you hardly ever find in Cranmer's work even occasional beauty. Once or twice a phrase stands out, but in the great mass of what he has left he is as dull, turgid and confused as all his generation were ; repeating himself, writing at vast length, using exaggerated terms, and seeming incapable sometimes of finishing his sentence at all. But when he says to himself : " Now I have something special to do ; here I am on my mettle, I must produce some final thing "—*then* he constructs with a success only paralleled by the sonnets of Shakespeare.

I say " constructs." Though we could not do the same ourselves, yet we can see how the hand is at work and how every word is thought out, each rhythm discovered, and the contour of the whole cameo carved. There is not in all that he has thus left of perfect English one lengthy passage ; most of the Collects, which, with the isolated phrases of the Litany are his chief triumph, consist in single sentences—but they are sentences which most men who know the trade would give their eyes to have written. And since that endures which is carved in hard material, they have endured, and given endurance to the fabric—novel and revolutionary in his time, the institution at the root of which he stands—The Church of England.

* * * * * *

There was nothing in those early years to teach him revolt against the society his boyhood had known. He must or may have felt against it the natural revolt of the young against what seems to them dead formula. But England was not yet touched by what was going on abroad. He saw Chubbs, his first Master, pass, and another—John Eccleston—arrive, when he was but sixteen years of age, and Eccleston also was in the old dying tradition of repeated routine stuff, and Cranmer still learned of the things that had to be learned, and particularly his beginnings of the Humanities. In the refectory, with the dozen at the most that stayed there, he would sit twice a day at meals hearing a boy from the school, or perhaps some young fellow like himself, reading out the lection of the day in Latin— a droning, perfunctory thing—and all the common talk between him and those about him had to be in Latin, officially at least.

He plodded on. He can have had no money save what his widowed mother provided for him—even those on the foundation were paid nothing, and had only their livelihood and lodgings for support; he knew the life of the town; he carried on in the obscurity which only so very gradually lifted, and so late. We have seen how tardy he was in taking his degree—already in his twenty-third year before he could call himself Bachelor of Arts. But the new life from the Continent outside was beginning to pulse into England.

In that same year when the young, short, heavy, hesitant man of such small lineage, of so obscure a world, had been granted his degree and given at the same time his place as Fellow among the company which sat in the refectory there in Jesus College, the great Erasmus was giving his lectures: the great Erasmus was Lady Margaret reader, and the great Erasmus had aroused the Great Curiosity—that which was to quicken and to threaten the life of Europe.

But whether Cranmer ever heard or met him we do not know. It may be doubted. He never spoke or wrote of Erasmus as one known in the flesh, nor Erasmus of him. He was not, even later, when great public office had been thrust upon him, of a sort who from ambition or even from vivacity would catch on to his fellows.

Among the figures at Cambridge appearing intermittently in those years when Cranmer was increasing there his quiet local reputation as a scholar, one of the most notable—indeed, the most notable after Fisher—was Stephen Gardiner. A man of features distantly resembling Cranmer's own, but larger and more lively, with more decided eyes and the expression emphasized by strong bushy dark brows. There was no more typical Englishman. He was perhaps about ten years Cranmer's junior, vastly more famous, the son of well-to-do people, cloth merchants in Bury St. Edmunds. A cleric of course, he later proceeded, also of course, to his Doctorate. He was to concentrate on Law, and both for his learning and his power of advocacy to become famous, until in 1524 he entered fully into public life by becoming the secretary of the mighty Wolsey, and the next year Master of Trinity Hall. The younger men about the place knew that figure well enough, as Cranmer, though older, must have known it ; and one of them who was already making some little mark among them was Fox, later to be Bishop of Hereford, Gardiner's constant companion and subordinate and of about the same age. He had come to King's from Eton, reaching Cambridge much at the time when Cranmer was taking his first degrees. Both he and Gardiner were to grow up at Cambridge acquainted with Cranmer's name as a senior, and we shall see what that acquaintance was to effect.

Not in disputation nor in any public action did Cranmer begin his activities.

There was something else at that moment more important to him than any reading or than any speculation ; the young fellow had got entangled at the " Dolphin."

The " Dolphin " was perhaps the best inn at the University ; it was the place where the Fellows of Jesus College would put up a visitor if they could not find room for him under their own roof. It stood on the corner of All Saints Passage and perhaps where to-day are the Master's Courts of Trinity.

Cranmer had cause to visit the " Dolphin " for other reasons than the drinking of its ale ; the host was a tenant of his own foundation, Jesus, and the hostess had a niece (or some such relative or dependent) working for her. Of what character that niece was we have no record, but she bore the significant nickname of " Black Joan," to which some preferred " Brown Joan."

Under either appellation the young men had noticed her or she them.

Young Cranmer married her, whether in good time or too late we do not know. At any rate he married her, and she was with child by him. He could no longer live with his company; he left it and supported himself and this woman as best he could—lecturing on theology, wherein his interest had begun, and taking what fees he could collect. Among other places which allowed him to speak to pupils under their roof was the small Benedictine college which then stood much where Magdalene stands now.

Within a year this unfortunate woman died in child-birth and the child was dead; as for young Cranmer, after his escapade he seemed stranded.

He had forfeited his narrow fellowship, his beer and commons and bed and roof, in the little place called Jesus College; but after some interval, we know not quite how long, they re-elected him.

After all, he was one of them, and he had done no harm though he had behaved oddly. They took him back into their company, and once more he sat at that board, and once more he heard the reading by the lad from the pulpit twice a day at meals, and once more he attended every week the Mass of the Holy Name. He proceeded in due time to his Mastership of Arts, in 1515—still in slow advance; but it would seem that about this time (he was twenty-six) his reputation was fairly established. He was remarked for his learning. He was moderately appreciated in that restricted world, and had some reputation in theology, for his company were confined by statute to that study and to no other —it brought him no luck in the end!

The next year, 1516, came an event, a landmark: for in that year—the year before Luther's famous challenge—there burst upon the world the New Testament of Erasmus, that " New Instrument " which he had worked at so assiduously, lonely in the top room of the tower at Queens' during his ungrateful four years, now half forgotten by him in his foreign residence and growing fame throughout Europe. It had been translated into this final edition, and it set the heather on fire.

III

THE ACCIDENTAL ENTRY

IN the year 1516 Cranmer was twenty-seven years of age. His local and modest reputation for scholarship was established, yet no influence that we can trace attached to him; he made, it seems, no close friendships, or at least none that are recorded in the increasing life of Cambridge. He must have read continually, still bent with his very short sight over the pages of the libraries, increasing his store; but with no power of putting himself forward, with no desire to do so: following the rut and content to follow it.

But there was a force at work throughout Europe which could not but reach even him at last; and a storm was about to arise the swell of which would be felt even in Cambridge, before it broke upon England.

The Greek New Testament of Erasmus with its arresting challenging notes and its commentaries which questioned a hundred official and accepted things in the practice of religion was working like yeast. The egg was laid which Luther was immediately to hatch—but Erasmus himself said bitterly and truly, "The Egg was an egg to hatch forth a chicken, but what Luther hatched forth was something very different indeed." It was so. For out of that egg came a small dragon, which grew suddenly in size.

In this same year, 1516, much talked of acts appeared upon the surface of public life; acts which seemed of vastly greater moment than the academic work of one scholar; nor is there a better example in history, I think, of how it is the mind which decides the tendencies of man and of how little are the loud external things compared with the silences of the mind, than this same year in which the Greek New Testament was published with its new Latin translation side by side on each page and that swarm of footnotes which rose and took wing and spread throughout Christendom the rumour of change. What filled those days in the eyes of men born to, or achieving, power; what Wolsey (who was just entering the magnificent portals of his fame) would have told you was essential at that moment; what the young King Henry thought of chief consequence; what the Emperor Maximilian made the subject of his plans; what Pope Leo, the Medici, in this fourth year of his pontificate schemed for as Sovereign of the Papal States and in part attained; what young Francis I gloried in as he remembered his splendid victory of last year beyond the Alps—all these seemed to be the meaning of the time. All to-day have sunk on to a lesser plane. Henry of England had come back from his first game of war (in which he had taken care not to risk his life but had revelled in pageantry), he had already suffered the first consequences of his blundering in foreign policy, he was in the midst of his quarrel with his Spanish father-in-law and rejoiced to hear of his death. Francis was firmly established in Italy, the victor for a year past of Marignano; Maximilian had crossed the Brenner to recover the Milanese and failed; and as for Wolsey, now the leader of England, he had received the Cardinal's hat with splendid investiture in Westminster Abbey, surrounded by the great Prelates of England.

These were the things that seemed to count; yet the book of Erasmus which was selling up and down Europe, struck off from Frofen's press at Basle, was more important by far. In it was struck the note of appeal against the authority of the living Church, the Church as it was, the Church teaching. It was not the first by many of such challenges to that by which men had lived for century upon century, but it was the most direct and the most vivid and the most scholarly appeal to that other authority of Scripture which the Church herself had given to men and which was henceforward to be used against her.

The Book of Erasmus was more than that ; it was an origin for Textual criticism and speculation upon authorship. It questioned the authenticity of Epistles. It interpreted at will the meaning of texts—specially of the famous Petrine texts, of doctrines and of fundamental words. Erasmus " marvels," he says, in his note upon Matthew xvi, 18, that the Roman pontiffs should draw their claims from the passage ; and throughout the book he puts into a summary as it were, or into a climax, all that vigorous satire and attack which he had been directing for years not only against the abuses but against the heart of the religious organization of Europe. For Erasmus held, in that earlier riotous mood of his, before he had been sobered by the sight of Revolution in action, that a corruption of religion had been at work from the very beginning, even in the earliest discussions upon the nature of the Incarnation, even in the first definitions before Nicæa. So much and such great work had been done in that room at the top of the tower of Queens' half a dozen years before!

That Erasmus intended the consequences of his labour or foresaw them we can certainly deny ; he had gone to all lengths in his use of scholarship and of wit. His fame had intoxicated him, the immensity of his labour had delighted him ; but he felt within his inmost being the necessity for unity, and destruction he abhorred. Yet it was he that lit the fire. In the next year came the German upheaval, the roaring protest of Martin Luther and the tidal wave.

Cranmer, there at Cambridge, gave no sign and, so far as we can tell, was not yet moved. His was a mind without initiative, reluctant to undertake any action, delighting in the personal exercise of form, concentrated upon an art wherein he was to be supreme. But he went not out to meet influence, good or evil; he submitted himself to it; only, when he was engaged too deep, it was as difficult for him to draw back as it had been first to advance. So in these years wherein we know nothing of what he did we may presume that he did nothing: he heard the great controversy arising, he must have followed it, for theology was his subject and examination in it his task; he must have felt the sympathy which all scholars then felt for the new scholarly movement, but what he felt as yet in doctrine—if he felt anything—we do not know and need hardly inquire. Others around him were making that atmosphere which later he was to breathe. To him, as to England in general, all this German storm was still alien—but not for long.

Young King Henry was never more national than when he engaged (he prided himself on his theology, for as a second son he had been trained for the Church) in controversy with Luther, nor was he ever more sincere. And Fisher, the soul of Cambridge, attended at the burning of the Lutheran books which Wolsey had ordered at the Cross of St. Paul's. But out of all England a sort of focus in Cambridge itself formed an exception: there a little nest or cell of Revolution was forming and a few were gathering for rebellion. Their example would spread.

On the site where now stands the Bull Inn stood in those days the "White Horse," the property of St. Catherine's Hall. In this Inn gathered, often by night, those who more and more inclined to question and to doubt. These few began to taste of the new spirit which the University about them—most of its members from routine, many from vested interest or from conventional tradition, but the greatest from their faith and strong intelligence—disliked, feared and would combat. One might compare those nightly meetings in the White Horse Inn (with its convenient back

entrance towards the river lane for coming and going
unperceived) to the Socialist groups of Oxford in the
days of my own youth when Socialism was new and
actively detested there. The novelty of the revolt
appealed to adventurers, so did its fancied intellectual
superiority and its call to enthusiasm. The meetings,
though careful, were not exactly secret; men talked
of the place as " Little Germany," so they were well
known enough : and there you might have seen, in those
evangelical discussions, in those hot denunciations of
all that was evil in the time and of much that was very
good, a knot of men, all Churchmen, scholars as yet
remote from the populace; John Rogers, Skip (later
chaplain to Anne Boleyn), and, chief among them all,
Barnes, Prior of the Augustinian Friars, which was
Luther's order. Whether Cranmer ever went in to
hear the debates of the little group as some have surmised,
we may doubt ; there was a slight element of risk about
them which would not have suited him, also it would
have given him a prominence he did not desire ; but he
was already breathing that air, sympathizing vaguely,
as a scholar, with scholarship ; the discussion of Greek
texts, the disputed rendering of ancient words was his
concern.   .

Was Peter indeed that rock on which the " Ecclesia "
was to be founded ?—Or was not that " rock " the faith
of Peter only, or even Faith at large—the Faithful ?
And what had a luxurious worldly court of a Medici
in Rome to do with Peter, kneeling there, fifteen centuries
past, enthusiastic at the feet of the Lord ?   And
" Ἐκκλησία " ? Was that word properly " Church " ?
Was it the " Holy Church," " Holy Mother Church "
of his boyhood, or was it not rather " congregation "
—no more than the general mass of those who followed
the Gospel, or even a few gathered together ? And
the centre of it all, the " Eucharist " ? What was that
but the Greek for thanksgiving ? Where was there

43

warranty in all that Greek for what the people held of
the Sacrament. And the *Mass;* the *Mass;* the very
heart and meaning of Europe, offered up on countless
altars, generation upon generation, for the living and
the dead ? Where was it to be found in those original
Greek phrases, fallen from the lips of Christ, in the
words of which Christ was revealed ? *There* should
Christ Himself be found, not in the bread over which
any one of busy official clerical thousands, of a mere
profession, a wealthy interest corrupted and greedy
muttered words of a morning.

But Cranmer neither spoke nor wrote of these things
which were moving around him. He passed seven years
listening, not compromised. Then, as the next tardy
step in the regular business of his life, he must take
orders. He must himself be a priest and so pass to
promotion and his Doctor's degree, which would give
him his final status.

All was learnt, rehearsed and performed in due order :
he was consecrated to the office which should bring
Christ Himself daily to the Altar. His hands were
blessed to hold that Host which some disputed and a
few in his world already blasphemed. He began the
Masses which he was to say, at first regularly and
domestically, later in high pomp. He must say them
with increasing, inward, concealed disgust, and on and on
year after year throughout his manhood till the approach
of age, to elevate the Victim in his hands for adoration.
The date was 1523 and Cranmer was thirty-four years of
age.

On Christmas Eve, 1525, in St. Edward's Church,
Barnes, the leader of "Little Germany" preached a
certain sermon.

Why did that sermon make so great a pother ? It
was of a sort which some few generations before men
would have taken for granted as one of the regular
homilies of the day ; there was little of doctrine about it,

a great deal of common morals—mainly an attack upon
the sloth and avarice and incompetence of the clergy.
The Middle Ages had been full of such sermons. It
had been a commonplace for nearly two hundred years
to denounce the evils of the times and to clamour for
" Reform " in the sense of betterment. Why should all
this now have a new significance ?

And here we must pause, and ask ourselves what
exactly was that movement, vague and enormous,
running through Europe, revolutionary and violent over
the whole district of the Germanies, beginning to be
heard in France and even here in England, or, at least,
at Cambridge.

We all know what came of it—there came of it the
historical thing called the Reformation; the establishment of the Protestant culture, the break-up of the old
religious unity; the independence of nations—at first
rather of Princes, from the old common authority of
Europe. There came from it the intense zeal for
separatist doctrines and still more for new morals
which everywhere marked the Protestant mind; and
there came from it also, but particularly in England, an
economic revolution whereby the wealth of the Church
and communal institutions associated with the Church
—colleges, hospitals, guilds—were seized by the rich
men and their rulers.

All that came of the Reformation (and was not accomplished without wars and massacres upon every side),
the final break-up of Europe, the final independence of
sovereign Princes from any common European authority,
was not achieved for more than a hundred years. Only
when it was achieved, in the middle of the next century
(the date 1648, the end of the great German religious
war, is a convenient landmark), was all that we now mean
by the antagonism between Catholicism and Protestantism irrevocably established. Into these beginnings
of the great movement we must read no such clear-cut

moods, nor such sharp definitions between one part of Christendom and another. But to understand why men began to feel as intensely as they did—and some to act —we must take a modern parallel; and a strong modern parallel is the quarrel against Industrial Capitalism to-day.

Protest against Industrial Capitalism from one aspect or another is universal : so was the protest against the condition of European religion at the beginning of the sixteenth century. One man in one mood will attack Industrial Capitalism for its destruction of beauty ; another for its incompetence ; another for the vileness of the men who chiefly prosper under it ; another for its mere confusion and noise ; another for its false values ; it was until recently most fiercely attacked for its impoverishment of the workers, its margin of unemployment and the rest—indeed so fiercely that it was compelled to seek palliatives for the evil. With a mass of men it was attacked from a vague but strong sense of injustice ; it allowed a few rich to exploit mankind.

In the midst of all these innumerable forms of a common protest and universal ill-ease there has grown up one definite body of doctrine whose adherents are called Communists and who desire the total subversion of what has been, hitherto unquestioned among civilized European men, the general doctrines of property and individual freedom.

In the same way the lethargy, the corruption, the avarice, the worldliness, of the official Church after the Black Death—this is, in the last two centuries of the Middle Ages—the increasing divergence between its profession and its practice, what might be called " the irreligion of religion," moved men to protest for all manner of reasons. The protest was as vague as it was universal, as confused as it was vague, but none the less intense for being vague and confused. The scandal of a divided Papacy—of great endowments which had been intended for the furtherance of holiness being treated as mere income to be grasped by the fortunate —the great political power possessed over men's daily lives by the ecclesiastical courts (independent of the civil power and yet daily more and more despised)— the machinery for a common moral government of Europe maintained while Princes were becoming every year more independent and nations more conscious of themselves—the scandals of pardons and the open selling of spiritual things upon every side—the scandal everywhere of clerical lives going side by side with the profession of a sacred caste and of its immunity from common penalties : all this made the protest universal and yet differing in degree and in object.

If you call every man who was at issue with the religious evils of the time a Reformer, then all Europe was made up of Reformers—save the sullen or cynical or merely stupid members of the privileged ecclesiastical body who stopped their ears and shut their eyes. But in the midst of these emotions, which in places had led to violent and open attack upon the official organization of the Church, its ceremonies, its discipline of celibacy, its religious orders ; which had led to violent denunciation of the Papacy as the key-stone of the arch, there was a spirit growing which was separate from the original general mood. It was a spirit which also gave itself the name of " Reform " but it intended something very different from Reform : it intended the establishment of a New Thing. It was to find its open expression at last, and its organization and personal being through the genius of Calvin—but not till ten years had passed from the date of which we speak, and not till twenty years after the capital date which had seen the publication of the New Testament of Erasmus.

If we return to the modern example of the revolt against Capitalism, we shall grasp the rise of that religious revolution four hundred years ago and the violent reaction against it.

To-day, because the protest against Industrial Capitalism has risen to great heights, it is felt to be threatening the very existence of society. In the same way the protest against official religion had, by 1525, reached a revolutionary degree and men began to fear for the stability of society. Hence the reaction against Barnes's sermon.

Industrial Capitalism may be defined as the corruption of a system which has always been admitted by European men—the system of private property. It has flourished under the protection which law and custom have extended to private property in essence, yet it has degraded property, allowing the swallowing up of the small man by the big one and the concentration of control in few and unworthy hands. Nevertheless, from the idea of private property did it spring, and by the remaining sanctity of private property is it protected. So also is it with that accompaniment of private property as an institution, the freedom of the family and the individual; freedom to make contracts and decide upon one's own activities. The great proletarian body of working men, now in such violent protest against the capitalist system, owe their existence to such freedom —though by the very exercise of that freedom they have largely lost it. They were free to accept such and such wages, or to refuse them; to drive their own bargain; in practice this has reduced them to the half-slavery we see around us. But freedom is still our social theory— and by its very operation we are creating those great monopolies which are the negation of freedom. Most men who protest against modern capitalism would still preserve property and freedom. Some, more clear-sighted than the rest, demand reforms which shall re-establish the old freedom and the old well-divided property among men and undo the evils of modern capitalism by returning to what were always the first principles of our civilization. But there is another spirit abroad which would undo the evils of capitalism by destroying the right to property and by destroying freedom. It would vest control in the officers of the State, reducing all men to a common slavery for the advantage of equal distribution and for ending the existing injustice. *That* demand, growing in volume, successfully rooted at last in one great state—Russia—made openly by small well-organized minorities on every side, threatens the very nature of our society : and against the Communist and his ideal society is now at war.

So it was in the parallel case of the early Reformation. The mere demand for reform began at last to seem to many an undermining of all that upon which European culture had been built. To denounce the vices and corruption of the clergy savoured of denouncing the Church itself which had made Europe and by which Europe still lived ; and the fear was the better founded because there *did* exist a growing body which *did* desire to destroy the Church—which aimed, not towards the purifying of the clerical body, the restoration of its due functions and zeal, but towards the denial and the destruction in doctrine and practice of the Catholic Church. Against this new protestant thing Society declared war.

Between the spirit which aimed at such destruction and denial, which zealously denounced the Mass for an abomination, attacked the whole sacramental system and was for sweeping away the sacred character of the priesthood, and the last lukewarm grumbler against this or that clerical due, this or that piece of simony or pluralism, there were infinite gradations. But more and more as time went on did the thing turn into a battle between two opponents—those who would preserve intact the great structure of the old Faith, its Liturgy and morals and affirmations of doctrine—

E   49

and those who would build up something quite new and different to act against it, to dethrone it, to take its place : and the Mass was the test.

In this year 1525, the thing had come to no such pass ; all was still in confusion, the line of demarcation between the two camps was not yet drawn. But the dread of disruption was in the air, and instinctively those who desired to preserve what had made Europe were ready to make war against what promised, in their eyes, to destroy Europe and indeed all society.

Therefore it was that such a sermon as Dr. Barnes, the Augustinian, preached on that Christmas Eve in St. Edward's Church in Cambridge, though there was in it no heresy, no denial of doctrine, was treated as though in spirit it was subversive : and men were beginning to take sides.

All authority was on the side of the Church, the great mass of people outside the Germanies were on the same side—especially were the English, with their conservative temperament and their attachment to institutions, upon that side ; but then also the imaginative strength of the English mind and its adventurous quality recruited men into the other : as yet a small body but one in which was burning intensely an appetite for change. Cranmer, the secretive scholar, hesitant, interested much more in his art of letters than in controversy, peering upon the manuscripts and newly printed books, interested and perhaps confused by the clamours that were rising, took no part but was moved on in his mind against the corporation he had joined. The Masses he said were said against the grain. The Church, its organization, its hierarchy of which he formed a part and to which he had pledged himself by oath, were growing distasteful. He had already begun to pray secretly for the relaxation of ecclesiastical power and particularly for the denial of the Papal claims. But he would risk nothing, nor openly appear in the new path which some few, more bold, were treading : he was wholly unfitted for perils as well as for rewards.

The months passed and left him still secluded : he was still outwardly of that England which was in the great mass following the old routines.

Then whispers reached Cambridge of something astir in London. When he heard, as did all men, of this new political interest it must have seemed to him at first but a distant thing connected with the Court and no affair of his, until it grew to occupy general discussion and to be in the conversation of all.

The King, no longer young (he was now, like Cranmer, in the middle thirties) was meditating some private policy on which there were rumours of every kind.

It had nothing to do with the religious debate : Henry was orthodox of the orthodox and had advertised himself openly as a champion of order and all the old strict scheme. He was devout. On the very central test of the Sacrament of the Altar and of the Mass he was even, being of an impulsive temper, enthusiastic.

What was he about ? In the next year, 1526, the formless rumours began to take shape, though few apprehended them ; in the next, the year 1527, came the great news—now certain : Henry would propose the repudiation of his wife, Catherine the Queen. The public pretext was that Catherine having been, nominally at least, his brother's wife, he was not lawfully married to her himself.

The elder Prince, Arthur, who had been called her husband for a few weeks, was only fifteen when he died. Henry had married Catherine as a maid. She had been devoted to him all these eighteen years. But Henry would now be rid of her, and the ground put forward was that old ceremony of a quarter of a century before.

To Cranmer, I say, remote in Cambridge, this Court news could only have been news like any other—save for one point : it involved a discussion in moral theology, the Catholic doctrine of marriage ; therefore it came directly into his field, for Theology he professed and taught and he examined in it.   On *that* side indeed his attention could not but be aroused.   Here was a professional interest. The examiner and lecturer in such things, the man who was teaching others in his humble way and had been honoured with a particular post in that department was immediately concerned and his mind must be at work.   With such a character as his, that mind would take at once whatever was the official side.   Warham, the saintly Archbishop of Canterbury, had listened to the King's professed doubts upon the validity of his marriage ; the all-powerful Wolsey was known to favour what was now called " The Divorce," for he would build upon it to further his foreign policy and secure a new marriage for the King which should confirm the French alliance by giving him for his new wife a French Princess.

Men were speaking also of the strong fascination and control which a young woman of the Court, Anne, the daughter of the Boleyns and a niece of the Duke of Norfolk, exercised over Henry ; but as yet, save at the Court itself, all that this fascination might mean was missed, and even at the Court its consequences were seen by very few—hardly beyond the circle of the Boleyns themselves.   The Great Cardinal himself had no suspicion of what was to come.

For the gentle, simple and dignified Queen Catherine all men felt sympathy.   They were familiar through portraiture and report with her broad smiling presence, her fair features—never beautiful but most pleasing— her admitted goodness.   She had worked well in the past, as Regent during Henry's brief absence on the wars abroad ; the great victory of Flodden more than ten years past over the Scottish national enemy had raised her in all men's eyes, for she had been in power when it was won and she had made the dispositions which rendered it possible. Nearly six years older than her husband, she had guided him well, and the long enduring affection between them had enhanced her position. She was the daughter of the great Spanish King who was dead, she was the aunt of the new Emperor. Her misfortunes endeared her to the English people. She had borne child after child to her husband and had suffered disappointments, for all those children save one had died in infancy or had come still-born, and her miscarriages were known. One heir alone remained, the hope of the country and of the still precarious dynasty, the little Princess Mary, to whom also the affection of the people went out.

Henry's new policy was exceedingly unpopular; the more would he need support wherever it could be found.

It was upon St. George's Day, the national feast, April the 23rd, 1527, that Henry had first declared himself; very privately to begin with, afterwards more openly. And what he was saying was this:

He was disturbed in conscience. The death of all those children, the absence of a male heir, he called proofs of Divine displeasure, and there were those about him and expecting reward who pretended to believe him.

It was clear that there would be opposition at Rome. The Emperor was very powerful. There had come a moment when his troops—without his leave, in an accident as it were—had sacked Rome and made the Pope, Clement VII, their prisoner. When Clement was free again, and moved by one strong set of political arguments to favour Henry's policy of divorce, he was yet also moved by considerations equally strong to hesitate. Germany was half lost to the Papacy; the Princes outside the Germanies, notably the powerful King of France, were threatening to declare their independence of Peter. There was talk of a Patriarchate of the West. Must the Pope lose England too? Would he not lose it if he denied Henry's claim? But then again, he must maintain the dignity of his office ; he was universal judge. The doctrine of indissoluble Christian marriage was a very sacred thing and he was the guardian of it. The woman whose repudiation upon the plea that her original marriage was void, because the Pope had had no right to give the dispensation for wedding a dead brother's wife, was a great Queen, and the people of England at least supported her ; and where would the Papacy be if the Pope himself admitted that its rights of dispensation could be questioned ?

There was in those days a famous monastic community living in Sion House upon the Thames. A monk of that community had made, in this year 1527, a pregnant suggestion and had laid it before the King. Might not the *Universities of Europe* be consulted, and their decision—supposing it were in favour of the King's claim—be opposed to the obstinacy and delay of the Head of the Church ?

The Universities were the oracles of the time; in them the Canon Law was taught ; by their Doctors of Divinity the details of moral theology were thrashed out ; their decisions had over and over again been of chief weight when the Great Councils, which had been summoned during the divisions of the Papacy, a century before, had assumed the right to end the distractions of Christendom. Their voice might well be predominant now : let them be appealed to.

It is possible that the suggestion had reached the ears of those who were disputing on the matter at Cambridge ; it is probable that Cranmer had heard of it ; at any rate it was an obvious suggestion enough under the circumstances of the time, and it was a suggestion which flattered the corporate body to which Cranmer belonged.

But it was not in Henry's character to do anything quickly and with decision. Though he was impulsive, vain, and feverishly excitable when he thought himself thwarted, though he was passionate in obtaining things which he desired—especially if they were things of appetite—yet he always delayed in matters of policy; hesitating between various courses, putting off, as sensual men who are essentially weak always will, a final decision. Moreover, the great lines of State policy were in the hands of others. Wolsey was still master of the King as of the Kingdom, and although his sovereign had now partly passed under the control of another (for Anne Boleyn's influence already rivalled or was greater than the Cardinal's), Henry had not yet summoned the resolution to do anything of public moment upon his own initiative.

Therefore that proposal made so early in the affair, in 1527, to take the opinion of the Universities of Europe and to use it, if it were favourable, for putting pressure upon the Pope, lingered. Two years passed and nothing had been done. It would be so much better if possible to do the thing in the regular way and to get the decision from Rome. It was the line of least resistance, though resistance was there.

During 1528 the effort continued. Anne's part in it was now publicly known. It made Henry's action in the eyes of the bulk of his subjects more odious than ever. But officially-minded men and especially men professionally connected with technical questions of theology were remote from public opinion in these matters—and of such was Cranmer.

There was in that same year, 1528 (when, by slow steps, the Pope was being shepherded into appointing a Court to try the case), an occasion upon which Cranmer might have met prematurely the King under whom his public life was to be launched. He was sent up to the Court by his college to plead in the matter of certain rights of property for the college interests, and there he met one who was also to be of high moment in his life— Thomas Cromwell. That strong, close, determined and unscrupulous character had already become a manager

55

for Wolsey, perhaps the chief manager of his affairs, and it was with him that Cranmer had to deal during his visit to the capital. There did he set eyes for the first time upon the powerful lowering face, with its deep-set small eyes, heavy jowl, and unrevealing level brows; the face which later was to spread such terror throughout England. Thomas Cromwell was the older man of the two, as well as far the more dominating; and in meeting him Cranmer first came up against those forces of Government admission to which at once flattered and terrified his shrinking scholarly soul. He was successful in his mission; he returned; he had made his first slight contact with the great world of public affairs, but only thus, indirectly, and in a minor matter He remained obscure.

There came the news to Cambridge of the great final events which were to end in Wolsey's fall; the Pope had consented to appoint the Court for which Wolsey had been working so hard, he had consented that it should sit in England under the King's eye and influence, he had named for Judges in that Court where they should act as his Legates—in his name and exercising his power —two men who were both of them in their different ways English Prelates: Wolsey himself, the Chancellor and ruler, Cardinal Archbishop of York and Bishop of Winchester as well; from the Pope's own side, the learned—the universally respected—Campeggio, master of the canon law, Advocate at Rome for English affairs and endowed with the Bishopric of Worcester.

The Pope did more, in his eager desire to retain the allegiance of England in those times when the allegiance of every Prince to him was shaken; he gave a document to Campeggio, a formal Bull, in which he admitted (a further weakness) that *if* the marriage between Prince Arthur and Catherine had been a true marriage—that is, if the boy in the brief interval between the wedding and his death had consummated the marriage—then by ecclesiastical law Papal dispensation could not hold; and more than that still, he gave Campeggio a written promise to take with him that he would abide by the decision of this Court, which he had set up under the King's influence and under men who received the revenues of English Sees; he promised not to allow a further appeal to Rome whatever the decision should be.

We do not know the exact terms either of the Decretal Bull which spoke of marriage with a deceased brother's wife as unlawful or of the "pollicitation" as it was called, the promise not to recall the case to Rome; for, by a further piece of deplorable weakness which he took for diplomacy, Clement VII forbade Campeggio to make either document public or to hand either to anyone in England; he was to read them in the presence of the King, he was to refuse to give them up or to have them copied. Also, when he had read them he was to destroy them; which he did.

It is likely enough that there was inserted into each document some phrase which limited each condition so that the Pope could plead his technical right to break the implied pledge contained in each. At any rate, he went thus far, and the impression was universal that when the Legatine Court should have come to its conclusions the affair would be settled. The impression was equally strong, seeing how the Court was to be composed and where it was to sit, that Henry would have his way. Still Clement played for time. Campeggio, who had the excuse of age and suffering, for he was tortured with the gout, journeyed north as slowly as possible; excuses for further delay were made after he had arrived in the island; but at long last the Court opened, in the early summer of 1529, sitting in the Hall of the Black Friars on the western side of the City of London over against the river.

Its proceedings filled all men's mouths, and at Cambridge, as at each other centre where men conversant with the arguments discussed the matter, it seemed that a verdict such as Henry desired was at hand. Through the last days of June, through the first days of July, the case continued, but upon the 23rd of July, 1529, further great news came to startle those who were expectant of the result. Campeggio suddenly adjourned the Court, pleading the practice of Rome and the summer vacation observed by the lawyers of the Curia, the Pope's Court. Other news, yet graver, had not yet reached England but was on its way—already, a fortnight before, the Pope had decided to recall the case to Rome and to allow Catherine's appeal. For she had refused to admit the authority of the Court, on the ground that it would be influenced, being composed of Henry's own Prelates and sitting under his eyes and in his realm.

The thing came like an explosion, for Wolsey concurred. He was publicly insulted, and it was certain now that Anne would have her way; that the Cardinal would fall and that she alone would have possession of Henry's conduct and mind. None could doubt that the great change had come, and that by her and through her Henry was determined on a new course. For to attain the divorce in one fashion or another Anne was determined. She would be Queen.

While these things were toward, in that hot height of summer, the recurrent terror of those days—the plague —had appeared. And Henry to find safety from it had left his capital and moved from place to place, ending on the 4th of August at Waltham, where was the great Abbey which Harold, the last Saxon King, had founded just before the Conquest. It was far enough from London to be safe, near enough for the Court to receive dispatches rapidly and to send orders to officials. This presence of Henry and his Court at Waltham was critical to the fate of Cranmer.

He happened at that moment to be living in the house of a certain gentleman called Cressy, in or near

Waltham. This man was in some way connected with him, for it was said that Cressy's wife (they were both of them of much the same rank as Cranmer—small landed people with arms) was some relative of the Cranmer family. Cranmer was acting in Cressy's house as tutor to his sons during the vacation, a work which the lesser academic men of his sort often undertook, work which had been the beginning of the great Wolsey's career many years before, when he had performed the same office in the great household of the Dorsets—through whose favour he obtained his first appointments. But Cressy's house was not of this sort, it was humble enough, and suitable to Cranmer's own inconspicuous position.

There were at that moment in Waltham with the King, that is, upon the 6th of August and during the days following, two high officials whose names we have already met, Gardiner and Fox, both of Cambridge, both ecclesiastics, upon whose services Henry and Anne Boleyn greatly relied. The more important of them, Stephen Gardiner, was a man of powerful intelligence, of great activity, devoted to the Crown, thoroughly official, with a well-ordered mind and strong will. Fox, also an official, equally devoted to the Crown in that capacity but with less initiative, stood with him there at Waltham. Both he and Gardiner had been used by Henry and Anne to put pressure upon the Pope in the discussions of the past years, and Gardiner in particular had spoken with violence and insistence to Clement's face, insisting on the King's demand; and through this act had become all the more grateful to Anne and the man who was now so thoroughly in her power. Fox had been used in the same work.

Now it was so ordered by Cranmer's fate that these two men should be sent to lodge in Cressy's house. When the great company of the Court moved, as it constantly did, up and down the country, especially when the King was hunting, as he now was, and had to combine his amusements with public business, there was not house-room for all save when the King happened to be staying in one of his own greater places. Here at Waltham it was necessary to billet out the greater people, at least, in houses fit to receive them, and such a house was that of the gentleman Cressy, who was ordered to receive these two principal officials of Henry's train.

So all things converged towards what was to come. Fox and Gardiner were Henry's chief agents; they were Cambridge men to whom the local Cambridge reputation of Cranmer both for learning and for literary ability and power of exposition were known. They were thrown with him under the same roof at the moment when, after the failure of the Legatine Court to decide the issue, some new policy must be undertaken. And in Cressy's house, Cranmer talking—as everyone then talked—of the great affair, was heard by Fox and Gardiner to repeat the suggestion already entertained these two years past that an appeal to the Universities of Europe could put a powerful weapon into the King's hands. They carried the news to Henry. He heard it and did nothing. Though new conditions had arisen which made the repetition of this suggestion (by a man whom he now heard was of some standing in Cambridge) of special value, Henry postponed action, as he always did; moreover, he must presumably first consult Anne Boleyn.

So Henry left Waltham and weeks passed, but the advice remained in his mind. Cranmer had taken unwittingly the first step that was to lead him to his very high exaltation, to his ultimate effect upon the religion of England; and to his own doom.

IV

THE TESTING

SO Henry the King halted. He was for ever hesitating, and drawing back, temporizing, save in those moments. when he exploded under impulse and did something violent—usually against those whom he felt to be managing him, and against whose management he had rebelled, though unable to shake it off.

It was as early as the first days of August, on the 9th of that month, that Gardiner and Fox had brought him Cranmer's renewal of the old advice to consult the Universities of Europe. But August passed and nothing more was done. In the interval he must have heard of Cranmer's qualifications, of his reticence, lack of enemies, wide reading and suave address. It is to be presumed that Henry had also been told what a good penman Cranmer was, that Cranmer's Cambridge reputation had been gone into, and that someone— would it not be the Boleyns ?—had thought of him as a useful advocate.

But the summer passed and the autumn; it was already winter before Henry made up his mind even on the minor matter of using Thomas Cranmer's abilities for writing out a brief.

It was not till the early dark days of November that the King sent for him. So Cranmer came to the Palace at Greenwich, where it stood—a vast long pile of building, battlemented, three stories high—and towering above it, near a dozen turrets, ending in that sort of inverted cup shape which one may see on so many Tudor buildings—notably on Henry VII's Chapel at Westminster, and repeated with wearisome repetition upon the modern Houses of Parliament. Into that teeming and noisy world of the Court came this timid and gentle-mannered middle-aged scholar; all his leanings towards the religious revolution which was sounding abroad in Europe and had sent its echoes to Cambridge kept well within his own breast. He came in and saw the King.

What he saw was a large fat man, not yet quite forty (in his thirty-ninth year), coarse, with a straggling thin reddish beard on his very broad, flat face, small deep-set grey-green eyes far apart under very slight eyebrows upon either side of a rather shapeless nose. The face was not yet brutal; it was intelligent; there was in the whole carriage of the body a strength which the horrible disease from which the man suffered had already affected but had not yet undermined.

There is a record, not contemporary but sufficient (for it was a moment that would linger in the memory), of what passed between them.

Henry said to Thomas Cranmer—the short and sturdy figure risen from his knees: " Were you not at Waltham in company with my Almoner (Fox) and my Secretary (Gardiner) ? "

Cranmer humbly answered that he was.

" Had you not converse with them concerning our matter of the Divorce, now in question after this sort ? "

And Cranmer answered: " That is right true, as it please your Highness."

Then Henry said: " Well, I well perceive that you have the right scope of this matter " (that is, the right view of it). " You must understand that I have been long troubled in conscience, and now I perceive that by this means " (he was speaking of the appeal to the Universities) " I might have been long ago relieved from the same if I had this way proceeded." So Henry —with great prolixity of words, as was his wont; and he went on : " Therefore, Master Doctor, I pray you and nevertheless, because you are a subject, I command you—all your other business and affairs set apart, to take some pains to see this my cause to be furthered, according to your advice, as much as it may lie in you."

So was Cranmer given his commission, and so did he enter great affairs.

It was a great honour, but it was also some peril. Cranmer would much rather have been back among his books. He dared suggest that the two Universities of England, Oxford and Cambridge, should first take this thing in hand and make out a case; so would Cranmer be free of so much responsibility. But to that suggestion Henry answered:

"You say well, and I am content therewith. But nevertheless I would have you specially to write your word therein."

So the thing was sealed, and the unwilling Doctor of Divinity was taken by the shoulders and set with his face down that road which henceforth he must follow.

In the Court at that time Anne Boleyn was of course never far from the King, and her father was in attendance. Henry sent for him. That courtier and diplomat, brother-in-law of Norfolk, continuously great figure in the King's affairs, Thomas Boleyn, for four years past a peer, the man who was waiting so eagerly and so secretly to see his daughter Queen, came at Henry's bidding.

The King said to him, showing him the reluctant scholar:

"I pray you, let Dr. Cranmer have entertainment at your house at Durham Place for a time."

So it was that Cranmer went up river on the tide to the water steps of Durham House, and under that roof, where at last he would be at peace and separate from the noise and movement that fitted him ill, he wrote and wrote in his slow careful fashion through the weeks that followed.

He was in no hurry to end, nor was the King, for that matter, in a hurry to press him: the King because he would still linger, wondering whether he would or would not—Cranmer, we may be sure, always willing to postpone. Anne bided her time.

There under that roof, in his priest's dress and perhaps already, what he later certainly was, chaplain to the young woman who was the eldest daughter and who had thrown her net over the King, saying his Mass in the chapel there, Cranmer became the intimate and the servant of the Boleyn family, whose fortunes were to be tightly woven in with his own. There would he see Anne daily when she returned from the Palace, dark-haired, with black and brilliant eyes : the insistent presence of Anne, with her French speech and sharpness, her readiness for mastery, her indifference to offending others, her quickness against offence to herself.

It was well on into the January of the next year, 1530, before the brief was concluded, and already Henry had dispatched his first envoys to begin consulting the Universities of Europe. Once more the King sent for Cranmer when he heard that the writing set him was accomplished ; the brief was clear, and its thesis was what the King desired : " It was against the law of God and therefore not open to dispensation by the Pope to marry the wife of a brother after that brother's death." Henry read the matter and approved. He said to Cranmer this time, " Will you abide before the Pope* by this that you have here written ? " and Cranmer answered, " That will I do, by God's Grace, if your Majesty do send me thither." But first he was ordered to Cambridge, where copies of what he had set forth on paper had been sent to the authorities in Church law ; he himself following after to make certain of the votes and opinions. Later it was said in his praise that he had brought over half a dozen of the Doctors of Divinity to approve of Henry's case.

* In our only account of all this written by a contemporary, but much later, the Pope is called " Bishop of Rome." I do not believe that the King would have used that phrase in the early days of 1530.

It was perhaps at the end of that month, January, or perhaps at the beginning of the next, that he went off in the train of that host of his, Boleyn, Lord Wiltshire, to whom and to whose daughter he was now bound, for the journey to Italy. There that host and master was to be Henry's Ambassador not only to the Pope but to the Emperor. It was an embassy impudent enough! One in which the father of the woman who had captured Henry and was pressing for the repudiation of the Emperor's own aunt, the Queen of England, was empowered as Henry's representative to ask the Emperor to yield! So went they off in a body, with Wiltshire at their head, the clerics about him. They went southward slowly enough, if only for the sake of dignity. It was a pace that suited Cranmer well (though *he* would not be consulted), until, upon the 13th or 14th of March,* they entered Bologna, where, not three weeks before, Charles V had received the Imperial Crown from Clement's hands—the last of the Emperors to be anointed and installed by a Pope.

The large walled university town into which Thomas Boleyn and his train, with Cranmer amongst them, rode in that Italian spring down the broad Emilian Way, with the Apennines hard by against the west, was still resounding with the arms of the Hapsburg, filled with his retinue, his German, Spanish, French, Italian men-at-arms; the last festivities of the great Coronation lingered in the market-place and the streets, under the huge simple brick oblong of that Cathedral in which the splendid ceremonial had passed.

They came late for what they had to do; a week before they had ridden in through the gate Clement had issued the official document ordering Henry to take back his

---

* The only evidence I know of the exact date is the letter of Casale written on the 12th to the effect that the Ambassadors will arrive on the next day or the day after that.

wife and forbidding any new marriage to take place before sentence had been pronounced.

The importance of that document may be exaggerated. It was only a matter of course: the Pope had not pronounced and therefore it was reasonable that he should warn Henry against the consequences of action until sentence was passed. Also a brief of this kind was revocable. There was nothing final about it. It was what is called nowadays a " gesture." If it looked unfriendly to Henry's cause, it must be remembered that the Pope was playing continually one side against the other. He had to soothe the Emperor, but he had also to retain Francis of France, the Emperor's enemy. To retain Francis he had to retain the much less important allegiance of England, the cause of whose King the King of France was pleading.

The arrival of the English Ambassadors was badly timed, their body was still more badly composed, and its composition was an excellent example of the power Anne Boleyn wielded over the unfortunate Henry. To send her own father to the Emperor with the demand that he should turn against the honour of his family, when, in the words of Catherine, " Anne was the scandal of Christendom," was an ineptitude. Yet Henry had obeyed and had sent Anne's father on that mission.

The English Embassy came into the presence of Charles, and Cranmer heard the strong reprimand with which Boleyn was received. For as that courtier, all of whose fortunes turned upon his daughter's capture of the English King, opened his mouth to speak, the Emperor called in a hard voice, " Stop. Let Boleyn's colleague speak, not he; for you," he shot at Boleyn, " are party in the cause." (All this was in French, the tongue in which Charles V thought and spoke, and in French was Boleyn's answer.)

Boleyn took the broadside stolidly. Indeed, all we

know of this man (which is very little) shows him to be stolid. He had proved himself stolid in doing anything he was told by his master : he was to prove himself stolid six years later when he allowed the vilest accusations against his daughter to pass without protest and her death to be decreed with no plea for mercy from his lips.

Boleyn answered to the Emperor that his office as Ambassador had nothing to do with the interests of Anne, but with the service of his master the King of England—he was there to speak for his Sovereign, not for his child. He was authorized to offer something like one million pounds of our money as compensation for Queen Catherine, and to restore her dowry and to give security for an ample household and maintenance for her ; to which Charles replied that he was not pre-pared to sell his aunt. He said, what was necessarily the opinion of all Christendom behind him in that day, that the cause was before the only lawful tribunal, that of the Pope : he would accept its judgment. If it were against Catherine he would hold his tongue. But if the Pope's decision were in her favour, then, and only then, would he support her with all his powers.

It was a quarrel rather than an Embassy, but in the midst of that strain Cranmer, though he was the Boleyns' man, though coming from under the Boleyns' roof and soon to be (if he were not already) Anne's chaplain, moved quietly.* He seems to have excited no anger against himself (it is true his position was subordinate) ; he had perhaps already given evidence of that courtesy in manner which later was to lead him on further into his evil fortunes.

For Fate was serving him as well for the moment, as ill for the future, as it was serving Anne, and his suavity, which was native to him, his timidity, which was still

---

* Gardiner has shown that Professor Pollard is wrong in saying that Cranmer was not Anne's chaplain. We have the evidence of Charles' envoy in England.

more deeply a part of himself, was paving the way for
his use in larger affairs. He must have wished himself
well out of it all, but he was caught; and caught by that
very urbanity for which he was most praised.

This effort to arrange things with the Emperor having
failed, the next business was to consult the Italian
Universities. It must be remembered that the scheme
had behind it the full authority of Wolsey; Wolsey
had fallen months before and was now living in trembling
expectation, hoping against hope for the King's favour
to be restored, yet knowing that his case was desperate.
None the less, the momentum of his policy survived
his misfortunes. Everyone knew, even Henry, bad as
his judgment was, that what Wolsey had decided to be
a good move should be a move to follow.

While, therefore, the other Universities were being
consulted it was now the business of these men in
Italy, having arrived in the south, to consult the Italian
academies.

They had obtained a brief from Clement in which
the members of the Universities were bidden to speak
their full minds upon the lawfulness or unlawfulness of
marriage with a deceased brother's wife.* Boleyn and
Lee, the King's Almoner, who was of that company,
went back by way of France some weeks later. Stokesley,
who had also been among them and had been nominated
to the Bishopric of London, was left to deal with the
University of Bologna. He had plenty of money with
which to gather opinions, so, of course, had also the
Emperor's agents. But Stokesley did something better

---

* Professor Pollard expresses his surprise (on page 44 of his "Thomas
Cranmer") that any of the Universities in Italy should have favoured Henry's
contentions seeing that Clement had prepared a Bull forbidding Doctors of
Divinity and other officers from maintaining the invalidity of Henry's marriage
before the sentence was pronounced. Professor Pollard may not be acquainted
with this brief in which the members of the Universities were bidden to pronounce freely, but he ought to have been—or, if he was not, he ought not to
have been so positive.

than merely bribe; he got a secret, hurried, irregular decision from Pallavicino and four others of the Carmelites signed on the 10th of June, and bamboozled Henry with this as being the decision of the whole University of Bologna; something which highly delighted the King, not only because Bologna was one of the greatest Universities of Europe but also because it belonged to the Papal States.

In the University of Ferrara Croke, another of the band, had singular adventures. The Doctors of Divinity could not agree. The document signed by those who voted for the King of England was forcibly carried away by the learned Doctors of the other side. It was recaptured and sent on to Henry as the decision of the University as a whole. When it came to the Doctors of Civil and Canon Law there was a hitch. Croke offered £500 or rather more. They sneered at it. He offered half as much again, but by this time they had grown frightened and said they would have nothing to do with the business.

From the University of Padua Croke did get an answer in favour of Henry; we do not know how it was obtained, but we do know that it cost rather more than £500.*

At Venice Croke and Cranmer together worked in the cause, but Cranmer, writing shortly after from Rome, deplored their lack of success.

Cranmer was ordered on to Rome. It had been discovered that his non-combative manner and quiet address could do something in favour of Anne. He had already begun by challenging, after the fashion of the time, any Doctor of Divinity in Rome to debate with him the root matter (as it had now become) of whether marriage with a deceased brother's wife were forbidden by the law of God or no. He went down

* Professor Pollard puts the matter thus : " Ferrara, Bologna, and Padua determined in the English favour."

from the north of Italy to Rome in that boiling summer of 1530 and fell ill, as well he might, recovered again, and wrote (the month was July) to tell Henry that he had but small results and excusing himself by saying that in Rome itself no one dared speak for fear of the Pope—which was not true, for the discussion was general, but a natural thing to say to Henry.

He got nothing from Clement VII. What Henry and Anne wanted him to get was at least a brief in their favour, but Clement played him off against the Imperial interests and the Imperial interests against him, marking time because time was the one element which might possibly work in favour of the distracted Head of the Church—torn as he was during the great religious revolution of Europe between his desire to preserve the mighty friendship of the Emperor and his particular solicitude for Henry, whom he had so greatly befriended and who had stood so strongly for orthodoxy during the violent beginnings of the Lutheran revolt.

But Clement did what he could. He flattered Cranmer, and Cranmer's employers Henry and Anne as well, by giving this chaplain of Anne's a high and fairly lucrative post, making him what was called Penitentiary for England.

Cranmer did not leave Rome till the September of that year, 1530. On the whole he had failed.

But we must note these points :

First, that he played quite a minor rôle, in which, if something was expected of him by Anne and the King, it was only because they knew (and especially did Anne, in whose daily intimacy he had lived) something of his literary capacity and scholarship. Next, that he was also now known to them both to be so pliable as to make a willing instrument in anything they might choose to do. Also that this soft and quiet manner of his would make him a specially useful instrument in negotiation with Charles, for it was only too easy to exasperate the

Emperor—insulted as he was by Anne's position at Court and by the gross indignities put upon his aunt, the Queen of England. Lastly, let us note that his colleagues in the Italian embassy had begun to remark Cranmer's favour with the woman who was all-powerful with the King. They flatter him in their letters home, and they profess to regard him as having shown superior skill to themselves. They, especially Croke, confide in him—because they now know that through him the ear of Anne can be reached and that Anne is ruling.

So Cranmer came back to England and was given as payment for his services a slice of ecclesiastical revenue —the revenue attaching to the Archdeaconry of Taunton in Somerset. Taunton was also the borough for which Thomas Cromwell, now the manager of the King's political affairs, having stepped into Wolsey's shoes, was nominally member in Parliament. Not that it mattered very much where he was member for, these things were, in the case of a man acting directly from the King, a mere official label. But the name of Taunton brings the two men together. This Thomas Cromwell, whom Cranmer had first met three years before in the little obscure affair of the College property, was to be yoke-fellow with Cranmer in so much that follows! A wolf and a sheep-dog in harness!

That next year, 1531, was the year in which Convocation, after lengthy debate and compromise in which the King had to retreat somewhat from his original position, admitted Henry's title to Supremacy over the Church of England, " So far as the law of Christ allows it."

Because of what followed this declaration has loomed very large in English history. It was important, but of nothing like the importance generally given to it. There was no repudiation of Papal Supremacy. The declaration was novel, but in nine things out of ten only conformed to the admitted position of the Sovereign, who had the practical regulation of everything in his kingdom, who nominated to all the great Abbacies and Bishoprics and clerical posts. The recognition of his practical Headship must have seemed to the average layman a matter of course; though to put it down in black and white that a layman was thus chief in Church matters was a shock to the trained Churchmen—and they felt it. But Warham, the aged Archbishop of Canterbury, though reluctant, and admitting his dread of the King's absolute temporal power, did not think it a breach with the past, nor for that matter did Henry himself. Nor did the Pope. The Pope was still head of the Church Universal; recognized fully as such by Henry and so regarding himself and so acting. The real break was to come much later, and after, as before, this act on the part of Convocation in 1531 things went on much the same.

Anyhow, Cranmer had nothing to do with it; he was not a member of Convocation and he does not seem to have taken any indirect part in the business at all. What he was asked to do, and it was of some moment, was to report for Henry and Anne upon a document most disturbing to their plans—I mean the considered argument against the Divorce drawn up by Reginald Pole.

Reginald Pole was in a very different class from anyone else connected with Henry's policy of divorce. He was, through his mother, as much a Plantagenet as Henry. Henry had both favoured and feared this younger cousin who stood in the heart of the Court. He was universally respected, and his power of judging the inner motives and the real facts of this unpleasant business of Henry's infatuation was something utterly different from the guess-work of outsiders, and the merely official subservience of the bureaucrats. His voice, should it sound publicly, would be heard all over Europe; no one would doubt his sincerity, and what was more important, no one would doubt his knowledge of the most secret details. We all know what difference there is between a man in the heart of a wealthy governing clique, a man belonging to it socially from the experience of his daily life, and a man of lower position outside.

Now Reginald Pole, strong as were his convictions and upright as was his following of those convictions, had been very reluctant to break with the King. He even served the King during the soliciting of the Universities of Christendom. He had worked to get decisions in France, and particularly from the great University of Paris, in favour of Henry, which Francis (as Henry's ally against the Emperor) had compelled his subjects to give. But Henry had himself asked Pole to give his views on the question of the divorce, and Pole had performed his task not only faithfully but, I think one may say, magnificently—at great risk, with lucidity and determination.

This private pamphlet of Pole's, intended at first for Henry's eyes alone, came as a heavy blow. It spoke of things which only Henry and Pole and very few others could have known; it especially emphasized the overwhelming part which Anne had played in the affair. It struck at Henry's very heart by testifying from Pole's own knowledge as an intimate and close relative, that the initiative had come not from Henry himself, the victim, but from this masterful woman.

Cranmer, now admittedly an expert in the affair of writing an exposition, read the book and was gravely affected by it. He reported that it was of such strength that if it were published the whole people might turn against the King. They were already angry. They were already strongly in favour of Catherine's cause. Since the Queen was popular, and her daughter, the heiress to the throne, the young Princess Mary, was an idol, the hope of the kingdom, Pole's revelation, if it were to appear, said Cranmer, might be fatal. Cranmer's advice was taken, and for the moment the dangerous thing was suppressed. We must remember this intellectual and political conflict between the hired scholar and the Royal cousin who was later to supplant Cranmer himself in the Archbishopric.

Early in the next year, on the 24th of January, 1532, came the next step, and a considerable one, in Cranmer's progress. He was instructed to go abroad again and act as Orator to Cæsar, that is, to be virtually Ambassador to the Emperor Charles V in his own kingdoms.

In theory the Emperor, being superior to all Kings, could not have an Ambassador present in the Court of any inferior, but only an Envoy; similarly no King could send an Ambassador to the Emperor but only someone to " plead for him " before Cæsar. It was but a technicality; the real point was that Cranmer was thus chosen to put the case as well as he could before Charles, to mollify him as well as possible, to get some compromise upon this proposed repudiation of Charles's aunt—sprung like himself from the great line of Spain, and like himself one of the half-dozen high crowned heads in Europe, against whom such indignities were proposed. At the same time Cranmer was to play upon the revolt of the Princes of the Empire. Each of these was a little King in his own district, and many of them were now using the religious turmoil, the Lutheran movement and all the religious enthusiasms behind it, as an engine not only for seizing the wealth of the Church but also for denying the nominal power of the Imperial Crown over them.

So Cranmer went off on his embassy. He hardly understood the scale of the task committed to him, and certainly not the further responsibilities to which it might lead.

V

THE CALL

CRANMER went off to the Germanies—a singular example of bad judgment upon the part of the two people who were to find him so useful a servant —Henry and Anne. He had that single qualification of a mild and popular manner ; he would not offend Charles. He would not exasperate the tension already existing. He had also what was for Henry and Anne the best qualification of all, that his will would be entirely submissive to the will of royalty and royalty's mistress. There was no danger in such a servant of separate initiative. Henry, when he thought of Cranmer, was quite rid of that uneasy suspicion with which all strong characters filled him—that they might in the end play the master and could only be got rid of by an outburst. Anne would be equally certain that there was no danger of Cranmer's advising Henry, whether on foreign or domestic affairs, in a direction different from her own. He would do what he was told.

He had not only to woo the Emperor round, if that were possible, to an acceptance of Henry's divorce policy—or at least to neutrality in it ; he had also to get into touch with the Lutheran princes and suggest to them secretly the support which Henry and the French King Francis were prepared to give them, under cover, in any rebellion they chose to raise against the Imperial crown. Further, he was to try and get the Lutheran divines of all shades who already had so much power in Germany to accept Henry's policy. " Surely," they thought in the Palace at Greenwich, " Surely it would be easy enough to get Luther and his clerical followers to approve of a plea which constantly appealed to the Bible and as constantly embarrassed Rome."

Lastly, he was to try and get better terms for English trade in the Netherlands—what to-day we call Belgium and Holland. The Netherlands were a part of Charles V's dominions inherited from his Burgundian ancestor, and the London merchants who found their principal market there were anxious to improve the trade.

The whole thing broke down. An abler man than Cranmer, or, at any rate, one abler in the province of negotiation and intrigue, might have effected something, though he would not have effected all. He might in particular have had success with his fellow-priests in Germany, who were also fellow-doubters with him— they were already rebels openly against Catholic doctrine: he as yet only in his heart. Yet he got no result at all; and the only thing he brought back from that connection with the Lutheran ferment was one of its younger ladies.

The clerical body in Germany which had revolted with Luther against Rome had many reasons for opposing Henry's policy. They were not crafty men; they did not think out policy; they acted mainly from personal reasons and from emotion. They could not forgive Henry's championship of the Papacy in the early days of the revolt: Henry's book, especially directed against the head of their movement, a book attacking Luther by name. That book had put a stamp on him. Moreover, he was strongly Catholic. He stood permanently in their eyes for that overt executive power supporting tradition which it was their whole business to undermine. He had been a King, standing with all the force of his Kingdom against them. Further, Henry, though now at some friction with the Papacy, was at no friction with the Mass and was devoted with an intense personal conviction to that one Catholic doctrine the denial of which was the pivot of all their efforts. For Henry was a strong believer in the Blessed Sacrament, loved the Mass and worshipped the Real Presence of Our Lord on the altar. Such orthodoxy was the only thing of any importance on which he remained steadfast during the whole of his life, while being in all other matters pulled hither and thither by vanity, appetite, fits of rage and sudden whims. Henry stood for the Mass—and to destroy the Mass was the main business of the anti-Catholic Reformation.

To some extent also they felt with their race (for you cannot call it their nation). The Empire had come to be German, and the Lutheran movement was a very German thing. Charles was not sufficiently German for them ; he was a French-speaking Burgundian. Catherine was a Spaniard. But they were proud of the Hapsburg blood, and Henry's insult to the Hapsburgs in the person of Catherine moved them. Then, again, Henry's policy was all mixed up with a discussion on the Papal power of dispensation—admitting it here, questioning it there, but basing all the action of the divorce upon the conception that such a power was in the nature of things and that the only point to be determined was the limits under which it might be exercised. But the Lutheran movement was for destroying the Papacy and denying its power altogether.

These were the obstacles against which Cranmer would come when he had to deal with the vigorous angry men who were leading the great religious revolt. Had he been quite other than what he was he might have played a skilful double game, making out to them privately and by hints, without too much committing himself, that Henry would ultimately be on their side and representing to his master at home that they were thinking of yielding to his ideas out of respect for him.

Of all such finesse Cranmer was quite incapable. His was a character that would contradict itself without hesitation at the orders of a superior, but not one that would enjoy or practise, or even pretend to the practice of, two contradictory policies for a common end ; yet to practise the pretence of two contradictory policies is the essence of diplomacy. And sometimes a pretence of three is even better than a pretence of two.

I have said that all he got out of the Lutherans was a lady, and that fruit of his mission was certainly startling.

The thing happened thus. In his painfully useless efforts to conciliate the Emperor, Cranmer, having joined the Court at Ratisbon, followed it to Nuremberg, where Charles was to negotiate with the anti-Catholic Princes. That awful menace which overhung Christendom and seemed to the men of the time so much more important even than the religious quarrels—I mean the Turkish threat to destroy our civilization—directly struck at the Germanies. The Turk had overrun Hungary ; he threatened the valley of the upper Danube ; if he conquered there as he had conquered lower down the river all our race and culture was at stake.

So fearful a peril worked upon both parties, the Emperor and the Princes ; it made the Emperor willing to delay, for the moment at least, in his plan of conquering the religious rebellion. It made him willing to give, in a sort of truce, licence to the revolted Princes and States so that they might keep the spoils of the Church on which they had laid hands, and follow what doctrines they would. As for the Princes, it gave them a reason on their side to rally to the common German cause and therefore to meet the Emperor half way. Cranmer, who trailed after the Court as a sort of passenger, effecting nothing, had to be with the Emperor in Nuremberg.

Now Nuremberg held at this time a prominent member of the new Gospellers ; a priest of course, as they all were originally ; an Augustinian as Luther had been, and Barnes at Cambridge. The order was fruitful in such. Also (it was a mark of these ex-priests of the Lutheran movement) he had early broken his vows of celibacy. This man, who came from near by the city, took to himself the semi-Classical name of Osiander, his original German name being Andrew Hosmer or Hosemann or Heligmann. He was a rough, coarse, energetic fellow, not unlearned, and still comparatively young—nearly ten years younger than Cranmer. He had entered the priesthood at the earliest canonical age, in his twenty-second year, attained some fame as a preacher, joined the Lutheran movement, and, of course, married within five years of his ordination. As with so many of his colleagues in the movement, the vulgarity of his language and the violent self-assertion which went with his driving power, while they made him odious to opponents, only raised him the more in his own world. His fame was further swollen by his vehement irruptions into the theological controversies of the religious Revolutionaries, and amid all that welter of discussion he started a line of his own, or at any rate somewhat divergent from that of Luther, the master.

Cranmer fell not only into his acquaintance but into his intimacy. There could be no doubt on which side the dynamic energy lay: the Osiander family with its loud tone, or Cranmer. So Cranmer got too intimate with them, and behold he found himself married to the niece of this man, very much younger than himself, a girl called Mary, or Anne, or perhaps both.

I say " he found himself married." We have no details ; we can only judge from the man's character ; we do not even know enough about Mary (or Anne) to tell what part she played : whether she were a victim of her uncle or a puppet or a principal. There, again, we have to guide us only the general knowledge that in most cases where an elderly man is thus caught the initiative does not, as a rule, lie with himself but with the more vigorous younger blood. Especially would this be true when, as in the case of Cranmer, the action was dangerous in the extreme to the older partner. It was dangerous in the extreme for Cranmer, a select cleric of Henry's, to marry : for Henry was violent against the marriage of his priests, in that year 1532. A very dangerous action is hardly undertaken by a shrinking man unless he is captured. Anyhow, Cranmer was caught, and he was something of a catch considering the official position which he held and the steady clerical income with which Henry had endowed him.

Consider the enormity of the occasion. We must remember what the conditions were. That a cleric already advanced in a political career should take a mistress in those days was nothing abnormal ; that he should take a wife, that he should go through an official ceremony of marriage, was a proclamation of open rebellion. England was Catholic, under a government which rigidly defended the ancient discipline ; there could be no question of an English priest being allowed to marry ; it would have meant the heaviest penalties and later it would have meant death ; it would certainly be intolerable in the eyes of the King.

We may get a modern parallel to the idea by considering the position of a civil servant to-day. By all the discipline of the Civil Service a member of that profession is forbidden to take part in active political life. In private he may express the strongest views on any national question, but he must not appear upon a public platform, he must not speak or write upon one side or the other. It would break him if he did. The parallel is very distant and very pale, but it will serve to explain what I mean when I say that Cranmer's step was an enormity. The English priest in Henry's favour and used by him on public work could have what adventures with women he chose, just as the civil servant to-day may, in private, express what opinions he likes ; but *marriage* of an English priest in 1532 was quite another matter. It would be the end of Cranmer if it should become known to his employers.

Therefore we can draw two conclusions of great

importance to the understanding of Cranmer at this moment. The first is this :

The marriage must have been clandestine. Some few people, of course, must have known of it, but it must have been so secretly conducted that there should be no danger of its reaching Henry's ears ; more, it is clear that Cranmer had yielded to the management of others, to the example and roughness of Osiander or to the subtlety of the girl—or both.

The second is that Cranmer could have had no idea of what Henry and Anne would later have in mind, and what is more could have had but little ambition for any high place in the Church.

On this latter point, indeed, we need no such proof ; it is clear from the man's whole character that ambition formed no part of it. He did not thrust himself forward ; he was drawn—not for his own good or of his own will.

It is one of the most distressing things about this strange story of a life so singular, that we know so little of this foreign woman whom Cranmer picked up in 1532.

Mrs. Cranmer (to give her her full title) is without a portrait and almost (but happily not quite) without record. Yet she must have meant a great deal. Did they become closely attached ? We do not know. And yet we ought to know, and not knowing we are without one of the great factors in that life. A man does not marry at such an age (he was forty-three), he does not make a second marriage, he does not make such a marriage at grave risk to himself and his future—without the thing being of preponderant effect.

He was a priest of now nearly ten years' standing ; he knew that his marriage would not be tolerated by his master ; he made it twenty years after his first extravagant affair with Black Joan—and on what adventures he may have had in between we have not a word, only Pole's stern denunciation of his sensuality. And yet we have upon her and upon his relations with her hardly more than a couple of lines. Would that there were a brief life of this perhaps placid German, but there is none. He brought her over secretly to England, and travelled with her, as was said, hidden in a tub.

She would presumably have lurked a while in the corners of Lambeth. An irregular alliance by the greatest of clerics was no new thing. But a wife for any one of Henry's clergy—let alone for the man whom Henry's mistress, the woman who governed him, had picked out for her service—was something not to be borne. Perhaps she did not pass as his wife; certainly she could not pass publicly as his wife while Henry lived, and at the end of his reign Cranmer sent her away for some years.

She was presumably young when the marriage took place; she long outlived the husband whom she had so oddly met and matched and who must have been old enough to be her father. After his dreadful death she seems to have waited in her obscurity—well provided with revenues out of the suppressed Abbey of Welbeck. Then she married again, choosing Whitchurch, her husband's constant companion and friend, the intensely anti-Catholic printer with whom the household was closely familiar. He died in the early years of Elizabeth, and she and her excellent provision of fortune tarried but a little time before finding a third husband in Richard Croft. Long after, this German woman died, still unknown, her character and nature unrecorded.

So much for Cranmer's mission to the Lutheran Divines.

As for his negotiations on the Netherlands, the Emperor had got out of the difficulty by giving all the authority there to his sister as Regent.

As for the Lutheran princes, the arrangements due to the Turkish peril would have made any success of Cranmer's in that direction difficult, though it would have been possible with sufficient skill to leave an impression of Henry and Francis being ready to support any future movement of theirs. As it was Cranmer did nothing here either.

It was now nine months since he had been entrusted with this subtle mission. He had had his commission in January; September, 1532, had come, yet nothing was done, and with the autumn Charles began to move southwards to visit Italy and see the Pope again upon his way to Spain. Cranmer dutifully followed in his train. It was lucky for him that the Emperor did not move fast on his way south, for Cranmer, though a healthy man for his years and first-rate with horses, preferred short stages.

It is amusing to note in the writing he sends home from this journey his perpetual dread of accident. They went by way of Pontebba, and just before crossing the Alps into Italy he writes (the 20th of October) a long letter to Henry which is capital reading. He makes no secret of his nerves. There have been horrible portents in the sky—a comet and a flaming horse's head. What is worse, the countryside is full of disbanded soldiery from the forces which the Emperor had gathered against the Turks, and the farmers are exasperated against them (and therefore presumably against all travellers). He gives with horror the news of a murder which has taken place on the road which " by the Grace of God " he must travel the next day.

He followed down into Italy and came with the Emperor to Mantua, where we find him in November. But meanwhile things had been happening in England which were to push him one more thrust forward in his unwillingly adventured life. Cromwell had cowed the Church. Convocation, its supreme legislative assembly, had actually consented to accept the interference of the lay power in the making of its Canons, and there had been devised by this high political genius a scheme whereby the Papacy might be moved in Henry's favour at last.

For in the session of the Parliament which met a little

before Cranmer's departure from the Germanies, Cromwell had imposed, in spite of some resistance, a law which gave the Crown the option, when it chose to exercise it, of preventing the Annates from being paid into the Papal treasury and keeping them in its own pocket.

The Annates were a Papal tax laid on the Bishoprics, amounting to the first year's revenue for every appointment. It came to no very great sum (about £100,000 a year in our money on the average), but the loss of it would be felt by Rome and the loss of prestige more severely still. Note that the thing was *threatened* only. The confiscation of the Annates was only held over as a threat to make the Pope decide in favour of Henry.

Meanwhile Henry, with Anne to decide him and with Cromwell guiding all, was persuaded during this same year 1532 that he must obtain the annulment of his marriage in England from the highest ecclesiastical authority he could. There seemed to be no end to the Roman delay, and to Anne it must have seemed useless to depend further upon it. The obvious thing to do was to get the Primate of England, the Archbishop of Canterbury, to hold a Court, try the case, and declare the annulment.

That would present the Papacy and Europe with what the French call " an accomplished fact " ; a thing done and therefore to be reckoned with and not to be got rid of by argument.

The obstacle lay in the character of Warham, the revered Archbishop of Canterbury. That old and really good man, the one man in England whom, besides More, Erasmus had sincerely praised, would certainly not *now* lend himself to any such scheme. Five years before, when the thing had first been suggested to him and before the tension between the English government and Rome had begun, it might have seemed to him natural enough for an English court (in which he would obviously play the chief part) to decide the issue ;

which would then have been sent for confirmation at Rome. But now that Rome had dealt with it as a principal it was quite another matter. To annul the marriage in England *now* by the authority of Henry's Primate would have meant a challenge to Papal authority, and against that Warham was quite determined.

Indeed he wrote a very fine protest to assure posterity and such as were intriguing around him at the time that he had never intended, by accepting the Temporal Supremacy of the Crown in England the year before, to break with the unity of Christendom or with the Holy See. England was still in communion with Rome and with Christendom.

What was to be done ? At first there seemed to be an idea that Warham could be got rid of, as Wolsey had been, by the monstrous trick of pleading Præmunire. It had worked once ; it might work again. But it was risking a great deal—and, after all, Warham could not last long : he was dying. When he should die he could be replaced by some nominee of the King's to act as was desired.

Who was that nominee to be ? Who was to be the next Archbishop of Canterbury, appointed for the purpose of declaring the annulment in spite of Rome and in spite of the Pope's prohibition, issued to all ecclesiastics, forbidding them to decide a cause which was now before himself.

Gardiner's was the obvious name. He had been the King's secretary ever since Wolsey's fall ; he had worked energetically and even roughly in the cause of the divorce, pleading before the Pope himself with something like menace. But Gardiner was too strong a character for Anne to favour or Cromwell to brook. He had already shown himself a champion for certain Church privileges, and even though he might lend himself to the new plan he would still be a great man in a great office, and such a rival would never have suited Cromwell.

Gardiner was devoted to the Crown, he was a regular official, but he was not subservient.

There was one man, quite unfitted for such promotion, neither of the calibre nor of the standing for such a place, but a man who was Anne's own and who would quite certainly do anything he was told. That man was Cranmer. It would be a startling appointment, not because Cranmer was as yet only an archdeacon—there was precedent for the promotion of a prominent cleric below the rank of Bishop—but because he did not stand in the public eye of England and of Europe on that plane. He was not thought of publicly as a candidate. He seemed an impossible successor to Canterbury, and certainly he himself would have been the last to dream of such a succession. Yet that was the decision taken. And Warham himself seems to have had wind of it, wondering on the edge of the grave what was to follow when he had left this bad new world into which he had survived—the last of the great unbroken line since Augustine.

Warham died on the 24th of August (1532) just when Cranmer, far off in the Germanies, had been sounding the Protestant Princes. Within a week, on the 1st of September, Anne (now officially admitted as consort) was given the semi-royal title of Marquis under the style of Pembroke. A month later, on the 1st of October, Chapuys, the Emperor's envoy in London, had learnt that Cranmer was to be recalled. For what purpose he does not say and presumably did not know. Neither perhaps as yet did Cranmer himself.

Hawkins was to be sent to replace Cranmer at the Emperor's Court. He took a long time to reach it, following on the movements of Charles; but at last on November the 18th he came to Mantua, presented his credentials to the Emperor and showed Cranmer his letter of recall. On the next day Cranmer started homeward.

He took his time, this man of slow stages, and there was no reason why he should not. He was three weeks reaching Lyons. There he was picked up by another of Henry's officials, Vaughan, on the 10th of December; and Vaughan saw to it that he should move a little more quickly northwards, though he probably did not reach England until January. On the 27th of that month (Monday), 1533, Chapuys wrote again to Charles V saying that Henry had told Cranmer he was to be Archbishop. He had done so within a week of his return, and Chapuys further remarks how astonished everyone was at the appointment.

The Court to which Cranmer thus returned was in a very different state from that which he had left almost exactly a year before. Henry had taken Anne on a royal progress to France, where he had met Francis and had insisted upon the lady being treated as a Royalty. He had sent to his wife Catherine demanding her queenly jewels, which he had given to Anne, and Anne was now living with him regularly as though she were his wife. What is more she was already with child, on which account Henry married her before dawn on or about the Saturday before Chapuys wrote his letter, January 25th. The marriage was solemnized quite privately, in a small room in the west turret of that new palace of Henry's in Whitehall which had until lately been York House, the Palace of the Archbishops of York and therefore of Wolsey, but taken by force from him (the first considerable piece of Church loot), before that minister had fallen. The marriage was kept very secret, and such few as got to know of it later concluded at once that Cranmer had been the celebrant. They thought, perhaps, that he alone would have lent himself to such an office. But Cranmer had not been taken into the plan. The celebrant was Lee, to whom Henry later gave the Bishopric of Lichfield and Coventry.

So the great decision was taken and Cranmer was

marked out for all that was to follow. He yielded, of course. It is right to use the word "yielded"; he had not desired that dangerous elevation.

Meanwhile Henry was convinced that the Pope would, in the last stage of the long-drawn-out affair, come down upon his side. He thought that Clement, in playing him against the Emperor and the Emperor against him, would upon the whole decide for a favourable sentence. By the end of January Bonner had written that the Pope would take that line, and allow the case to be settled in England. He was not so certain but that he thought it necessary to offer the Pope's Nuncio in London a great bribe, which was refused. But he showed the Nuncio every honour, and there was a famous scene on the 8th of February when he put that Papal Envoy on his right hand in the House of Lords, all the great Chamber filled with the scarlet robes of the peers and everything done to make the occasion impressive. The Bulls which it would be necessary to obtain from Rome in order that Cranmer should be duly consecrated Archbishop were given without hesitation, though Clement, like everyone else, knew very well what Cranmer's appointment meant, and, what is more, he had been specially told by Chapuys —had he needed telling! It seemed natural to think that the Pope would be relieved by having the responsibility taken from his own shoulders.

Henry advanced £25,000 on the 6th of February to the Archbishop-Elect, to give elbow-room for all that had to be done in the new promotion, fees, etc. Anne went about publicly boasting that she would be Queen and saying with odd impudence, "she was as sure as death the King would marry her," and well she might be: she made that boast on the 15th of February, 1533, and already three weeks before the King *had* married her. But that word "death" was ominous; her death was indeed sure, but it was to come sooner than nature had intended or than she dreamed of. The last of the Bulls had left Rome on the 3rd of March and the passage to England was a matter of about three weeks.

It is important in all these critical days to avoid extravagant theories, the worst and most foolish of which is the lending to Henry of an extravagant subtlety and dark hidden cunning such as he had never shown in his passionate and wayward life. Equally foolish is it to lend to Clement and the Papal Court in general a sudden new mood of rustic simplicity wholly at variance with everything we know of Italian diplomacy and of all Clement's character and action since the beginning of the affair.

We must go by the plain facts of the case : Clement knew perfectly well what the Archbishop was being nominated for—he was being nominated to pronounce a divorce in England. Henry himself believed and those about him believed, and for that matter the Emperor's Ambassador also believed, that the clearly apparent relief of tension which should follow on that move would end in the Pope's accepting the local sentence against the marriage with Catherine—not, of course, officially but in practice. The Pope would avoid extreme measures : he would blame the act but not produce a rupture.

Clement's conduct had afforded grounds for that idea. It is probable that if, even at this late hour, the Pope had spoken strongly, or, better still, that if he had refused the Bulls, the divorce might have been blocked ; but Henry was backing up the Papal foreign policy in an important point and his ally Francis, the French King, was helping him. The Emperor's great anxiety was to come to some sort of terms with the religious revolution in Germany, and he therefore desired the speedy summoning of a General Council of the Church which might decide matters in his favour—for the Lutheran revolt had already become a half-successful rebellion against himself. Now, to have a General Council at this moment was not at all (unfortunately !) what the Papal Court desired. Henry opposed the calling of a General Council, and the French King suggested an alliance between his family and the Medicis, proposing to marry his son and heir to the Pope's niece.

Over and over again during the long business of disruption in Christendom came moments when a perfectly clear, straightforward and honest policy would have preserved unity, but when small temporal, personal motives prevented the adoption of such a policy. A General Council early in the business might have saved Europe : it was held at last—but too late.

The English Government continued to pay Annates to the Pope, including those of this very See of Canterbury ; and on both sides, at Rome as in London, there was an atmosphere of truce.

It is exceedingly important to remember that it was in such an atmosphere of truce between Henry and the Pope that Cranmer took up the position for which he had been so strangely and unexpectedly chosen—not for his services but by the Boleyns' influence. One effect of this truce was that a law forbidding appeals from the Church Courts in England to any higher Court overseas was passed with comparative ease ; it was, after all, in the line of scores of other such efforts which had studded the various age-long relations between the Papacy and the Christian Princes. It was probably regarded as permissive, like all other similar legislation, Præmunire and Provisors included ; anyhow, whatever chance of clerical resistance there might have been, this atmosphere of truce between the two powers prevented it.

Henry, then, and all who were working this highly unpopular business of the divorce, regarded the Pope for the moment as an ally. And Clement did nothing to undeceive them. But to make assurance stronger for the future, Cranmer had orders to safeguard himself secretly against the oath of Allegiance which, on consecration, he would have to take to the Pope—an oath that was a matter of course and had been in existence from time immemorial in the English Church. That oath was, moreover, the prime condition without which the Bulls could not have been obtained from Rome and without which, therefore, Cranmer could not have been made Archbishop at all.

On the 26th of March, being a Thursday, four witnesses were summoned privately to the Chapter House of the Church of St. Stephen's—that is, of the Church of the Royal Palace at Westminster. A notary was told to come with them in order to make record of what passed. Behind those walls and with care to hide everything from public notice, Cranmer made a secret declaration that the public oath of obedience to the Pope which he would take upon his enthronement he privately regarded as not binding him to prevent any such changes as the King might propose to effect in the ecclesiastical affairs of England. In other words, he gave due notice that he was prepared, if necessary, to break his oath at the King's orders. It was only after this singular proceeding that he took the public oath of Allegiance to the Pope at the High Altar, as had all his predecessors for so many centuries, and so bound himself and assured the English people against schism.

We must be careful to give its exact measure to this piece of perjury. We must not regard it as proceeding from Cranmer's own initiative ; he would have been the last man to have taken any such risk. He simply obeyed the orders of what was the nearer and the stronger power. We shall find him perpetually taking such orders in the future, and contradicting himself without hesitation on all matters, the most profound, the most honourable, the most sacred. He was acting as the servant and nominee of Henry and Anne, and he dared not do other than what he was told.

That is no excuse in morals for his contemptible act, but it explains the perjury in terms of Cranmer's character and not in a fashion which that character would never have had the strength to undertake.

It has been claimed that there was precedent for such " Perjury in advance." Francis the First having been taken prisoner at the battle of Pavia, eight years before, had solemnly sworn to observe all the shameful conditions to which his captor bound him, including, among the rest, the dismemberment of his kingdom; and before taking that oath the young man had established a similar private record of protest that he intended to break it. But it was very truly pointed out by Pole in his later denunciation of Cranmer, and by Cranmer's accusers in the last ordeal before his death, that the precedent was not a parallel. Francis the First was prepared to break an oath which he had taken under constraint, and an oath taken under constraint was not, in the moral code of Europe, binding. Cranmer was taking an oath voluntarily. He was not compelled to become Archbishop of Canterbury, and to swear allegiance to the Pope was on his part the act of a free man from which no secret reservation could relieve him. To this he might have replied, but did not, that to disobey the King's appointment would have been so dangerous that he *was* morally compelled.

At any rate, weighted before history with this perjury, but not publicly before the English people or before Europe (for nothing was known of it outside), Cranmer was duly enthroned as Archbishop of Canterbury on Monday the 30th of March, 1533, and the game began.

VI

THE DIVORCE TO ORDER

DURING the days of Cranmer's consecration and enthronement as Archbishop of Canterbury and Primate of the Church in England a step was taken preparatory to what he had been promoted to achieve. The two legist classes in Convocation, the Canon lawyers and the Theologians, were asked to answer separately two questions. The Theologians were asked whether a Papal dispensation could permit a man to marry his deceased brother's wife if the original marriage had been consummated. The lawyers were asked whether the evidence which had been recorded for Wolsey and Campeggio in the Legatine Court four years before were sufficient to prove that the marriage between Catherine and Arthur had been so consummated. Three days after his consecration Cranmer appeared at the head of the body which was thus deliberating, the votes were taken, and there was in each division a very large majority for Henry's demand. Out of the eighty-five theologians only nineteen opposed and out of forty-four Canon lawyers only six. Six weeks later the Convocation of York followed suit.

Then there took place one of the most extraordinary and at the same time one of the most amusing pieces of official business in all the history of official business, rich as official business has always been in absurdities. It has been wittily said that God, in permitting men to be wicked, has happily made them stupid—to which it might be added that Divine Providence has also been very good to us in making wicked actions often so particularly funny.

On the 11th of April, before he had been Archbishop a fortnight, and little more than a week after the voting in Convocation under his presidency, Cranmer sat down in Lambeth Palace and solemnly wrote the following letter to the King. I put it into what I trust is legible modern English, and I hope it will please my readers as much as it does myself. It is good proof, by the way, of what we have already noticed, that Cranmer's exquisite prose was a thing of occasion ; that when he wrote as a theologian it made no pretence to distinction, and here we find him writing as an official—that is, turgidly—keeping to the official style with no effort at beauty :

Please it your Highness—that where your Grace's great cause of matrimony is (as it is thought) through all Christianity divulgated, and in the mouths of the rude and ignorant common people of this your Grace's realm so talked of, that few of them do fear to report and say, that thereof is likelihood hereafter to ensue great inconvenience, danger, and peril to this your Grace's realm, and much incertainty of succession ; by which things the said ignorant people be not a little offended—and for as much as it has pleased Almighty God and your Grace of your abundant goodness to me showed to call me (all be it a poor wretch and much unworthy) unto this high and chargeable office of Primate and archbishop in this your Grace's realm, wherein I beseech Almighty God to grant me his grace so to use and demean myself, as may be standing with his pleasure and the discharge of my conscience and to the weal of this your Grace's said realm ; and considering also the obloquy and bruit [rumour], which daily doth spring and increase of the clergy of this realm, and specially of the heads and presidents of the same, because they, in this behalf, do not foresee and provide such convenient remedies as might expel and put out of doubt all such inconveniences, perils and dangers as the said rude and ignorant people do speak and talk to be imminent, I, your most humble Orator and Bedeman [official prayer-monger] am in consideration of the premises urgently constrained at this time most humbly to beseech your most noble Grace that, when my office and duty is, by Yours and Your predecessors' suffrance and grants, to direct and order causes spiritual in this your Grace's realm, according to the laws of God and Holy Church, and for the relief of all manner of griefs and infirmities of the people, God's subjects and Yours, happening in the said spiritual causes, to provide such remedy as shall be thought most convenient for their help and relief in that behalf ; and because I would be right loath, and also it shall not become me (forasmuch as Your Grace is my Prince and Sovereign) to enterprise [engage] any part of my office in the said weighty cause without Your Grace's favour obtained and pleasure therein first known—it may please the same to ascertain me in Your Grace's pleasure in the premises, to the intent that, the same known, I may proceed for my discharge before God to the execution of my said office and duty according to his calling and yours : beseeching Your Highness most humbly upon my knees to pardon me of this my bold and rude letters, and the same to accept and take in good sense and part.

From my manor at Lambeth, the 11th day of April, in the first year of my consecration.

Your Highness' most humble
Bedesman and Chaplain,
Thomas Cantuar.

This precious epistle, specially asking for leave to do what he had been nominated as a servant to do, is remarkable for many things, but for two in especial. First, that it is all made up of one sentence, perhaps the longest passage in the English language without a full stop. But second, and more important, that it is at a level as abject as one would have thought possible in a Prelate addressing a layman and a King. And it is here that our amusement is heightened by learning that even so it was not humble enough for the King's ears.

For Henry himself sent it back corrected, with emendations better pleasing to his conception of the Royal office. The most comic of these emendations is the changing of the words " upon my knees " to the words " prostrate at the feet of Your Majesty," which seems to have given Henry some deeper Papal thrill. While it is also funny, but I am afraid blasphemous as well, to see that he added at the very end a passage where Cranmer is made to call solemnly upon Jesus Christ that his only motive in asking the King's leave to do something which had been arranged between them weeks before was his zeal to try the case truly and impartially.

The letter, thus edited, was sent back across the river to Lambeth. We have both copies remaining : the original and the second one added to by Henry— all written out in Cranmer's hand.

Henry sent an answer to this letter which he had himself revised and strengthened. He granted the boon which the Archbishop so humbly demanded. He gave him leave to go on with the affair, and took care to remind him at the same time that he was no more than a servant and that he, Henry, was not " subject to the laws of any earthly creature."

The winding up of the farce proceeded as rapidly as the canonical forms of that " Holy Church " to which Cranmer had just protested his allegiance permitted.

Catherine was at Ampthill, a royal manor which like so many others, fell later through the religious and

Whig revolution, into the possession of the landed class which was to oust the monarchy. Henry had already given her notice that her title would be changed, that she should no longer be called Queen, but Princess Dowager. To this she had twice answered that Queen she was, and Queen she would remain.

Ampthill lies four miles off the great Roman road leading from London to the Irish sea, and the nearest market town to it is Dunstable. The Queen was "cited"—that is, warned—of the approaching trial and given notice of its terms and summoned to appear. The venue of the trial was to be Dunstable, and Cranmer opened his Court there on Thursday the 8th of May at the Convent in that little town.* Cranmer had with him the Bishop of Lincoln as an assessor. The Bishop of Lincoln was the King's Confessor and was supposed by many to have started the idea of the divorce in the King's mind, though he himself protested against the accusation. Gardiner, Bishop of Winchester, appeared as Counsel for the King and seven others with him.

Would Catherine appear? At first sight the answer to that question may seem unimportant, but Cromwell, who should have known, evidently thought it was of the first importance; for he ordered Cranmer in a private letter to keep the determination of reaching a sentence there and then dead secret, lest, if it got out, Catherine should again openly appeal to Rome; he, Cromwell, judged that if she did so all his plans would break down. A regular service of posts was established between Dunstable and the Government (which was only thirty-five miles off, say three hours), and the whole thing worked under direct orders.

---

* The date often given is the 10th of May, because many have hurriedly made confusion between the first recorded act and the opening of the Court. The first recorded act being the proving of the "citation," the date of which *was* the 10th of May, but the Court opened on the 8th.

Cromwell need not have been so nervous. Catherine had asked the advice of the Emperor's Envoy, Chapuys, and he had told her not to recognize the Court, before which, therefore, she refused to plead. She was pronounced contumacious. Upon the next day on which the Court could sit (Monday the 12th of May), there was proved a second citation which she also refused to obey, and she was pronounced "verily contumacious." The Court heard arguments on the consummation of the original marriage during that week, and served the third citation upon the 17th of May, this time to hear the judgment of the Court.

Henry and Anne were in a fever to get the thing over as soon as possible. Anne was far gone with child, and it was important to have her crowned and to put the mass of Englishmen who were so bitterly opposed to the King's policy " in the presence of an accomplished fact." But Canonical rules are strict and they had to be observed. Wednesday was the vigil of the Ascension, Thursday was the Ascension itself, the first open day was Friday the 23rd: and on that day Cranmer read out the sentence—which was not his own but which Henry had dictated.

It is interesting to read the comment of an eye-witness whose report was drawn up for Cromwell's private eye. He tells us that " My Lord of Canterbury held himself very well and very uprightly, *without any evidence or suspicion of him to be noted by the counsel of my Lady Catherine* [my italics], if she had had any present." Which of course she had not.

Thus, then, did the impartial Thomas Cranmer pronounce his sentence after so much deliberation and weighing of evidence—which sentence had already been determined for him by his master. The marriage between Catherine and Henry was not valid; it had been null from the beginning; it had been carried out in defiance of God's law and was void.

But there was to be a third act to the farce—it was duly performed. It is perhaps even more laughable than that first exchange of letters across the Thames between Lambeth and the Palace and the Palace and Lambeth which had taken place a month before. Cranmer, having discovered after so close and thorough an examination that, after all, Henry and Catherine were not married at all, wrote to his King a " Godly Letter " begging him to cut short, while there was yet time, his evil and incestuous intercourse with his brother's wife. He must submit (hard though it might be !) to the decrees of his Creator. He must remember what punishment followed upon breaking them. And so the main matter ended.

But there was another little point to be considered. It was all very well for the Primate of England to declare null and void that marriage which had endured over twenty years and which had presented the English people with their very popular young Princess Mary, the heiress to the throne ; but if that young Princess and heiress was to be supplanted and some boy of Anne's was to be King after Henry's death, there must be a marriage between Henry and Anne.

Now we know that there had been a secret marriage, valueless in the eyes of the Church, but at any rate duly ceremonial, and performed by a priest before witnesses. It had taken place four months before.

Was another ceremony performed after ? Many have thought that it was, but if it were no record has remained. Cranmer's orders were to put it publicly on record as the decision of the highest ecclesiastical authority in the Kingdom that the King and Anne were married. They went no further. Where, how, or when the marriage had taken place he was not allowed to divulge, although by that time he knew. On Wednesday the 28th he was back in Lambeth, and in the low vaulted chapel of that palace he gave further sentence, deciding that the King's marriage with Anne was valid.

It was a foolish move on Henry's part, for it did not quiet the public suspicion. If the authorities would not give a date and place and evidence for the marriage it only made things worse to "confirm" it in this vague fashion. Anyhow, so the matter stood, and Cranmer—as chief spiritual authority in England— solemnly proclaimed the legitimate wedlock of Henry and Anne.

Here it is important to note the *pace*. The *pace* was being forced. The trial at Dunstable had been rushed through as rapidly as was possible consistently with canonical form. The sentence had been delivered on the very first open day, and its terms had previously been dictated by the principal interested party before the Court—the King. This legitimization of the marriage had also been passed within the briefest possible delay : the Archbishop in his Palace by Monday, the documents drawn up, presumably, on the Tuesday, the legitimacy of Anne's marriage announced on the Wednesday.

And the pace was kept up. Already the Coronation was fixed for the very next feast day, four days hence, Sunday the 1st of June, which was Whit-Sunday.

Anne slept the Wednesday night in the Palace at Greenwich, where Henry also was, and on the next day, the Thursday, went up river in state on the flood tide to the Tower ; flood tide on the Thames and flood tide in her fortunes. She went up on that flood tide in great pageantry—to show what new things were beginning in England. The majesty of the Queen of England had a gorgeous barge for part of its furniture, second only in magnificence to the King's, on which were blazoned the arms of Aragon. The Boleyn woman in her triumph had these pulled down and the coat which the Boleyns had rather absurdly suggested for themselves put in its place. When Chapuys, the Emperor's Ambassador, spoke in private to Henry about this insult Henry apologized and said he would have the arms removed ; but he did not—so torn was he between the desire to save himself in the eyes of Europe and his inability as yet to deny Anne anything. As the great painted vessel swept up on the flood tide* of that afternoon a whole procession of gay boats attended it, close on two hundred. So she came to the Royal rooms in the Tower, to the blare of trumpets and the boom of the saluting guns.

All the Friday she spent in her preparations, and on Saturday, in a magnificent triumphal procession, she went—all in white satin under her litter of white satin —from the Tower to the Palace of York House, Whitehall. Whatever the Court and the courtiers could do to make that doubtful pageantry splendid, was done. A long line of vivid colours, the windows on either side of the streets in the City all the way from the Tower to Ludgate, and in the sparser houses with their gardens on the Strand, rich with hangings, the trained City Companies in ranks on either side, the long file of horsemen headed by the French merchants, and, at the end, Anne herself, while there rode in front of her litter the man whom she had made and who was about to crown her, Thomas Cranmer.

But the populace was silent, the thing was wholly official ; none dared make overt protest, but there was no cheering nor any of the public acclamation which should salute a new Queen. That Saturday night, the 31st of May, she passed in the Palace at Westminster, and the next morning went on foot, still in a splendour of pageantry, down the few hundred yards to the Abbey. Even that distance must have been a trial to her, for she was ill ; but what was illness now that she was triumphant !

* It was high water between four and five o'clock.

Then Cranmer crowned her, and Gardiner was at his side.

Within ten days of her crowning a courier had come into Rome riding hard, and he brought news.* Sentence had been delivered by that Archbishop of Canterbury for whom Clement himself had recently sent the Bulls; the trial had been held in spite of the Pope's prohibition; the thing was done. Clement, on hearing that the thing had been done, showed great anger. Was that anger simulated or was it genuine? Was it put on to keep the Imperialists in hope, or was it the expression of real irritation? Sound judgment inclines, I think, to the view that the irritation was sincere enough, but not to the view that it was due to surprise, or witnessed to a settled policy of condemning Henry finally and breaking with him. All that went before and all that went after belies such an idea. Months and months were to pass during which the Pope continually postponed any real action and in practice accepted the situation.

But the irritation was genuine, I think, because the extreme rapidity of all that had been done in England was offensive to Clement. He had issued the Bulls knowing very well for what purpose they would be used; he had made canonical and legitimate the position of Cranmer as Archbishop, though without a doubt Cranmer was only being promoted in order to pronounce a divorce at some time; but Clement would have wished that as *he* was delaying perpetually, so should the other party —Henry—delay, in a sort of courtesy of temporizing, to give everyone time for something to turn up and for a solution to be found without a breach between the Pope and England or between the Emperor and the Pope or between the Emperor and Henry. The driving

---

* The rapidity with which the news was communicated was remarkable, and leads to the supposition that it was expected. It meant posting with relays every day and covering more than sixty miles a day, as well as allowing for the delay in crossing the Straits.

power that had broken through all such calculations was Anne's will, for it was that will which had forced the pace.

All that summer it seemed to Cranmer that the dangerous path down which he had been led was now become a secure highway ; with the wealth and the glory of his office fully confirmed to him, the man of the Boleyns, a Boleyn on the throne and about to give the kingdom an heir, an heir which his own sentence had legitimized and whom perhaps he would later serve as he had served the father.

For the honour and circumstance of his office his timidity cared little and little also for its emoluments ; the scholar would have avoided responsibility if he could, and never cared for money as he cared for his art or for his secret and now strengthening hatred of the Catholic Church—but at any rate he was secure, and to a man of such a temper that was the most of all he needed. Of course the price of this security was continued sub- servience ; but subservience came native to him and he would do all that he was bid.

* * * * * *

There was in those days a young priest of the name of John Frith. He was a Kentish man, the son of a tavern- keeper in Sevenoaks. Let none marvel that one doomed to such a fate as we shall read was the son of a tavern- keeper ; the ale-room was in those days the gate to many a career, as it had been to Cromwell and was later to be to the Cecils. Tavern-keepers could afford to educate their sons. Let none marvel again that a man doomed to such a fate was a priest ; you will find that priests were commonly the leaders in these quarrels with their Church.

This young John Frith could argue upon matters of the spirit with dexterity, and Wolsey or Wolsey's people had noted him for this while he was yet at

Cambridge; therefore they had brought him to Oxford with some idea of his joining Wolsey's new College there. Six years before, a gospelling spirit had moved him against the existing state of things and particularly against the corporation of which he was a member; and he had got into a sort of little secret group which called itself by the surprisingly modern name of "The Christian Brethren," and whose business it was to expose and decry the Christian brotherhood of the Church. He was arrested and held for a while, then released on condition that he should not go ten miles from Oxford; but he broke his bail and went overseas—finding money we do not know how, but it is illuminating to discover how easily men travelled in those days.

He came home about two years later and got into the stocks at Reading as a vagrant. Then he seems to have been preaching again heretically in the fashion of the Christian Brotherhood, and now in this year of 1533 he was haled up before Sir Thomas More to answer for his efforts at revolution.

He argued with Sir Thomas More; he was sent to argue before Thomas Cranmer, and was kept in the Tower pending a conclusion upon his case.

Cranmer next, with sundry assessors (among whom was the Bishop of London and Gardiner and also Boleyn, Anne's father), examined Frith at some length, but found him quite obstinate upon a particular matter, which was that the Real Presence in the Sacrament was a fable. Whereupon he was, very naturally according to all the practice of the time, handed over to his Bishop, the Bishop of London, for his case to be determined on; the Bishop of London handed him over to the secular arm, and upon the 4th of July, 1533, John Frith—with a companion who shared his opinions, Andrew Hewitt, a tailor's apprentice of London—was burnt alive at Smithfield.

There was in this little incident nothing extraordinary

at all. It might have happened to anyone who felt sufficiently convinced upon the doctrines which Zwingli, following in the wake of Luther but going further than Luther, had preached upon the Eucharist—to wit, that there was no Real Presence at all, and that the bread and wine were but memorials.

It seems that this young man John Frith and his colleague Andrew Hewitt had been specially persuaded to their opinions by the writings of Oecolampadius,* one of the more violent and uncompromising of the German enthusiasts against the religion of their fathers.

Now there is in this examination and condemnation of Frith and his companion by Cranmer a very great interest for all who would closely consider Cranmer's character and career.

The interest lies *not* in the burning. Cranmer would see that the man was burnt (not, indeed, by the Church of which he was the Primate in England, but by the secular arm to which the Church handed him over after condemnation), just as naturally as an English judge to-day would condemn a man to hanging for murder and hand him over to the prison authorities to be put to death in that awful fashion. Cranmer burnt Frith as later he burnt others and as at last he himself was burnt, by common form and as a part of regular practice. No, the interest of this first affair lies in whether Cranmer, here so acting, did violence to himself and was condemning one whom he secretly approved.

Was this one more case of so many in which the soul

---

* Lest any reader coming upon the name " Oecolampadius " should think he was some Father of the Church, reverend with the centuries and expressing the belief of our origins, I hasten to add that his real name was Hussinger or something of the kind ; but exactly what has never been determined. His friends thought it more pleasing to call him Hauschein, which is the German for " A Light in the House," and he himself thought it grander to put it into Greek, a language in which the word for house is " oikos," to which he added " lampadios " (" lampish ")—" A House-lamp-ish one." Hence Oecolampadius.

of the man was exasperated by the necessity for hiding his real self, performing an office which he abhorred; was it yet one more occasion of those in which he was inflamed and angered in the secret places of the soul which had to be kept so hidden? Did he not himself at that moment, 1533, doubt or deny as fully as John Frith that Jesus Christ was there present in the Sacrament of the Altar? Was he not filled with a suppressed revolt against what he had to do now, and would be doing for so many years—playing chief part in the solemn display, the high liturgy of the Mass; acting perpetually as sacrificing priest—as the high sacrificing priest of England?

He was. There was no new development in him after this time in the matter of Sacrament and Mass. He was fixed long ago. A man filled with new notions, breathing in his twenties an air of enthusiastic change, does not get suddenly converted at fifty-eight.* Cranmer was as sure as ever poor John Frith could be that the thing was a falsehood; what is more—a blasphemous falsehood. Yet he let John Frith go to the fire. He was party to it. He was not only party to the deed, he was a principal in it. And by this may you understand what Cranmer was, what he continued to be, and what in the end he became. For all these fourteen years, as long as Henry lived and refused to change, he, Cranmer, must play the false part, hide his strongest feelings, chafe and writhe inwardly. This is the key to all that followed.

There is a letter written by him to Hawkins which stamps him clearly enough and which he must himself have remembered on the dreadful day which was to come more than twenty years ahead when he himself was to run furiously through the rain towards the pyre laid for his own destruction.

* Cranmer was 58 in the year when Henry died, and till then professed orthodoxy.

Here it is in its significant phrases :

" Other news have we none notable but that one Frith . . . was . . . examined before me . . . whose opinion was so notably erroneous that we . . . were fain to leave him to the determination of his ordinary, which is the Bishop of London. . . . he thought it not necessary to be believed . . . that there is a very corporal presence of Christ within the sacrament of the altar. . . . I myself sent for him three or four times to persuade him to leave that his imagination ; but for all that . . . he would not apply to any council. . . . now he is at a final end of all examination : . . . and delivered . . . to the secular power where he looketh every day to go unto the fire. And there is also with him one Andrew, a tailor of London, for the self-same opinions."

Such was Cranmer's passing gossip in his letter to Hawkins, and I say that by all our experience of men, particularly of time-servers, while he was writing it Cranmer himself in his heart agreed thoroughly with the man whom he had thus given over to the flames.

He was a man in his forty-fourth year ; it was twenty years since he had been under the influence of men speaking just such things, and had agreed with them ; he had been, when his mind was forming, of that group at Cambridge where these things had been said with such persistence and so reasonably ; he had been but in his early twenties when the first writings of Erasmus which had suggested just such things were in the mouths of all his group. He had mixed in the Germanies with the men who spoke thus. He had secretly married into them. All his past as well as all his future shows clearly how his mind had set and that his fixed hatred of the institution which he desired to destroy included hatred of its central doctrine, the Real Presence, a detestation of the Sacrament of the Altar and of the Mass. He had to keep it under till the end of the reign—when he was fifty-eight; but then, when he was free at last to vent his bitterness, he stands revealed and we see uncovered what had been concealed for all those years.

Yes, Cranmer knew well enough what he was doing when he condemned " one Frith " and " one Andrew, a tailor " to the fire. And it is essential in our reading of the man to remember that.

He had done so as an official ? It was part of his business ? It was part of the routine which he had to carry out as Archbishop ? No doubt. Let that be his excuse for those who find it sufficient ; but let it be remembered.

It was his business to see that heretics should be burnt as an orthodox King demanded, and if within his heart of hearts Cranmer inclined to what those heretics maintained with a boldness which he dreaded, that was no reason for not carrying on the functions of his office. Did one deny the Sacrament ? Why, he must go to the fire ! Nor did Cranmer hesitate to write with his own hand that such an opinion was manifestly erroneous. Did another obstinate fellow of humble birth stubbornly maintain that the Eucharist was but bread ? Cranmer would argue with him—he could not do less, and there was not a drop of cruelty in the man—but if he would not recant, why he too must go to the fire.

Those were the days also in which the Archbishop consented to a rôle for which he was much better fitted, a rôle of police-cunning and entrapping ; for it was in this summer that he played the part of agent in catching and entrapping Elizabeth Barton in the toils—of which later.

In general, though he was doing sometimes cruel work which was repugnant to him, and at other times mean and repulsive work which ought to have been repugnant to him, all went well. There had not even come that final break with Rome which, because it was a decision, Cranmer would have dreaded like any other decision. There had still been played between Rome and Henry's Court a continued comedy of delay, in which Cranmer had little to do : an intricate many-sided set of intrigues. But there had been no irrevocable step taken.

Cromwell, to make himself the more powerful, had sent Anne Boleyn's uncle, the Duke of Norfolk, off on an embassy to France to try and persuade Francis against meeting the Pope as he had arranged. Henry had sent his envoy to that meeting and had appealed from any decision of the Pope's to a General Council. The Pope had, with full publicity, annulled all that Cranmer had done and ordered the undoing of it by the chief culprits, that is Henry, Cranmer and Anne, before the end of August ; he had issued a brief of censure—but all this was only for delay. It reads to us who know what was to come as something more decisive than it was. The door was left open and deliberately left open. Rome deliberately held its hand. Why lose England ? Time might still bring relief. Catherine might die. Anne's strange power over Henry might vanish as such things do.

Henry's uncertain vacillating temper and now too prolonged familiarity with Anne had led to bickerings and to short quarrels, but still the position seemed to stand firm ; they had only to wait for the child that was to come. As the hour of Anne's delivery approached Henry's spirits rose and Cranmer's assurance with it. It would be plain sailing. The child would certainly be a boy. The astrologers had made sure of that, so the King had no doubts. Down in the Palace at Greenwich in the first days of September the event was awaited ; when Sunday morning, the 7th, came it was at hand. And somewhat after three o'clock in the afternoon of that day the child was born. It was a girl.

VII

THE FIRST PERIL

IT was a girl : and they christened her Elizabeth.
And now what were the chances of Anne ?

We must keep in mind two things which determined the whole of Cranmer's position in these years ; the first is that Henry's policy was not an assured thing : it was floating ; it was reversible. The second is that Cranmer's fortunes seemed to himself and others to be wholly bound up with those of Anne.

Henry had not determined finally to break away from the unity of Christendom and to repudiate the authority of the Pope. He never determined anything finally. He vacillated and changed continually all his life and was always at the mercy either of sudden impulse from within or the domination of a steady and stronger character from without. Cromwell, one may well believe, had a fixed policy and was working for the steady aggrandisement of the lay power and even, if it were necessary, for secession from Christendom. Certainly he had no religion to urge or restrain him. Even he, however, was concerned with an immediate policy and with no such distant ends as were, without intention, reached.

Anne, therefore, might be repudiated in a fit of anger or of tedium or of disgust. Twelve months before, in the late summer of 1532, she had held the King completely bound. He could not live without her ; he was fascinated, caught, unable to exist apart from her constant presence. Not many months after his satisfaction, all that had begun to change ; there had been little troubles. However, the child that was to come was the all-important thing, and as they awaited it together the man and the woman carried on. Now the child had come, and it was not the male heir which might have given

Anne a fixed position. Negotiations were still going on between the English government and the Papacy, with the French government as a sort of intermediary and friend of the English, urging the Pope to further delay and to compromise. The detestation of Anne among Henry's own subjects, the popularity of the injured Queen and of the true heiress Princess Mary, a girl of now seventeen, was another force which might make for a sudden change.

Then, as for Cranmer's position, we must remember that he was wholly the Boleyns' creature. Even if he had not been, as I think probable, in some way connected with them before the famous original interview with the King at Greenwich four years before, he at any rate had been an intimate member of their household ever since. He had been their chaplain, their confidant, in some way and for a short period a sort of tutor to Anne herself. He had written their brief for them; he had travelled with them, and he counted in everything, even now that he was Archbishop, as their nominee, a dependent of the Boleyns.

If Anne should fall, what would happen to him? There was no more security in his position than in hers. It is true he was not likely to give rise to one of Henry's violent outbreaks and he would never dare to work behind the King's back as others did, or, like them, to deride Henry: no, not even among his intimates. But if there were a general breakdown of the Boleyn influence, and if Cranmer were swept away when that storm should burst, it would be quite easy to get rid of him. There was nothing awe-inspiring in his person and nothing much left of sanctity in his office. The King would not hesitate to get rid of this " *ad hoc* " Archbishop as he had hesitated in the case of Warham; he would take some plea, any plea would be good enough, and by death or by the simpler process of a forced resignation dismiss this temporary servant and appoint another in his room.

Hence, anxiety ; and what really saved the situation was a combination of two things : the thoroughly bad diplomacy of Henry and the steady policy of Cromwell. The thoroughly bad diplomacy of Henry muddled up all the remaining negotiations with the Papacy and the King of France, and got things into a tangle from which no compromise between Henry and Clement could issue ; while Cromwell, with his fixed determination always in mind to increase his own power and to advance towards the spoliation of ecclesiastical goods—which would vastly enrich himself—used every opportunity to exasperate the quarrel with Rome. He was to attain his end in less than a year and a half, to be rid of the Pope, and to find himself complete master of all the clerical body of England.

Henry's bad diplomacy was a mixture of suspicion, sudden annoyance, and the increasing desire to put his foot down and show that he would not be trifled with— and to do this just when it would have been most to his purpose to have restrained himself. Francis I was doing everything to keep Clement in a mood of delay, and Clement was more than willing to go half way to meet him. The official censure against the marriage with Anne had been issued on the 11th of July, no decisive sentence had been pronounced and there was opportunity for indefinite postponement, for which Francis, anxious above all things to keep the English alliance against the Emperor, steadily worked. Yet it was in such an atmosphere that Henry impetuously spoilt everything.

Clement was the guest of the King of France at Marseilles, and it was there, in the very Court of Henry's ally, that the public insult was delivered of threatening the Pope with an appeal to a General Council. All had been ready for a re-trial of the case : after this such a re-trial would be difficult or impossible.

Francis was almost as much moved by this public

insult as was the Pope himself ; he complained to the English envoy that there was no dealing with his master. The more he, Francis, tried to work a reconciliation, the more was done against it ! Then Henry naturally, like all impulsive people who blunder, put the blame on the shoulders of the very man whom he had offended. He said that Francis was betraying him ; he had passionate outbursts against the French Ambassador, and he became so inconsequent and self-contradictory that Cromwell and Norfolk had to apologize for him behind his back lest there should be an open rupture, for an open rupture between the French and English governments might turn Francis into an ally of Charles V.

All this played into the hands of Cromwell, and, of course, played even more directly into the hands of Anne. It suited her perfectly that there should be no further delay or compromise with the Pope. And with her insistence and vehemence, in spite of the fluctuations in her hold on her now satiated lover, to whom she had failed to give an heir, she carried most of her points in domestic policy.

The chief of these points was the degradation of the Princess Mary. Henry loved the girl. All during her childhood she had been the heiress upon whom he had doted, and even while he dreamed of the possibility of a brother, she was the real hope of his throne. It was essential for Anne to degrade her.

First, the order was given that the Princess Mary should serve in attendance upon the baby Elizabeth (to whom Cranmer had acted as godfather) at Hatfield. Further, she was put under the guardianship of Anne's aunt, Lady Skelton, and because Lady Skelton was attracted by the dignity and courtesy of the girl, Anne passed all bounds, insisting upon her being insulted and saying that she ought to be thrashed to break her spirit— for it was a characteristic of the Boleyn woman that her tongue was quite unbridled. She was one of those who might hope when she could no longer hold a weak man by appetite to cow him by violence of language.

When Henry rode out to Hatfield one day to see the Princess, Anne—feeling that his strong affection for Mary might turn his wavering spirit—sent messengers to prevent the father and daughter meeting. She had her way. But how strong public opinion was, and how indeed it was further exasperated by such conduct, there were plenty of incidents to show. Fox, the King's Almoner, the man who had been most steady in his support of the divorce, privately congratulated the Princess on her refusal to give up her title and her mother's claim, and the populace of the locality would come and cheer her under her own windows and tell her she was the rightful heiress to the throne.

But Anne still had her way. Everything worked with her : the King's exasperation both with France and the Pope, Cromwell's determined policy, and the difficulty men always find in retracing their steps.

Meanwhile, Cromwell was able to use after his own fashion an incident which would strengthen the forces which made for a break with Rome and therefore for his own ultimate domination over the Church as well as the laity of England. This opportunity lay in the visions and prophecies of one Elizabeth Barton, a maid-servant living in a village about a dozen miles from Canterbury, who had turned nun and professed to have supernatural revelations. She had been a well-known figure for some years before there was any question of divorce ; she was now, as might be expected, whether she were under hallucinations or no, following the popular stream and affirming that her informants from the other world were as angry with what Henry had done as his own people were. Many men and women of great position had seen this Holy Maid of Kent ; most of them had been greatly impressed with her sanctity ; a great number of them had accepted her revelations as genuine.

Among these was that aged, saintly and universally respected scholar, famous throughout Europe, Fisher, Bishop of Rochester, who had been tutor to the King in his youth, and whom we have seen prominent over Cambridge thirty years before. He, without a doubt, respected the prophetical claims of Elizabeth Barton.

Thomas More had seen her also (for that matter the King had seen her), but Thomas More had not been as much impressed by her as Fisher had. As she was in the neighbourhood of Canterbury, where Cranmer for the moment was staying looking after the affairs of his palace, it was convenient that Cromwell should make him an instrument for the plan he had in mind, which was to use Elizabeth Barton's opposition to the divorce for the purpose of intimidating opposition in general. In this negotiation he unexpectedly discovered talents in Cranmer which he had not known to be present— talents useful in a secret agent—talents of intrigue. No one would have thought that Cranmer would display such capacities after his diplomatic failure in Italy and Germany; that he was suave and could soothe an opponent Cromwell knew as well as everyone else after three years of closely watching Cranmer's character. But that Cranmer could lead the unsuspecting into a trap, that he could cozen and reap the fruits of police-cunning, came as a novelty, and a pleasurable novelty, to a man like Cromwell, who needed aid of that kind continually. It was the beginning of a close alliance between the two men which lasted to the very threshold of Cromwell's fall and death. They were made one for the other; master and agent, pursuing for very different motives a common cause in the destruction of Elizabeth Barton.

Cromwell had sent down to Cranmer a list of questions which he was to put to the Holy Maid. Cranmer remonstrated, because he said that to ask direct questions would be to put her upon her guard. He preferred deceit, and his Dean of Arches, Gwent, who was present, has left us a vivid picture of his method; saying (in praise of the Archbishop!) that the unfortunate woman was entirely taken in by his manner. He pretended sympathy—a method which he was to use during all the rest of his public service in order to extort secrets from those who were to be ruined. " He does yet but dally with her," Gwent tells Cromwell, " as if he did believe every word, and so soon as he has all he can get out of her she shall be sent to you."

By these methods Cranmer got the unfortunate woman to make violent political statements, and was then able to send her on to Cromwell under arrest. She had prophesied the doom of Henry and Anne; she had said that if they married, Henry would lose his throne within seven months, and—here was the important point for Cromwell—there was got from her a list of all the people who had conferred with her : a list including some of the greatest names in England. With that list in his hand, Cromwell could use it as an instrument of terror all around.

He let Fisher know and he let More know that he held them. He tried hard to drag in the Queen herself, Catherine of Aragon, and the Princess Mary, but admits that he failed. Yet it did not suit his book to strike at once, least of all the woman herself, from whom information was still to be obtained. It was enough for him to discredit her and to keep his list of victims in reserve, for each after she had been degraded would still remain guilty of having toyed with treason. On the 25th of November, 1533, she was made to stand on a high scaffold in front of St. Paul's in London to admit imposture and to have a sermon preached at her. But her life was not touched. Cranmer, who was proud of the part he had played, wanted something more drastic and more thorough, but Cromwell would allow no such interference of Cranmer's vanity with his own cold reason. It would have spoiled his plans.

Balked of this victim, Cranmer chafed; he turned to his chief activity and wrote a book against her. He imprisoned a monk who had countered with another book. He continued to urge the trial of Elizabeth Barton—but Cromwell disdainfully and strongly bided his time.

During that winter, 1533–34, the rift between the English government and Rome grew broader, and at the meeting of Parliament (which was Cromwell's instrument) preparations were put in hand for declaring the King's new marriage valid by statute as it had already been declared ecclesiastically valid by Cranmer many months before, while in Rome the last stages towards pronouncing a final divorce were toward.

On Monday the 23rd of March, 1534, the Bill for the Succession which Cromwell had laid before the House of Lords passed its third reading. Princess Mary was no longer heiress in law : the baby Elizabeth was heiress, the succession was settled on her ; it was High Treason even to publish any words which should slander the validity of the marriage with Anne, misprision of treason even to speak critically upon the matter, and an oath could be administered to anyone of age which they should be commanded to take under the same penalties. That is, anyone of age could be compelled to swear that Mary was no longer heiress nor Catherine Queen, but Anne the true Queen, legitimately married and the baby Elizabeth legitimate heiress to the throne. To this proposed statute was added quite arbitrarily, without debate or vote and simply by order of the government, the form of the oath, which was all-important for what was to follow—and in this oath the authority of the Pope was by implication denied.

This all-important statute passed, I say, its third reading in the Lords (it became law shortly after) on

Monday the 23rd of March, 1534. On the same day in Rome at 5 o'clock in the afternoon the doors were opened on that Consistory Court wherein had sat the Cardinals to decide finally upon the validity of Henry's marriage, and the sentence was announced. By an overwhelming majority they had decided that Catherine was the true wife. The news was greeted in the Imperialist ranks with high enthusiasm, salvos were fired and the thing was celebrated as a triumph.

That was a matter of course. But more remarkable was the abstention from voting of the French Cardinals, and more remarkable still the voting in favour of Catherine by those native Cardinals who were known to be in the French interest. Indeed of the whole body only three had dissented, and even these had not voted against Catherine but had only proposed further delay.

Clement still hesitated ; he still desired a reconciliation with Henry if it were possible, but he could not neglect so formidable a decision with a majority so imposing. He forbade the publication of the sentence—which had not force in Church law until it was published—before Easter.

While all this was proceeding Cromwell was using the Parliament to strike where he had determined to strike, against the opposition at home. It was formidable ; it was in a sense universal, for it covered pretty well the whole nation outside the official world and that small body of men who mixed up their will for a religious revolution with the cause of Anne. Earlier in the session Cromwell, pursuing what was to be his particular method of getting condemnation without trial by a Bill of Attainder, brought in such a Bill against Elizabeth Barton and certain of her clerical supporters, of whom the most prominent names were Sir Thomas More and Fisher. They were attacked under the accusation that they had known of the treason of the Holy Maid of Kent and had not revealed it.

The Holy Maid and those who had been mentioned with her were put to death at Tyburn on the 21st of April. More and Fisher were at first dealt with differently. Fisher was allowed to go free on payment to the Crown from the funds of his diocese of something over £7,000. More's name was erased from the Bill; and among those who pleaded that it should be so struck out was Cranmer, moved by we know not what emotion; it may have been a sympathy with high scholarship, perhaps a dread of consequences, or perhaps a mere following of Cromwell, who had also proposed that policy.

But the erasure of More's name was not designed to save More; it was designed to save the Bill. For though it is difficult to imagine a case in which even the House of Lords in the present phase of the reign would have refused a demand put to them by Cromwell in the name of the King, yet this was a case where such a refusal might have been offered. There had already been one or two hesitations of this kind.

It mattered little whether More's name was erased or not. What Cromwell envisaged was the making an example of him to further the taking of the Oath. And on the 13th of April, a little before the butchery of Elizabeth Barton but long after the Bill had been presented to the House and passed, long after this curious erasure of More's name, More himself, with Fisher at his side, was summoned before the Council.

It is significant that the Council was sitting at Lambeth in the Archbishop's Palace, for what was to happen turned directly upon religion.

More was examined first. He said that he would swear to the succession, but that there were parts of the oath—meaning the implied repudiation of the Pope's supremacy—to which he could not swear. Fisher came next and answered in much the same fashion but more lucidly. He said that he was being asked to swear to two things : one a matter of civil law and of temporal

interest only—the succession ; to that he was prepared
to swear. But the other was a matter of Divine law
and of religion, and to that his conscience forbade him
to swear. In other words, he did not think it his duty
to refuse the Oath of Fealty to a bastard who had been
legitimatized by statute, but he found it impossible
to deny the supremacy of the Pope over the universal
Church. Cranmer had pressed More hard in the
examination, and it is significant that at Cromwell's side,
and agreeing with him, was the Abbot of Westminster,
and this last said certain words which should never be
forgotten. To which More made an equally unforget-
table answer.

For the Abbot of Westminster said :

" You ought to think your conscience erroneous when
you have against it the whole Council of the nation."
And More replied, " I should if I had not before me a
still greater Council, the whole Council of Christendom."
In that objection and in the answer to it you have in a
flash the new quarrel between nationalism—the religion
of the State, the worship of England—on one side,
and Catholicism upon the other.

Further, let it be remembered that these two men
thus standing out were exceptional. In the general body
of Englishmen, strong as they were for the legitimate
Queen and the young Princess, the true heiress whom
they adored, there was no particular feeling for the
Papacy. It was generally regarded as a matter of course
that the Pope was the Head of the Church, but of a
direct and necessary connection between their immemorial habits of worship and belief and the exact
definition of Papal power they had no clear grasp as
yet, and still less any enthusiasm for it. The King might
quarrel with the Pope if he liked and then be reconciled
with him again, as had the King's predecessors over and
over again, and pretty well every other Prince in Christendom. To run the risk of death for a subtle distinction

upon the nature of the Papacy was to play the eccentric ;
and that is why so very few, and of the more highly
placed only these two, were sufficiently sure of their
convictions and of their courage to maintain the position
they did.

More had been called early, in deference perhaps to
his great position as a former Lord Chancellor, and he
argued the case like the lawyer that he was—how the
Oath was not in the Statute and therefore was not legal,
how he spoke only for himself, etc. But he had also
said that he had secret reasons for not taking the Oath
which he would only divulge to the King, and what
these were we know not.*

More after this refusal was let free to think it over,
and he walked about in the long garden of Lambeth
Palace where it stretched pleasantly beside the broad
river, turning up and down the walks till evening ; but
he remained of the same mind. At evening he was
ferried across to the further bank, where he was to lie
in the custody of the Abbot of Westminster. Fisher
had already been sent to the Tower ; four days later
More joined him there.

It is remarkable that on the same day that More
went to the Tower, Cranmer again tried to save him, and
this time, I think, upon his own initiative ; for, whereas
the erasure of More's name from the Bill which had been
but a matter of form was accepted, Cranmer's present
plea was of no effect at all. Why did he make it ? To
say that he made it from a general mildness of temper
cannot be true. No one was keener on condemnations

* Perhaps he referred to his discussions with the King years before, when the
King himself had maintained the Divine origin of the Papacy while More had
doubted it. Some have thought that he referred to an impediment of blood
which made Anne's marriage necessarily invalid by Divine law because her
sister had been Henry's mistress—we shall see how the same idea arose later at
her condemnation. But I do not see how this could have been More's reason
on the present occasion, because he was quite ready to take the Oath of
Succession and only stopped short on the implied denial of Papal jurisdiction.

than Cranmer when he thought them politic or to his
advantage. For though he was a mild man he was not
mild in our modern sense; he had no abhorrence of the
ordinary procedure of his time : he had burnt people,
as we have seen, cheerfully enough, and was to burn
others and to plan further burnings. Yet in this case,
as on one or two other occasions in his life, he was for
mercy. He proposed that More's acceptation of the
succession should be regarded as sufficient and that on
the other matter he should not be pressed. After all,
he had remained silent. But Cranmer's opinions were
never of much weight with stronger men and of none
with Cromwell : his plea was not listened to.

In the last steps which had to be taken for the completion of the break with Rome and for the exertion of
the King's supremacy Cranmer was little concerned. He
was content now to be the subordinate of Cromwell's
policy—and it was, for that matter, to the advantage
of his shadowy position that the last link with the Holy
See should be broken.

That happened in the November of the year (1534),
when a Statute was passed the terms of which were
uncompromising and which wound up the affair. Both
Houses of Convocation had given the official vote that
the Bishop of Rome had no greater jurisdiction in
England than any other foreign Bishop : Cranmer's
own body of Canterbury, in March ; York, in May.
And later in the summer towards the end of June the
Universities followed suit. The subordinate part which
Cranmer played in all this is best exemplified by the
violence of his sermon in which he calls the Pope " Anti-
Christ," and there you have his permanent interest—
that desire for an attack upon the whole system of
Catholicism which was the one permanent motive in his
mind—as was the exact opposite the one permanent
motive in Henry's.

To call the Pope Anti-Christ was a familiar form of

invective in the mouths of the German religious revolutionaries, but in the mouth of the Archbishop of Canterbury it was a new thing. He took the opportunity o
Henry's quarrel to release his inmost mind. He darec
not, of course, proceed further to any declaration agains
those doctrines which were so dear to his master—
notably the full doctrine of the Eucharist, to him alread)
odious, to Henry very dear. All he attempted wa
merely negative. He sent out a pastoral letter bidding
men refrain from discussion upon matters which th
reforming theologians were discussing, such as Masse
for the Dead and the Invocation of the Blessed. He eve
(which is not without a touch of humour) bade me
refrain from debate upon the right of priests to marry
and the humour is enhanced when we remember tha
it was in this very year, 1534, that he sent over to Ger
many for Mrs. Cranmer, that niece of Osiander's, wh
had suffered, or proffered to him, his elderly romance.

And here, with the arrival of Mrs. Cranmer, we mus
admit a certain speculation and doubt which is no
without interest. How did Henry treat the affair
Of priestly marriage he would have none ; the con
cubinage of the higher clergy was a practice to whicl
he can no more have objected than any other great publi
man of the time. It was deplorable but it was admitted
much as in the wealthy society of London and Pari
to-day adultery and divorce are admitted, but bigam
refused. Henry cannot have been still ignorant of tha
secret marriage now two years old. Probably he pre
ferred to treat it as though it were no marriage ; bu
at any rate there must be no Mrs. Cranmer openl
ruling the household at Lambeth ; she was to be kep
in reserve. I have mentioned the story which con
temporaries believed, which passed into current history
which has naturally been criticized by Cranmer's admire
but which is probably true enough, that, under th
necessity of hiding, Mrs. Cranmer travelled in a sort o

tub, and that once when the tub was put wrong side up she was constrained to protest. It may be so. The matter is of no great importance. What is interesting is to see the way in which the unfortunate man's predicament was looked at.

He continued to serve. When, in the following January, Cromwell was made a sort of spiritual vice-gerent for the King Cranmer bowed to that extraordinary power, as did all the other Bishops; but he was prepared to do more. He was even enthusiastic in the degradation of his order and the submission of the Church to the lay power. This was best seen in the following September, when he undertook to send a circular letter to all the Bishops under his jurisdiction, telling them that the Crown had suspended their powers, and that these must be renewed from the Crown again. It was a most drastic declaration, not only that Henry was now experimental Pope in England, but that his Church derived from him. Just as hitherto a Bishop could not be canonically Bishop in England until the Pope had officially installed him, though on the King's nomination, so he was now not a Bishop in the eyes of the law save by the action of the King; and it was Cranmer himself who underlined this, who dotted the i's and crossed the t's, he, the head of the clergy— acting, of course, for Cromwell. It was particularly pointed out that the office of Bishop was not regarded as necessary to the government of the Church, but rather was convenient, in order to spare the King's Vicar-General the trouble of looking after details. Cromwell could not be everywhere at once; hence Bishops. It was a singular example of the extremes to which the new doctrine was leading; and all this Cranmer admitted as Cromwell's agent.

With Cromwell now active master of the Church over which Cranmer nominally presided, Cranmer went into the background—content to support passively in general, actively in particular, whenever he should be called upon, all that might be officially desired.

When in this same year, 1535, the visitation of the monasteries began—the first muttering of that storm which was coming, of that spoliation which Cromwell had already planned—Cranmer did go so far as to write feebly about his own monastery of Christ Church at Canterbury, the seed-plot, as it were, of the great office which he held, the corporation which had had in early days the active right of electing the Primate of England and which still went through the forms of such election. He made no effort to safeguard the future. All he did was to ask particulars of the policy as it would be applied in this case—even so, Cromwell did not trouble to answer him.

Cranmer had also to take an active part in the settlement of those who were made to leave the monasteries because they were under twenty-four years of age, the responsibility of finding them employment lying between him and Cromwell. He, therefore, was a party to the spoliation as certainly as he sympathized with it. But he had no initiative to take in the matter, for Cromwell had supplanted the Bishops. In the same way he stood silent when More and Fisher were sent to the scaffold after so long a delay; he watched the beginnings of the terror; it must have powerfully affected such a mind as his, but he gave no sign. If he still felt hesitation over the sacrifice of those great men he dared not express it.

His preoccupation was not with Cromwell's flank attack on the Church, nor even with the nomination of Bishops of the reforming kind, such as Latimer, under Cromwell's influence (though he approved); his mind was rendered anxious by something more immediate and more personal.

What was the position of Anne? Upon Anne, he still felt, all his future safety depended; and Anne's own future seemed doubtful enough. The very heavy disappointment which Henry had received when she gave him a daughter instead of a son got worse with the succeeding months. She tried to recover her hold upon him by pretending that she was again with child in the spring of 1534—which was not a very useful lie for it was bound to be discovered, and when it was discovered it made Henry less amenable than ever. He was already beginning to think of another favourite (not Jane Seymour—that was to come, but so far there was no talk of *her ;* it was some other unnamed woman, and who it may have been we do not know to this day).

In the February of 1535 Henry had thought of getting rid of Anne altogether. His connection with her had led to nothing but a series of troubles. There was the standing tension with France. There was the new Pope (Paul III) ready, perhaps, to issue an excommunication. There was bad financial trouble ; and in the summer came continual rain and that which was disastrous in the little agricultural England of that day, a ruined harvest. Fretting him all the time, and more than fretting him, was the increasing unpopularity of the Court ; and Henry, too vain to take any part of the blame, was sure that Anne alone was the sole cause of it. She was indeed the cause of it, for much the greater part ; and of all these troubles getting rid of Anne would free him. That the heads of More and Fisher should fall was some proof that she had partly regained her ascendancy at that moment, but she had gone too far when she urged that the man whom she now but intermittently controlled should put to death her rival, Catherine, the legitimate Queen, and the daughter whom he still loved, Mary.

But, long before the end of that year, 1535, Anne really was with child once more and her chances revived. They were to *seem* yet greater, and her position almost

secure again in the public eye, when, in December,
Catherine began to show signs of illness. It was
at the beginning of the month that the legitimate
Queen had fallen ill. She recovered. On the day after
Christmas she suffered a relapse, and yet forty-eight
hours after seemed better again. Chapuys was with
her, the Ambassador of her nephew the Emperor. He
remained with her until Tuesday the 4th of January,
when she seemed to be in really good spirits, but as he
was starting off on the Wednesday morning, the 5th of
January, he asked her doctor, de Lasco, what he really
thought of the case; and de Lasco told him that he
believed a poison had been at work: a slow poison,
administered apparently with her drink at long intervals.
When Chapuys reached London on Saturday the 8th
(he had gone very slowly from Kimbolton because he
expected news which might hurriedly summon him to
return) the servant came back with the news that the
Queen had died on Friday the 7th. What had
happened was this:

A little after midnight between Thursday the 6th
and Friday the 7th, having already got a little sleep
after combing and plaiting her hair, Catherine woke
and asked what the hour might be. When they told
her, she waited a while and then asked again, saying that
she wished to hear Mass, but it was not yet the canonical
hour. Her Spanish Confessor, George of Atequa (who
held the revenues of the Bishopric of Llandaff), proposed
to say Mass for her although the canonical hour had not
come; but the Queen told him he must wait till it
should arrive; and when it was four o'clock the Mass
was said in her bedroom, the responses to which she
herself gave; and after it he gave her communion.
After this she fell to prayer, calling upon those around
to forgive Henry and to pray that he might return to
right living. Then she summoned that doctor of hers,
de Lasco, and dictated two letters, one to Chapuys and

one to her husband, which last she signed, " Catherine, Queen of England," and which contains that famous phrase, " the desire of my eyes is to see you again." At ten o'clock she asked for and received Extreme Unction. She was still able to make the responses, and this being accomplished she remained at prayer, until, at two o'clock in the afternoon, she died.

I have said that in the public eye it seemed as though this death would be to the benefit of Anne. The news when it came to the Court, on that Saturday, January the 8th, was most indecently received ; the King saying openly that now he had no more fear of war, Anne's father and brother as openly proclaiming their relief and crying what a pity it was that Mary had not followed her mother's example.

On the next day, the Sunday, all was festive, the King in his best and Anne's baby daughter Elizabeth brought to Mass with all manner of glory, flourish of trumpets and train of attendants ; and at night a ball, where the King took the infant in his arms and carried her round the room, showing her to all and sundry.

I say " in the public eye," but hardly in her own estimation ; for Anne had every reason to be anxious indeed. In spite of her condition Henry was treating her brutally, and she was not capable of treating him with respect. She made scenes. There was something like violence between them. On the 29th of January, 1536, she miscarried—and the child would have been a boy.

Now, indeed, things were beginning to look difficult for *her*, and Cranmer knew what that would mean for *him*.

The death of Catherine had been misinterpreted by Anne. She had cried, " Now am I queen indeed ! " with that bitter, loud voice of hers and that growing acerbity ; for in spite of her dominating will and quick wit she was of narrow judgment. There was now pitted against her not only a will stronger than hers but an intelligence indefinitely superior ; I mean the intelligence of Cromwell. For Cromwell had at last determined to be rid of her.

Cromwell knew (and even Henry must have known, for if he had not grasped it Cromwell would have told him in time) that to be rid of Anne—and with Anne of his increasing troubles at home and abroad—he must first be rid of the unhappy Catherine. Then only could he be free from his complexities with an open road before him to act as he willed. Then only would the standing menace of Imperial enmity be dissolved and the English government free to ally itself as it would in what looked like the renewed great struggle between the Empire and France. Then only could Cromwell proceed to that imposition of his own full power over the Church, to the seizure of the monastic property and much of the clerical wealth—with only the unarmed spiritual opposition of Rome to meet and that opposition not supported as it had hitherto been by the might of Charles V.

Did Catherine die a natural death ?

Our histories have taken that for granted, but contemporaries had grave doubts, and the wisest of them were the least satisfied. They thought with de Lasco she had been poisoned.

Suspicion of poison was so common in the sixteenth century where great people were concerned, it is an accusation so easy to make, so difficult to prove, that everyone will at first be inclined to pay little attention to the suspicion. I certainly do not propose to decide it, nor even to examine it here, but I think it is important to the history of England to state the case. Chapuys, the Emperor's Ambassador, not only himself thought she had been poisoned, but noted how many others thought so.

The body had been immediately embalmed, but

embalmed by a man in the confidence of Anne and of Henry; the dead woman's doctor was not allowed to be present. Immediately after the embalming the body was enclosed in a leaden coffin and no one saw it again. In a hurried letter to Cromwell, sent during that same afternoon, comes the phrase, " the which must needs shortly be done, for they may not tarry "—yet the Queen had died of nothing that could advance corruption and it was the depth of winter. Her doctor again asked to be present; he was refused. Still more remarkable, the Bishop of Llandaff, her chaplain, who by all custom should have watched by the body was not allowed to do so. No witnesses were permitted. What is more, the man who was sent to embalm her, after he had told the Bishop of Llandaff what he had seen, and especially the condition of the heart and how everything else was healthy, bade him, as might one who could not bear to keep a secret in his own breast, to tell no one further. But the Bishop told the doctor, and when the Imperial Ambassador sent a few days later to find what the truth might be that doctor said that there could be no doubt of the poisoning and repeated that he had believed it all during the course of that uncertain illness. There was further mystery. Chapuys after a great deal of trouble got leave for the doctor to see the Princess Mary, in order to find out details of her mother's death—but when they came they were forbidden to see her. When the doctor tried to go home to his native country— Spain—every difficulty was put in his way, as in that of the Bishop of Llandaff, who had said Catherine's last Mass and given her her last communion. *He* tried to escape in disguise, was caught by Cromwell's spies, and thrown into the Tower.

Why was it so important to keep these men from going abroad?

If Catherine were poisoned, who poisoned her? Suspicion would fall at once, of course, upon Anne, for

Anne had openly demanded her death, and on the surface of things it would seem that she would be the principal beneficiary by it, and indeed she had said she would be. Chapuys thought it was Anne, but he also thought that the King was an accomplice.

Now, if murder was done it could hardly have proceeded from Anne, because, so far as she was concerned, the thing came too late. It would have been of more service to her a year before or even earlier than that.

As for the King, he might, in his usual unreasonable, unconsidered, passionate way have proposed to act by Attainder against the unfortunate woman whom he had wronged ; but if he had attempted so monstrous an extreme there would be little doubt in the mind of any cool observer that he was running the risk of rebellion. Public opinion was exasperated in the highest degree ; that one act might make it boil over—in spite of the reign of terror which was now in full swing.

If there was one man in England who could see things as they were and also had power to act it was Cromwell. If the murder was done—it remains uncertain—Cromwell was the man that did it. He was the calculator ; he was the man who fully understood how Catherine's claim, while she lived, roused the Emperor and the English people and therefore bred more and more peril both at home and abroad. But whatever he may have done in the matter of Catherine, Cromwell was also now determined to get rid of Anne, as being an obstacle to his full power, as making alliance with the Empire impossible and as being a disturbing element in the actions of the excitable and uncertain King.

Cromwell, in his plans for the destruction of that now distraught and wayward woman, Anne Boleyn, knew that he held a trump card. Henry's incapacity for fixed life had been taken advantage of again ; a new woman had been thrown at his head.

Some months before, during the summer of 1535,

Henry, hunting in the west of England, had come to Wolf Hall, the modest squire's house of a man whom his father had noticed—one Sir John Seymour. The family had seen to it that he should take ample notice of the daughter, Jane.

She was an ugly little woman, pale, and about twenty-five years of age. Whether she had kept her virtue is doubtful, and it was cynically remarked by contemporaries that if she had not it would be all the better for the foolish King—who could then find plenty of reasons for divorcing her if it ever came to yet another marriage. She caught him by a sort of kittenish way she had, which, in spite of her looks, netted the loose King: that and proximity in a small house. For it was not the first time he had seen the young woman; she had been a maid of honour to Catherine.

After Anne's miscarriage on the 29th of January, when Henry came upon her, and, in a fashion characteristic of him, began heaping reproaches on her for not having given him a boy (saying that he saw well he should never have an heir by her), she, with her accustomed violence, had counter-insulted him, telling him that it was his fault—he had so angered her with his infidelities.

We know what effect reproaches had upon the temperament of Henry. In the next month he advanced Jane Seymour's elder brother Edward, then about thirty years of age, to be a Gentleman of his Privy Chamber, and Jane, either understanding or well coached, knew how to play her hand. When Henry sent her a purse of gold she returned it with protestations about her sacred honour. Whereupon the comedy was played of Cromwell giving up his room in the Palace communicating with the King's by a secret passage. In that room Edward Seymour was lodged, and there Jane could now privately receive the King.

Henceforward the intrigue against Anne was in full

blast. It served the Seymours' ambitions, it served the King's silly vagaries, but the man who really conducted it was Cromwell. He must have given to it as much attention as to that other twin plan of his which was then reaching its last stages : the plan for destroying the monastic institution in England, of seizing its wealth to the profit of the Treasury and especially to the huge increase of his own fortune.

Cromwell had gone so far, towards the end of April, that he actually mentioned his design against Anne to the Emperor's Ambassador in that Easter-tide, and thenceforward things moved quickly. On the 24th of April a Commission was appointed, with general instructions, Cromwell one of the members upon it and therefore the chief member—and it was appointed because Cromwell had assured the King that he was in grave danger. There were conspiracies about (he said), and having so frightened the King, he began to collect his evidence against Anne.

It was not difficult. History will never be assured as to whether the accusations made against her were well-founded or no. But perhaps experts in these unpleasant things will ultimately decide that the woman had lost her balance. She had always been somewhat abnormal, and she seemed now to be lending herself to every kind of affair, promiscuously. There are apparently cases of the kind not uncommon with those who are of Anne's temperament and who have gone through what Anne had gone through. It is at least certain that, like her daughter after her, any admiration— the most outspoken, the most incongruous, the most grotesque—was eagerly received, and the more so as she was now losing whatever looks she had had.

Only five days after the appointment of the Commission a man hardly of gentleman's rank, one Mark Smeton, who played the lute in the Palace, held a conversation with her which was reported to Cromwell. Her question and his reply had been compromising. On the next day, the last of the month, he was arrested. The next day again, being May Day and in those times a great feast, there was a tournament at Greenwich and a gentleman of the King's Chamber, the Keeper of the Privy Purse, Henry Norreys, was to joust with Anne's brother, Lord Rochford. Henry and Anne were present at the tilting.

As the King rode back to London with his train he beckoned Norreys to ride up to his side and privately told him this : that he was suspected of adultery with the Queen. Let him confess and he would be pardoned. He protested her innocence and his own. Henry rode off, and Norreys was immediately arrested, as Smeton had been, and when he got to the Tower he found Smeton there. Late that evening Anne heard the news. Henry was away at Westminster. He preferred to leave the difficult work to others.

On the next day, the 2nd of May, she was called before the Council, and it was then at latest that Cranmer (to whom so far the news seems not to have come) must have heard it.

His peril now was extreme—and well did he know it.

As for Anne, *her* peril was manifest ; for the Council, including her own uncle the Duke of Norfolk, examined her rudely and she became hysterical. It was on the morning of this day, the 2nd of May, that she had gone through that ordeal. The tide was still at the ebb ; she was kept prisoner in her room till it should serve. Then, at two o'clock, the same hour in which Catherine had died those few months before, they put her aboard the Queenly barge from which she had stricken Catherine's arms only three years ago, and, watched by a great concourse, she was floated up on the first of the flood to the Tower. She went in by the Traitor's Gate.

Kingston, the Commander of the Tower, the man who had arrested Wolsey years before, received her and put her into the same lodgings which she had occupied on the day before her crowning. It was while she there lay, with the Sacrament for which she had begged exposed for her prayers near her room, that a letter from Cromwell reached Cranmer; it increased his terror. He, Anne's man, raised by Anne and like enough to fall with Anne, was ordered to Lambeth from the house in the country where he lay. He was bidden to await within the walls of his palace the King's pleasure, and not to presume to come to Court.

He obeyed, and on the morrow wrote a piteous letter, imploring the King not to confuse the Queen's case with his own; not to involve in her ruin the ruin of that new ecclesiastical establishment of which she had been the authoress and over which he presided. But before that letter could be sent he received a summons to cross the Thames and present himself in the Star Chamber, on the opposite bank. It seemed to be the end.

He went, and found the Lord Chancellor, with three others of the Council. What they said to him, how they examined him, we know not; certainly they must have desired to make him a witness in some way to Anne's guilt; at any rate they told him what proofs they had, or said they had.

Cranmer, thus at bay, prepared to save himself. He went back across the broad river to his Palace and added to the letter words admitting his belief that the woman who had made him, upon whom his career had been wholly dependent, in whose house he had lived as a chaplain and whose bread he had eaten as a humble dependent, was guilty. He added, in that letter, how he marvelled that one whom he had so much respected should have fallen to such things. But he himself had fallen lower—for he had abandoned honour to make sure of dear life. He was to fall lower still.

In less than a fortnight, on the 15th of May, Anne's

uncle, the Duke of Norfolk, with twenty-six Peers assisting, opened the Court against Anne in the great Hall of the Tower. There, sitting in a chair at the bar of this Court, the victim heard fully of what she was accused : that she had admitted five men to her intimacy, not only Norreys and Smeton had been her lovers but Bretherton, and Weston as well, and her own brother Lord Rochford. They found her guilty, and condemned her (on the disgusting order of the King) to an alternative death, by burning or beheading, according to his august pleasure—and so she was left in the agony of uncertain prospect.

On the Tuesday, the day after her condemnation, Cranmer went humbly (under orders) to see her, and to do worse than he had yet done. He was to worm what he could out of his protectress.

What he said, and how far he succeeded, we know not, but this we do know, that he played with her the same trick that he had played three years before with the unfortunate Elizabeth Barton. He pretended to be Anne's friend, he put her in good heart, for in this way can information best be obtained from those in terror. When he left her she was convinced that she was saved. She told her ladies that she understood she would be sent to Antwerp, and perhaps the bait held out to her was that her life would be spared if she would consent to a divorce. But all was kept secret.

On the next day, Wednesday the 17th, Cranmer held his ecclesiastical Court at Lambeth to decide with impartiality and solemn justice that interesting question whether this woman, whom he had so solemnly declared to be Henry's wife, were in truth his wife or no.

And Cranmer played his part. Henry's Proctors made no demur, and Thomas Cranmer casting up his eyes to Heaven, invoking the name of Our Lord and protesting that he had God alone before his eyes, pronounced sentence that the marriage between Henry and

Anne—his own especial marriage—was and always had been null and void.

A blank day passed. Of the Friday morning, the morning the woman would be put to death, there is a story told* well worth remembering. Cranmer paced up and down, up and down, the long garden at Lambeth beside the flowing river. Had he slept ? It was very early, in that summer weather ; the sun not long risen over the roofs of London down-stream beyond the bends of the Thames and the young flood just making, racing past beyond the lane under the Palace walls. A man had recently come to him, as though his soul were not already sufficiently seized with horror, and had added further horror. It was one Ales, a Scotch refugee, flying from the danger of persecution for heresy in his own country, one whom Cranmer had protected. The young fellow had had a fearful dream. He had seen Anne's head held up by the hair, severed from the trunk, bleeding—he could count the veins. With that vision in his heart Cranmer paced up and down, up and down.

Had any man told him when the hour would be ? They had kept her in suspense all the day before : she and her small neck. All night she had prayed and talked and raved, and raved and prayed and talked, and would not sleep. It was nine o'clock when the headsman of Calais cut off her head with the sword.

But Cranmer had saved himself.

* I say "told." The story is likely enough but the date less certain.

VIII

BACK TO HEEL

CRANMER had just saved his bacon. It had been a very close thing.

When he had been summoned from the country to Lambeth, sternly told not to approach the Court by Cromwell himself—his master and the master of the whole country too—bidden to await the King's pleasure (which meant Cromwell's pleasure), he was not far from death. He must indeed have trembled. He, the Boleyns' humble man, ready though he was to obey whatever powers were strongest, official though he had become, had found himself pitted against that much stronger silent force from which he had hoped for permanent if contemptuous protection—the will of Thomas Cromwell; for Thomas Cromwell it was whose influence, supporting that of the Seymours, had brought Anne Boleyn to the scaffold; and with Anne doomed to die, Cranmer would normally have been sucked into the same disaster.

But he had saved his bacon after all; and he had saved it by eagerly submitting to the King's peevish and angry desires. He had gone as far as it is possible to go in subserviency; he had betrayed the woman by whom he had become what he was, he had pretended to be her friend in order to worm out evidence from her, he had given her a false hope of life with the same object—he had gone down to a level as low as a man can reach in dishonour.

He had suffered indeed; but he had not done penance, he had not made satisfaction. If he who was of the New Learning and was so impatient of the old translation from the Greek which talks of " doing penance " instead of " repentance "—if he had understood that there is no

149

repentance without satisfaction, without undoing so far as one can the ill one has done, he would have known— in his conscience he must have known—that he was on the path to the Pit.

The woman was dead. She would have been dead anyhow. But he had actively helped on her death— and she had been his friend, protectress, everything. That pacing up and down on the fatal morning along the walks of Lambeth Palace garden was an agony, but it was not a penance. He had fallen.

Having thus preserved himself for the moment, he turned the more to the cultivation of Cromwell, and Cromwell graciously received him into favour again. After all, they had been allies, more or less, all these four years since first the obscure Cambridge Fellow had been picked out for public service, and especially in the three years since the divorce, still more in the eighteen months which had followed the complete separation from Rome. When Cromwell had begun his policy against the monasteries, Cranmer, being Primate of England, might by a word—though at great risk to himself—have put a brake on the wheel; it ought to have been his especial concern to protect that most ancient institution at Canterbury by which his office had come into being, though all his sympathies being now against the Catholic Church and in favour of the revolt against it abroad, were necessarily against the monastic institution; and in nothing more than its championship of chastity. Yet it should have lain with him to have done something to prevent the ruin of the monasteries and convents, a vital part of the great ecclesiastical body of which he was the nominal head.

There may be pleaded for him that little thing he did, his proffering a timid word of mercy for the Carthusian Priors. But he effected nothing and dared effect nothing. What is more, he allowed the spoliation of the secular endowments, including those of his own See. In the twenty years between his appointment and his death more than a third—more nearly a half—of the endowments of the Archbishopric of Canterbury had been robbed, and he, Cranmer, a priest, presided at and permitted the robbery in order to curry favour with the lay robbers.

Cranmer, therefore—Anne Boleyn being no longer there—becomes Cromwell's man. As such, quite apart from his own interest therein, he would have increased his subservience to the King. For, in whatever things Cromwell was acting behind the King's back, they were political, not ecclesiastical, and they were especially matters of foreign policy or private peculation. For in foreign policy Cromwell felt himself to be such a master and Henry to be so poor a judge that he acted almost independently—and as for private peculation, he took bribes with a regularity and on a scale surprising even in a politician. But Cranmer cared little or nothing for money. Also his business was purely ecclesiastical, and on that side the more he cringed to Henry the better for Cromwell's security. In whatever matters Cromwell acted independently of the King—and they were many and important—it did not concern Cranmer. That the King should be kept in a good temper was Cromwell's main interest, however much he despised Henry in his heart, and Cranmer always kept Henry in a good temper, for, alone of all those on whom the Tudor had to rely, Cranmer consented to be wholly at orders and to flatter without exception.

Even on the ecclesiastical side, however, there was this much in common between these two men, Cranmer and Cromwell, though for very different reasons. Each was intent on leading the King as much as he could into an anti-Catholic position ; each was for inoculating the Crown with the New Learning.

Cromwell's motive was wholly temporal. Save when he looked into the depths of his heart (did he ever do so in health ?   He was constrained to do so at last under terror of death), his attachment was to the religion of his childhood ; for the theology of the Reformation he had no respect, nor, for that matter, for any other theology when his worldly activities were at their full. He was for making money, for exercising power—that is, for being a master and very rich. He favoured the religious revolution because the greater the separation from the unity of Christendom and the more isolated the Crown of England, the greater his own domination and chance of more gold. The King had made himself a little local Pope, or rather had been made such a Pope by Cromwell—Pope over England—and he had made Cromwell his Vicar-General ; master of all Bishops and of all the clergy ; absolute lord of spiritual affairs in the realm. It suited well the ambition of a man finding himself suddenly in such a situation that the clergy should be humbled, and what could humble them more than the New Learning, with its explaining away of the Sacraments and its undermining the whole basis of the sacerdotal office ?   With its hatred of the Mass, the very function and power of the Priest ?

Cranmer's motive was quite other. He was not ambitious for power, he was not greedy for wealth, but in all his weakness and vacillations and servile attendance upon power, the solid inward kernel of his thought was still the passion to destroy that which he, with so many more outspoken, much more determined, men —careless as he could never be of consequence—now hated, the ancient ecclesiastical structure of Christendom. To replace it by what he and his called " The Gospel," to erect in its place what ultimately was erected —a personal religion based upon private emotion, and, when it sought authority, clinging to private interpretation of Scripture as the alternative to the external authority of the Church—this was Cranmer's inner motive. He desired what he could not then enjoy but

what he looked for in the long run, a day in which that
detestable mummery of the Mass which he himself was
constrained to celebrate continually in such pomp would
be done away with, and when the Sacrament of the Altar,
as Papists called it, should be shown for the base thing
it was—no more than bread.

Had Cromwell by some miracle been purged of avarice
and ambition he would have rallied to that which he
had overthrown and forgotten, but which he confessed
in the last hour—the authority and holiness of the
Catholic Church. But with Cranmer it was the other
way. Had Cranmer had the courage he would long ago
have been a martyr to what he long within his heart
accepted.

In this ambiguous attitude then, this dreadful difference
between the outward and the inward man, to which
Cranmer was condemned by his own miserable weakness
of will, he remained for all those years.

On one occasion, indeed, he could act without hypo-
crisy : the burning of Forrest. Forrest, a Friar, had been
spiritual director to Queen Catherine. It was a special
reason for Henry's hate. He denied the supremacy of the
lay King over the Church and he was hung in a cradle
of chains over the fire to which Cranmer had seen he
should be condemned. Latimer preached for hours an
enthusiastic sermon against him at his passion. But
Latimer and Cranmer were to meet again on another
day, and before another fire.

When Cromwell arranged that the Bishops should set
forth a sort of common formula of religion (commonly
called by posterity "The Bishops' Book"), Cranmer
aided him ; and though of course, with Henry on the
throne, it had to be an orthodox pronouncement, he
worked as much as he could upon the unorthodox side.
Upon its completion he fled from London in the summer
when the plague was threatening ; the King read the
document, kept it for nearly half a year, expended upon

it his entirely Catholic views of theology, and sent it back by Cromwell for the Archbishop to ratify.

The messenger found Cranmer at Ford, his country house near Canterbury, at the end of January. Nothing is more interesting than to read the comments which the Archbishop made; they have all remained for us to peruse with a smile. Cautiously, humbly, he tried his hand here and there at persuading the King to accept new doctrines by degrees; he does not condemn good works, but he does propose in careful language that Henry sets too much store by them. In the prime matter of the Real Presence (the forty-first clause) where Henry hammered and thundered upon the full dogma, he, Cranmer, however strongly he felt, remained silent. It was too dangerous to interfere in such a matter. He writes back to Cromwell protesting that in any suggestions he might have made he is not " a picker of quarrels with His Grace's Book." He only made them for " this intent, that because now the book shall be set forth by His Grace's censure and judgement he would have nothing therein that Momus could reprehend. And I refer all my annotations again to His Grace's most exact judgement."

Upon that last point there can be no question; whatever the King said Cranmer would echo. Thus was issued under Cranmer's outward approbation, Henry VIII's " Godly and Pious Institution of the Christian Man "—the new charter as it were, in England, of Catholicism *minus* the Pope; or rather with Henry as Pope, but in all other matters England Catholic.

Therefore you have therein the seven Sacraments, the Real and Corporal Presence of Jesus Christ in the Eucharist under the appearance of Bread and Wine, and, conspicuously, the " Hail Mary."

Of those twenty-one Prelates, with a long tale of Archdeacons and Doctors of Divinity, who put their names to it, Cranmer's comes first—" Thomas Cant."

leading the procession, with "Jo. Lond.," "Steph. Winton.," "Jo. Exon.," "Jo. Lincoln," and all the rest of the litany, ending up with him of Carlisle—and at the end, "Johannes Tyson, of Holy Theology and Ecclesiastical and Civil Law, one of the Professors."

So much as Cranmer could do for that destruction of Catholicism which he had secretly at heart he did. The Vicar of his own manor at Croydon he would boldly interfere with, for that unfortunate man had muttered something too much like the old acceptation of the Pope. He did what he could to prune down the number of holy days and observances, the popular festivities; he remarked with pain that it was difficult to enforce orders in this, much as he desired to do so, when the King's Court itself seemed so bound by the old customs. But he writes to Cromwell something rather touching in this connection, saying that he would have all the Bishops made responsible rather than the King, so that "the evil will of the people" (for there is no doubt what the people felt about these innovations!) "might be conveyed from the King upon the ordinaries," which means, in modern language, that the Bishops, the King's subjects, should act as lightning conductors for Henry deflecting the curses of the English from the Tudor head. But he dared not complain to the King himself of the Court's clinging to the old holidays; it was to Cromwell who sympathized with him that he made his moan.

There was to be in this interval one sharper trial, however, one harder piece of service which he had to swallow. For he was compelled not only to agree to but to take an active part in the burning of the unfortunate Nicholson, who is best remembered in English history by the false and assumed name of Lambart under which he tried to hide.

The year was 1538, just the moment when Cromwell was most hoping that something active might appear

on the King's part towards the New Learning; it was
the moment when, as we shall see in my next chapter,
Cromwell and Cranmer between them had triumphantly
managed to hoodwink Henry in the matter of the new
Bible. But in the main point of their intrigue they were
to be balked. On the Sacrament Henry was still fixed.
He, so impulsive, passionate, and therefore both wavering
and easily shepherded, could not be made to move upon
that point of doctrine.

It was a strange scene. This Nicholson (he had earlier
been imprisoned for heresy under Warham but released
upon Warham's death) was a man far advanced; a
pioneer in the rebellion against the ancient religion.
He had been a crony of that Frith whom Cranmer had
already so readily agreed to burn. He was a schoolmaster
in London and a priest; he knew that he was in danger,
and therefore did he take on the false name of Lambert
or Lambart. But his zeal was too great for concealment.

Taylor, the man who was later Bishop of Lincoln,
having preached a sermon at St. Peter's in Cornhill,
Lambart came up to him and presented a document
under eight (or ten) heads : eight (or ten) reasons against
the Real Presence.

It is worth remarking as illuminating the nature of the
times that Taylor himself had hal believed the same
thing, but dared not yet say so. Perhaps he thought to
save Nicholson, certainly he thought to appease the
King, by supporting for the moment the main doctrine
on which the King was determined. Taylor, after
consulting Barnes (who was also in his heart opposed to
the Sacrament), went to Cranmer, both because Cranmer
was the head of the Church and because everybody knew
that Cranmer would take up whatever position the King
desired and even be zealous in it.

What Cranmer said to Nicholson-Lambart we do not
know. Presumably he tried to persuade him to hold
his tongue. Cranmer, so thoroughly in sympathy with

the wretched man, could not have desired to be dragged further into the matter, but dragged further he was, in spite of himself ; for Nicholson—most unlike his judge —was of an heroic fanaticism and would not yield. He told Cranmer that he appealed from him to the King, and was at the pains of putting down his heresy very carefully in writing lest the King should miss the point of it.

Nothing could have suited Henry better. He was immensely vain of his theology. A Court was formed, Henry had himself carefully dressed in white satin (white, as being the colour of the Holy Ghost), took on the Papal office of supreme spiritual judge, solemnly mounted his throne in Westminster Hall, ranged upon his right hand his Bishops, upon his left his nobles, summoned the lawyers to attend, and held a great trial.

It pleased Henry's temper to make the Bishops, knowing as he did that some, being Cromwell's nominees, were not sound on the Eucharist, bow publicly to his inclination. They were therefore summoned, one after the other, to answer Lambart's objections to the Real Presence.

Cranmer was ordered to rise second and to take on the disputation immediately after the King, and Cranmer urged the unfortunate victim, with all those reasons which his own inward self denied, to accept the official truth : he was mild, he called the poor fellow " Brother Lambart "—but he did for Brother Lambart all the same.

No one could have seemed more orthodox than Cranmer upon that dark and short November day of 1538. If there were ten of Lambart's original objections, eight only were dealt with by the Court. Seven Bishops argued in turn after the Primate, and for five mortal hours the unhappy wretch was subjected to this ordeal until he was all bewildered and at a loss. But at the end of such a strain the King, who was already sufficiently incensed against the prisoner when he heard that he had been hiding under a false name, put to him this question :

" What sayest thou now after the instructions of these learned men ? Art thou satisfied ? Wilt thou live or die ? "

Even with his head thus confused and after such moral torture, Nicholson could not get his tongue to say that he believed what he did not believe. He did not deny the Real Presence, but neither did he affirm it ; he threw himself upon the King's mercy.

Henry answered : " Then thou must die."

Sentence was pronounced, and, immediately afterwards, on the 30th of the month, Nicholson *alias* Lambart or Lambert was burnt.

If any thought, as both Cromwell and Cranmer had thought and had hoped, that something might yet be done for moving Henry towards their anti-Catholic side, for getting him to admit some wedge into a crevice of the maintained traditional religion of England, what followed was to disappoint them still more.

There had been three years before, in the days of Anne's trial and after her execution, debate upon, and subsequent publication of, a sort of manifesto which was supposed to settle in open fashion the religion of the country, now that Henry had broken from Rome. In those debates the men who secretly favoured the New Learning had worked hard for some slight introduction of it : they had got only negative results. The document had been finally drawn up under the form of ten articles, perfectly orthodox, nowhere denying anything of Catholic doctrine or practice.

But Henry, feeling that even among his servants there was something of rebellion in the air, determined to enforce those orthodox views which were his own and those of the English people, and in the spring of 1539 he bade Cromwell and Cranmer, with ten Bishops to assist them, frame further articles which should make matters perfectly clear. The committee got rid of its responsibility by reporting that it could not agree, though in what way they were divided or what about we have no record ; but in less than a month the act was framed ; Henry put it before the House of Lords on the 7th of June; Cranmer voted for it (let that be carefully remembered) ; he voted for it on all three readings. It received the Royal assent on the 24th of the month and became law on July the 12th.

Now what were these six articles which Cranmer had thus dutifully assented to ?

The first was the fullest possible statement of the Catholic doctrine of the Real Presence, and ending with the words, " After the consecration there remaineth no substance of Bread or Wine nor any other substance but the substance of Christ, God and Man," and the Act reiterates that anyone who offends against this first article shall be burned—a provision already law but here re-emphasized.' He was to suffer forfeiture of goods also, as for high treason.

Communion in one kind was enforced by implication in the second article.

In the third Henry created a new dogma of his own, showing himself more Catholic than the Pope ; for he declared the celibacy of the priesthood to be imposed by the law of God—whereas under Catholic doctrine it is no more than an appointed discipline. What is more, Henry made the denial of clerical celibacy a crime ; to act against that third article or to deny it was to be henceforward a felony.

It was to be felony to impugn the vows of chastity taken by man or woman ; it was to be felony to impugn private Masses, which were declared agreeable to God ; and it was to be felony to impugn auricular confession.

To use a very modern form of modern English—that was that ; and to all *that* Cranmer subscribed.

Such were the very open definite definitions to which

Cranmer in particular assented ; and what was more, under the effect of the third article he hurriedly sent Mrs. Cranmer back to Germany.

But one thing Cromwell and Cranmer had effected in those years : they had produced by a very careful piece of manœuvring an English translation of the Bible, specially designed by its wording to help on the Reformation. They had tricked Henry into accepting it, and had published it abroad under his authority and with his recommendation—although that translation contained phrases which, had he read it, he would never have passed. The matter is too important to be treated as one of the other incidents of those four years during which Cromwell held power, between the death of his victim Anne Boleyn and his own ; for that translation of the Bible, the foundation of all that followed, has played so great a part in English history that it needs a division of its own.

IX

THE BIBLE

IN those ancient days when civilization was being renewed in its native land, the basin of the Mediterranean, from three to four thousand years ago, a group of hill tribes calling themselves Israel—after a revered ancestor—received, established or inherited a singular tradition. Their remnants, when first we see them in the light of clear history (not much more than two thousand five hundred years ago), were filled with a spirit already deeply rooted, passionate and convinced. The essential of this spirit was a claim to be the servants of the only true God, to be his chosen people and (what sounded much more important to outsiders who heard so strange a thing) the destined heralds of a Divine event. There was to come from amongst them a Saviour who should renew all things.

Not numerous but energetic, they inhabited a narrow and somewhat barren belt of high lands overlooking the coastal plain on the extreme east of the Mediterranean, with the ancient and mighty civilization of Egypt to the south and south-west of them; the ancient and mighty civilization of the Euphrates and the Tigris beyond the deserts to the east of them; and on the north, ultimately imposing their culture upon the world, the Greeks.

Partly because Israel was thus a meeting-place for the nations whose routes of commerce passed right along their boundaries; much more through their passionate energy, conviction and unique affirmations upon themselves, they attracted the notice of antiquity, to whom they were known by the name of one of their surviving tribes—the Jews, having their capital at Jerusalem.

This very small but remarkable people had gathered

(at various dates) their traditions into a sort of little library of books ; a selection of which were particularly sacred to them. To this collection the leaders of the Greek civilization which had overspread the whole of the eastern world, the Jews included, gave the name of " Ta Biblia," which is Greek for " The Books." The curiosity these writings excited caused them to be translated from Hebrew into Greek, and they were thus given some chance of survival. Though ninety-nine hundredths of ancient literature has perished, it is possible that this collection, or some fragments of it at least, would have come down to ourselves. But it is not likely that the whole would have survived, and it is certain that no special prominence would have been given to it but for a singular accident, which, in much larger matters than this of the Hebrew scriptures, has vitally affected the whole world. That accident was the rising, in the midst of the ancient civilization, of the Christian Church.

This institution sprang from the Jewish people themselves. It claimed to have been founded by a Jew who Himself claimed to be of Divine origin. He was—said His followers—that Messiah, that Saviour, whom the immemorial traditions of His people looked for. Save by a very small group of original disciples His claim was rejected, and regarded as so blasphemous that He suffered death by Crucifixion. But the society which claimed to derive from His foundation left the Jewish environment, planted itself everywhere amid Europeans, men of our stock, and flourished exceedingly.

It called itself from the beginning by the Greek name of " *ecclesia*,"* that is " Church," and was soon found spread by the enthusiasm of its missionaries throughout that united civilization which now extended from east to

---

* This word had long connoted in the first century, the time when the Church arose, a closely united society, the bond of which was the performance of mysteries after initiation, and which therefore had about it a certain air of secrecy.

west, identical with Europe, and known to us as the Roman Empire.

It was discovered, when it was of a stature to be noticed, upon all sides, arrayed under regular officers called Bishops, possessing a mysterious rite of Bread and Wine, and within perhaps two generations of its origin possessed also of a certain number of documents, recording in a fragmentary fashion the teachings of its Founder, more fully and in more detail His sufferings and death, and His instituting, on the eve of His crucifixion, that same rite of Bread and Wine known by the Greek name of the Eucharist. Others of these documents dealt with the missionary journeys of those who first propagated the general Church throughout the Roman world, and the letters which they wrote to the subsidiary Churches, those local bodies which built up the whole.

This set of documents witnessing to the inauguration of their Society, the Christians preserved as a sacred and awful record, to which they could appeal in matters of dispute and treat as a testimony of their Divine Founder, His teachings, His precepts, His example, His claims.

It was only natural that such a collection (The New Testament) should be famous and preserved. But what would seem most remarkable was this : that the Christian Church, spread throughout all countries and soon including all races, so that the tiny original Jewish group from which it had sprung was rapidly merged in the mass and disappeared, yet equally preserved the old Jewish books.

This new European institution, the Christian Church, though it had no stronger antagonists than the Jewish people (in whose eyes the Christian Messiah was an impostor and the cause, to them, of great misfortunes), maintained that " Ta Biblia," the old Hebrew Scriptures, were the revealed word of God. Those ancient writings, all dating from long before the advent of Jesus Christ, were given great reverence by Christians as foretelling the Saviour. They came to be called " The Old Testament," as distinguished from the more sacred and essential records of Jesus Christ Himself and His Apostles, " The *New* Testament "—that is, the new concord between God and man, the new witness of God's revelation to man.

Historically this curious development whereby the sacred books of opponents and even of enemies were preserved everywhere by the Christians proceeded from the fact that in the beginning of the Church when the faithful gathered for the Eucharist they were themselves no more than dissident Jews, who read the old Jewish Scriptures in their meetings as all Jews did. But the moral reason for the unique place given by the Christian Church to these ancient writings, their exaltation and sanctity in Christian eyes, was that they form as a whole one body of prophecy : a symbol of and, as it were, a tendency towards that Divine event which the Christians claimed to have taken place in the birth and career of their Founder.

In a word, the Christian Church caught up, preserved, propagated and made sacred what it called " The Old Testament " because it was, in the judgment of the Church, the introduction and the premonition of that supreme historical fact, the Incarnation, and therefore of the Church itself, founded upon that doctrine and event.

Through the agency of the Church the " Bible," as we call it (an English word derived from " Ta Biblia "), included all that ancient ante-Christian mass of the Old Testament which permeated the whole of our civilization. The stories told in it became universal throughout all Christendom and so remained century after century ; those stories were familiar to every one of the millions whom the Catholic Church instructed, and were repeated as the prefiguration of the life, passion and death of

Our Lord, the prophecies of His coming, the symbols of the Christian truths, darkly or more clearly expressed in things written or handed down before the Christian Church arose. Therefore the psalms or sacred hymns of the Jews as well, their Chronicles, their minutely detailed laws, their proverbs and treatises of wisdom, the rhetoric of their religious leaders or " prophets " —all these, contained in the old Jewish sacred books, were treated as matter upon which Christians also were to be fed, as witness to the intention of the Creator from the beginning to preserve one strain of revelation amid mankind and to lead up to the glorious moment in which the Messiah had come and given life to His people : the Christian Folk ; the members of the Catholic Church.

Thus it was, by such an adventure or accident (as the non-Christian would say), by such a Providence (as the Christian would claim), that documents cherished and handed down by the chief enemies of the Church were accepted as a chief part of the Christian culture, were bound up with the most sacred Church documents themselves, and solemnly pronounced to be inspired and Divine. All Europe was steeped in them for much more than a thousand years, the episodes which they related appeared everywhere in the mosaics of the Churches, in the illuminations of the service books, in the myriad carvings which adorned the temples of the Church. Thus the Bible stood fixed in the minds of European men from generation to generation.

To one contemptuous of or indifferent to Catholic doctrine, to the Pagan approaching it, even to the newly converted (as St. Augustine testified in his own case), this older portion of what the Catholic Church now called " The Scriptures " or " Holy Writ," might seem barbarous or incongruous. Much of its rhetoric was sublime, but more of its narrative was tedious ; there was little of that chivalry which would seem native to the blood of Europe, still less of that humour which would seem equally native to it. It was alien. Some of its passages were certainly obscene, others grotesque. It vouched for events miraculous and to the general mind incredible—yet it was pronounced on the awful authority of the Catholic Church to be Divine. Its sentences were quoted as oracles and appealed to in the settlement of all doubts, and the Canon of Scripture was made, side by side with, and only inferior to, tradition, the reference book of the Catholic Church.

Thus it was that by one of the most striking ironies in all our European story, that which had been given its character and value and even its survival solely by the authority and power of the Church, came, in the quarrel of the later Middle Ages and at its explosion in the sixteenth century, to be used as a principal weapon against the Church itself.

*   *   *   *   *   *

From the very beginning of debate upon, and settlement of, doctrine within the Church the text of Scripture, the Old Testament as well as the New, had been a court of appeal. By their own interpretation of texts, even obscure, the orthodox had supported the traditional views on the Sacrament, on the authority of the Church and its officers, on the whole Catholic scheme ; and by *their* interpretation the various sectarians had also from the beginning of the Church supported *their* own multiple and conflicting views.

To appeal to Scripture was not only no novelty, but no other appeal could be conceived, save, of course, to the supreme and final authority of the Universal Church. Where, therefore, that Universal Church itself was called in question, when men began, under the corruptions and strains of the later Middle Ages after the Black Death, some three generations before the moment which we call that of the Reformation, to question the authority and office of the Catholic scheme itself, to Scripture would they appeal. Scripture was claimed as a co-ordinate authority which might be set against that other living authority, the Church : though, but for that living authority Scripture would never have been known.

Those now inflamed against the restrictions of the age-old religion, the temporal claims of its officers, the excesses of the priests, their rapacities, the contradiction between their profession and their lives, the contrast between the machinery of Church life and what should have been its spirit, the wealth of the hierarchy—all these appealed to Scripture. The distaste for repression in every form, and especially the revolt against the priesthood in its sacramental function, its claim to separate privilege, its exercise of the Mass—all these various reactions against the great fixed body of Catholicism turned to the Scripture for support.

*   *   *   *   *   *

The principle that Holy Writ being of such pre-eminent and unique value should be familiar to all was, of course, as old as the Church itself ; we need not repeat what has just been said upon that. To translate Holy Writ from Hebrew into Greek for the eastern half of the Roman Empire, into Latin for the western, was a thing that came as a matter of course, and under these Greek and Latin forms thousands of passages from it appeared in every part of the ritual, in all books of devotion, in all sermons, everywhere wherever the Catholic spirit was abroad.

Into the barbaric languages, the Slavonic and the Teuton, into the Coptic, presumably into the Punic, it was translated ; and when, late in the Middle Ages, there arose the vernacular languages which took on fixity at last and had a literature of their own growing up from the thirteenth to the fifteenth centuries, there arose side by side with them, though somewhat later, a tendency to translate what should be the food of all Christian people into the vulgar tongues. The more essential portions, the psalms, the Gospels and much else had been translated over and over again into various dialects, but after the establishment of the great European idioms thus late in the Middle Ages, a tendency arose to translate the Scriptures as a whole into those local languages, and thus there was a Bible in the Bohemian-Slav dialect, a Bible in the northern French, a Castilian Bible and a Flemish one.

English, which was the latest born of the vernacular tongues, had its own popular translation which has come down to us and has been confused with the effort of Wyclif and his followers.

But almost coincident with this wave of translating the Scriptures from the main Latin version of the West into the local dialects which had become national languages, came a new development which was itself of the very first importance, and which we must understand lest we miss the whole meaning not only of the Reformation itself but of the strenuous defence which was put forth against it by the official Church.

This development was the new use of those very Scriptures which the Catholic Church had imposed upon the mind of Europe. They were used as a weapon against the Catholic Church itself.

There had always been heresies, that is, revolts against particular doctrines of the Church. It is a mark of the development of Christendom from the earliest ages, and the chief activity of the " Ecclesia " from Apostolic times to our own has been the marking down and denunciation and exclusion of affirmations contrary to the doctrines of which it professed to be the undying witness. The Apostle Paul acted thus against the Corinthians and in age after age the process continued.

But after the middle of the fourteenth century (say

1350), when the Black Death fell upon our Western civilization with its catastrophic effect, or rather when those who in youth had been subject to this effect grew up to manhood and formed the first generation affected by the catastrophe, there appeared what had not been present before at any time in the European story—a *general* protest against the Church as a *whole*. It was a protest which coincided with the corresponding process of hardening or, as I have called it elsewhere, " crystallization "—loss of elasticity—in the organization of religion. The strain and ill-ease arose because men had grown indignant at the contrast between what the Church might be and what it was in its externals.

The Papacy, the centre of all that organization and its chief, the institution which gave that organization unity, was shockingly weakened by internal dissension. Rival claimants had produced the Great Schism just at the time when those who had been children under the Black Death or who had received their most vivid impressions from the years following on that vast over-turn of society were conducting public life in Europe. There arose a persistent and insistent cry for " The Reform of Head and Members." The scandal of a divided Papacy, with one claimant supported by one set of Christian Princes, and another by another ; the progressive weakening of Papal authority under such a scandal (there were at last *three* men each claiming to be Pope and each followed by their own section of Christendom) must be put an end to.

Great Councils were called with the object of setting things right. They only made the confusion worse, and though the Papacy was chiefly in question, the whole structure of the visible Church also fell under criticism and the demand for rectification. The vast income of the clerical body in all its forms, often drawn in irritating fashion from the laity ; the power everywhere of the

Church Courts, scandalously used on occasion for the advantage of a privileged body and not for the advantage of the Faithful as a whole; the continued wealth of the great monasteries, though they were now halved in the number of their members; the worldly character of many of the great Prelates, getting worse as the spirit of the Renaissance spread—all this acted as a ferment.

Therefore it was that particular enthusiasts arose in England, in Bohemia, in France, vague and fluctuating in their various affirmations of new dogma, but fiercely agreed in their common denunciation of the whole clerical body, *and as a consequence in their progressive attack upon those points in Catholic doctrine or practice which gave the clergy their privileged and peculiar position and strength.*

The more violent of these enthusiasts would go so far as to attack the received and solemn doctrine of the Real Presence. They would themselves propound very different counter-doctrines. The same man (as in the case of Wyclif and many others) would hold and proclaim different opinions successively at short intervals. Often passions ran high upon practices which did not touch doctrine at all but were merely questions of discipline or ritual, as, for instance, whether the laity should receive communion in both kinds. But what has got to be remembered in order to understand the growing excitement which filled the fifteenth century (1380-1516) and and came to a head at last in the explosion of 1517 is that the root of the new thing which men held to be so great a menace was an attack upon the organization of Catholicism.

The movement did not begin by attacking this or that doctrine through rationalism or scepticism; it began by an eager desire to undermine the authority of the official Church. The questioning and whittling down of the full doctrine of the Sacrament, what became at last a fierce hatred of the Mass, what was throughout a denunciation of the Papal and later even of the episcopal office, denial by some of the priestly power of absolution, by others of the efficacy of the sacraments administered by bad men, violent recrimination against the monastic orders and particularly the Friars—all these things were the secondary effect of one primary cause: reaction against the structure of the Church: *war against the priest.*

No longer, as had been the case throughout the centuries, were particular heresies the peril with which Catholicism found itself confronted. It found itself confronted with a general denial of its own essential spirit—that is, of the sacerdotal function, of the sacramental system, and of the whole philosophy upon which such things reposed.

War against the priest had a weapon ready to its hand in the special use of the Old and the New Testaments, that is, of the Bible as a whole. Since Catholicism had created in man this universal respect for Scripture as the inspired word of God, to Scripture would those turn who desired to destroy Catholicism. For, used in a certain fashion, the weapon was of the utmost value to their effort.

There were three ways in which the Bible could be so used, three ways which were fused together in their action but which we must keep distinct in our minds because they are separate in quality.

In the first place appeal to the Catholic sacred books against Catholicism itself could be and was used as an appeal to primitive usage.

Secondly, if the authority of the clergy was to be removed, some other authority must be found: and the authority of Scripture, though the Church had created it, could be used to supplant the Church itself. Its single authority could be perpetually insisted upon, to the exclusion of all other, and therefore to the exclusion of the authority of Pope, Bishop and Priest, Bull, Sentence, Definition by Council, and the rest.

Thirdly, since Scripture existed in a form the language of which was no longer the common speech of men in the West (the Latin Vulgate, and at the end of the process, for scholars, the Greek Septuagint as well), Scripture could be made to stir up the populace against the Catholic Church by the use of translations specially designed for that purpose. The men who desired to innovate, the enemies of the priest who desired to upset the sacramental system and the hierarchy, would translate key words in such a fashion as to support their argument.

It is not historically true that this rising anti-Catholic movement began with a fervid desire to make the laity acquainted with the Scriptures. The laity were already permeated with the Scriptures and had so been for centuries and centuries. The desire was rather to use the Scriptures for a special and new purpose. Therefore, whenever the Scriptures were so used they were accompanied by commentaries and annotations the object of which was to undermine the respect for the Papacy, the priesthood and the hierarchy as a whole, the sacraments which they administered, the authority which they exercised.

The whole thing can be most clearly seen in that example which is most familiar to English-speaking people, the use of the Bible just before and after the year 1400 by the Lollards. There was already a Bible in the English tongue which had only just begun to be universally used by all classes in England. It could not be spread throughout the community as a document, it could not be possessed by a great mass of private houses, because a book of that magnitude transcribed by hand before the invention of printing was a very costly affair; but it was to be found in the libraries of the rich and of great institutions and was consulted by all those who could have access to the numerous copies of it which were to be found throughout the community.

Innovators, however, proposed to make a *new* translation of their own, with the object of emphasizing their tenets—or rather their negation of the Catholic position. But as a new translation alone, even with key words specially translated in a new way, would not have had sufficient effect, they worked by adding a long commentary which pointed out how, in their opinion, Scripture showed the claims of the hierarchy and the sacramental system to be false. It was even quite easy to do this without a new translation, merely by adding the commentary to the existing orthodox translation; but a new translation might be of some service by presenting in certain key words an idea which the orthodox translation did not give. The essential, anyhow, for those who planned a revolution in religion was to have plenty of commentary and criticism which would leave the reader to read into the Bible a disproof, either positive or negative, of the clerical claims and of existing discipline.

For instance, in the matter of discipline, there was celibacy of the clergy universally insisted upon in the Western Church. But in the Bible you find no trace of such clerical celibacy for the Jewish priesthood, and in the New Testament are allusions to marriage among the Apostles and to married officials of the early Church. Or, again, in that minor point of discipline, communion under one kind, the communion of which you read in Holy Writ is a communion under two kinds; or, again, in that major and central point of doctrine, the Real Presence in the Eucharist, the commentator would insist that the words of institution were not seriously intended but merely metaphorical.

For the matter of that, commentary as it progressed, could go on to deny pretty well anything it liked, and as we know, in the process of a few generations, it did come to deny everything which Christians had ever held. It is not difficult, by putting one's own interpretation upon their phrases to maintain that the synoptic gospels do not present Our Lord as God, and though the very first innovators would have been shocked by that particular private interpretation, such an interpretation began fairly early ; the first examples of denying the Divinity of Our Lord, and proving that denial from Scripture, came quite soon after the first outbreak under Luther.

The Bible, then, was the principal weapon to hand for those whose intention was to destroy the structure of Catholicism.

When they began to use it (from just before 1400 onwards) the authorities of the official Church met the danger by repression. It was the simplest and most obvious way and the way consonant to the whole mind of the time not only within the Church itself but among its enemies. All were agreed that where the truth was known speech and writing opposed to the truth should be suppressed. Since heretical translations were going about they must be sought for and destroyed.

The next step was to say that only orthodox translations should be used ; therefore Bibles must be examined and must be licensed. Moreover, since the chief method of attack against the Church was to read out loud to an audience from the manuscript Bible and to make anti-Catholic commentaries as one went along, the reading of the Scriptures also must be licensed by authority and forbidden to those who intended to use them for an attack upon the general Faith.

Hence you may see why, in the generation just before the outbreak of the main rebellion, the generation just before that of Luther, More, Erasmus, Cranmer and the rest, the generation who were born in the middle of the fifteenth century or rather after, the struggle turned upon the Bible. It did *not* turn upon whether the Bible were inspired and of Divine authority or not—the Catholic Church itself had given it that position, and but for the age-long insistence of the Catholic Church upon the Bible it would have occurred to no one to give it any authority at all; indeed, it would probably not have been heard of—but upon what it meant, and whether certain interpretations of its texts and certain translations of key words made with an anti-Catholic object should or should not be published. The vernacular Bible was there in orthodox form in many languages, but the official Church was increasingly restricting its use as a weapon against herself.

Now just at the moment when that generation prior to the Reformation was coming into activity and leadership, there spread the new invention of printing. The number of books was no longer restricted to a few expensive manuscripts; they could be produced by the hundred in a comparatively short time and at a comparatively small expense. A Bible, which used to cost two hundred pounds, might now be produced for ten.

We must not imagine that the invention of printing had its effect immediately; no new invention ever has. There is always a " lag." Printing was well established by the time this generation, born in 1440–60, had come of age, but the habitual use of printed books is not found until that generation had grown elderly. It was the next generation, the generation of More, Erasmus, Cranmer, Latimer and the rest for whom the printed book was normal. The restriction of Scripture used for private interpretation and as a weapon against the Church when Scripture meant a manuscript costing more than the average man could earn in a whole year's labour was one thing; the restriction of it when it cost one-twentieth of the old amount and when it could be produced, not in a few scores, but in hundreds and in a brief space of time, was another. You could print and bind a Bible at the end of the fifteenth century and sell it at a profit for a dozen pounds or less ; and this meant that a book which all men revered and which most men desired to possess could be possessed by anyone of the middle classes and by many of the populace. As in the case of the old manuscripts which had cost many hundreds of pounds each and which only a few could possess, the printed Bibles had also to be licensed and carefully watched. But it was impossible to prevent men who had heard a certain opinion propounded upon a set of texts from using their judgment as they read and perhaps adopting the novel and revolutionary ideas. What could be prevented, and in effect very largely was, by the authority of the Church and the civil state, was what Catholic tradition and authority regarded as false translations. What could also be prevented was the printing of commentaries emphasizing what such authority regarded as false interpretations.

There was in those days a man who was to prove of singular effect upon the English mind, not in his own life-time nor for a life-time after, but at very long range as it were. The name of this man was William Tyndale. He was much of an age with Cranmer—a year older ; he had been a Franciscan monk of that strict rule the Observants, whose house at Greenwich was rightly regarded as one of the great bulwarks of enthusiastic orthodoxy in England ; it was the house against which Cromwell at the crisis of the struggle on the King's Supremacy and the breach with Rome directed his earliest efforts ; the house whose members had given the reply, when they were threatened with drowning if they continued to support the Pope, that, " The way to Heaven was as short by water as by land." The place was a nursery for enthusiastic men ; but the enthusiasm of one of them turned contrary to that of the rest, and William Tyndale was that one.

He was a Yorkshire man, ugly, quarrelsome, zealous to the very limits of zeal, and in the years when his contemporary Cranmer was hiding within his own breast, in the obscurity of a Cambridge college, his growing distaste for the religion he must outwardly profess, Tyndale had broken bounds and was actively at work in the attack. He went to Hamburg in 1524 and there set up his press, helped by Coverdale (who could not bear his temper and later left him). Thus early he had made no doubt in his rejection of the Sacrament, and he was in the full swing of the tide which was carrying the German Reformation. From Hamburg he went to Cologne, where he printed a New Testament ; then to Worms, and in 1525 appeared his version in which a key word, by which such things must be tested, appeared with many others to show his purpose.

For there is in these things a test, as in all others ; a single point which though it is minute is decisive ; it is the famous text, Matthew xvi, 18, where Our Lord says : " I will build my Church." Tyndale, faced with that word " ecclesia," called it in English " congrega-tion." There was no Church, you see. The Church was an imposture.

This new stuff reached England in the next year, 1526. But Henry's government had been warned—this, remember, was even before there was any public talk of the divorce and when there could be no question of anything but strict orthodoxy for Henry's subjects : England was all Catholic and with not even an excuse among the boldest for innovation. The offending book, with its offending mistranslation, was so thoroughly suppressed that to-day only a few fragments remain. Meanwhile Tyndale did not make his position with Henry any better by stoutly opposing the divorce. For he was an uncompromising man and challenge was the breath of his nostrils. By 1530 he had brought out at Marburg the first books of the Old Testament, the

Pentateuch, in English; with commentaries of the most violently anti-Catholic kind, and in 1534 came another New Testament loaded with anti-Catholic attack throughout. Then, in 1535, came the whole body of the Bible—and in that effort William Tyndale showed himself the twin to Cranmer in talent as in years, for, like Cranmer, he had created the glories of English prose.

The rhythms of that work run through all successive recensions and adaptations of it. Tyndale did not know what he was doing nor did those of his time understand; but a long life-time after, when the men who were then little children were very old or dead, Tyndale's rhythms had begun to vibrate in the minds of a younger generation, and when at last the final version of the English Bible appeared—it was after an interval of nearly eighty years—the spirit of Tyndale still moved through its majestic cadences.

There you may see what the man did; unwitting. He did not live long, he had fought too hard, hated too much and was too much hated in return—he and his " congregation " Church. He had taken refuge in Antwerp and lay there in doubtful security protected by the privileges of that hostelry which received English merchants in the town and was called " The English House." Henry, " his natural Lord," did what he could to have him kidnapped that he might feel the royal vengeance for having denounced the Boleyn marriage. In that effort Henry failed. He had not the satisfaction of putting the angry prophet to death under the warrant of his own hand and in his own realm. It was done by others. William Tyndale was lured by a trick out of his refuge, the authorities of the Empire seized him, now that he was out of quasi-neutral ground, and on the 6th of October, 1536, he was strangled there in Antwerp and his body burned. But that mighty thing, the power of prose, was at work, and Tyndale's rhythms were to

come across the sea. The book existed, though the
man was dead, and there were men in England who
were determined that it should be spread throughout
the country and do its work against the Catholic doctrine
and tradition of England, still universal though they
were and still strongly protected by the English King.

Of those men, the two most determined upon such
an end were Cromwell and Cranmer.

X

THE HOODWINKING OF HENRY

IT was the business of Thomas Cromwell to get Tyndale's Bible somehow or other into England. Had he been King as well as master the thing would have been done long ago, for Cromwell saw better than did any other man of his time that the great economic revolution by which he himself and his relatives so vastly profited would never be secure until there had been a doctrinal revolution as well. A man quite indifferent to doctrine whether moral or theological, at least in all the conscious active part of his mind (whatever might lie hidden and forgotten deep below the surface to rise suddenly in the last hours), he saw quite coldly and clearly what was needed.

But Cromwell was not King. He was the man who managed the King; he was the man to whom the King had handed over the whole government of the Church, making him despot in every detail of its administration; but still, he depended upon the capricious, impulsive and now tyrannical Henry, grown at last to indulge a certain pleasure in cruelty, capable of any violence, already badly soured by the experience of deception and ridicule at the hands of the woman who had mastered him and whom he had savagely put to death: a man confirmed in his ideas of his own all-importance by the birth of a legitimate heir to his doubtful dynasty. That man, the King, was not to be shaken from points of doctrine—and the whole purpose of Tyndale's translation, the very object Tyndale had in making it and the object all had who desired to diffuse it among the English people, was to attack those points of doctrine.

How was the thing to be done? It was a question like the corresponding question in modern society, how is communist propaganda to be disseminated throughout capitalist society ? And that question would be far more formidable to-day if our capitalist society had an autocratic head, with laws which put to death at once anyone who denied the rights of property. Tyndale's Bible, which was written to support just those opinions which the Six Articles punished so severely, must yet somehow be brought into England, and the largest opportunities must be given for the circulation of its highly heretical choice of words.

Not only were the new doctrines to support which that Bible had been produced odious to the King, but Tyndale himself had been personally odious, as a fanatical opponent of the divorce. It was intolerable to Henry to think that a subject who had fled abroad should, from the security of his exile, oppose the will of his natural Lord and make him ridiculous before all Europe.

There was all that against Cromwell's intention. But Cromwell had genius. And he thought he knew thoroughly well by this time what material he had to do with when he shepherded, handled, and cozened his appetitive, unwieldy sovereign. Yes, so he did know his material well. He knew also how that material concealed an incalculable element, which was like an unstable chemical compound and might explode. " But surely " (thought Cromwell), " after eight good years of management I ought to know by this time how just to avoid the explosion."

And he was right. He did manage to insinuate Tyndale's translation into the country—after a fashion. He did not during that perilous transaction produce the explosion ; he kept Henry quiet, and when the explosion came it came on quite another matter, in which, as we shall see, Cromwell did at last miscalculate.

It was a godsend for Cromwell that such a man as Cranmer should be at this moment the ecclesiastical head of the Church of which he, Cromwell, was the effective official autocrat. It was not only that Cranmer by theological bias, by a now vivid anti-Catholicism, interiorly supported all Cromwell's policy, rejoiced at the dissolution of the monasteries, argued in favour of every revolutionary step in details of liturgy and discipline, and felt with all his heart in favour of whatever would further undermine the Mass, the Sacraments and the whole tradition of the national religion : but that Cranmer was an emollient. He was the lubricant whereby the difficult policy might be gradually forced in. For Cranmer stood well with the King as no other official about Henry stood. In him alone had Henry found complete unquestioning attendance and obedience. You will look in vain through the whole list and roll-call of those who, in any prominent position, were called upon to help Henry in the administration, to carry out public work, even merely to advise—you will look in vain, I say, through the whole list to find any one name of man or woman who did not, after some little contact with Henry, begin to despise him and to play their own hand—except Cranmer. For Cranmer never dreamt of such daring. Wolsey ; the old second Duke of Norfolk (the soldier of Flodden) ; Thomas Howard, the third Duke ; Boleyn and his daughter Anne and Boleyn's wife ; Cromwell of course ; Gardiner without question ; later Edward Seymour—and so on through fifty names ; every one of them finds out that vanity and lack of assiduity in the man whose orders they are supposed to receive. Each therefore proceeds to plan out a policy of their own and make some considerable advance in it. Some of them came to ridicule him openly behind his back ; in all of them Henry found, and was to find till his death, an element of irritation, because he felt the pressure of an opposing will. He felt that the normal human being (especially if at all ambitious) soon found him out and ceased to be wholly a servant—became too often a master.

But with Cranmer it had not been so. The man had always done exactly what he was told, and to people like Henry Tudor an exceptional experience of that kind is delicious. With Cranmer he felt safe; he might in a fit of petulance get rid of even so accommodating a dependent and agent, but it would never be through having suffered resistance from him.

Vividly must Henry have remembered in particular how only a year or two ago Cranmer had humbly but eagerly thrown over that which should have been particularly his own. The King had thought for one moment to destroy him because he was the Boleyns' man and the very creation of Anne herself—yet with what devotion had not this honest head-clergyman of his betrayed Anne; cajoled her by false promises; used his old friendship for a lever for making her commit herself, and so driven her to the scaffold. No, Henry would always brighten when his faithful Cranmer came into the presence. And that, I say, was the greatest asset that Cromwell had in his scheme.

But wait a moment. It would be impossible to bring in Tyndale's Bible exactly as it was. The meat of it, what gave it its chief character, was the perpetual anti-Catholic commentary, the bitterly heretical interpretation of point after point. This would have to be left out. Nothing but the naked text must appear. But that would have its value; for there were eager men (very few compared with the whole nation, but sufficient for the task in hand) who would know well when they read the work publicly to others or preached upon it or spoke of it in conversation, how to carry on Tyndale's spirit; to tell men that this statement in the Gospels was metaphor, and that such and such a word in the Greek or the Latin meant not what the Catholic Church said it did, but something other and un-Catholic. The specially sought words which Tyndale had used in his translation in order to suggest support of the new doctrines would still stand, though the commentary had gone. Yes, the naked text would suffice.

But there was one last and apparently insuperable objection. Tyndale's name was very publicly known, and better known to the King than to anyone. What Henry would do if an attempt were made to make him swallow that name did not bear thinking about—therefore the name must be suppressed. Tyndale's Bible must be smuggled in under a false name, and Cromwell must risk the chance that the King, in spite of his love of theology and in spite of his passion for annotation and marginal notes, would miss the operative phrases, especially that glaring use of " congregation " for " Church," and would not detect that the book put before him was virtually the same as the original book which he had banned ; it was unlikely that Henry would find out, for to do that would have meant an assiduous reading of all the book, which they might fairly calculate Henry would not undertake.

Coverdale, who, it will be remembered, had worked with Tyndale but had broken with him on account of his bad temper, had already published translations abroad based on Tyndale. He was given the task of revision. There worked on it also, presumably by order, another man who had become a religious refugee among the religious innovators in Germany, an intense anti-Catholic, a priest called John Rogers. With John Rogers manipulating the text one might be certain that everything would be done that could be done to keep the Tyndale spirit. But it would never do for either Tyndale's or Coverdale's name to appear when the King should be approached. They risked a forged name.

And risky it was ; if there was one thing that Henry detested among the various methods adopted for getting round him, ambiguity of title or name was perhaps what he detested most. The trick to-day is universal, but in those days it was comparatively rare—and the more effective. So long as the King did not find it out all was safe. It was a risk, but the risk was undertaken and proved successful; Henry never woke up to what had been done. Instead of the name Tyndale or Coverdale or John Rogers, the fictitious name of " Thomas Matthew " appeared upon the front page of the publication, and it was wearing this coat and after sundry minor slits and stitches in the fabric itself had been made, that Tyndale's Bible reached England in the year 1537.

Among the more enthusiastic and convinced in that well-to-do middle class which gave the strongest recruitment to the proposed religious revolution was a substantial man called Edward Whitchurch, a man with a good many thousands of capital available as free money for speculative operations. He was a member of the Grocers' Company and had a solid position in the City of London. Energetic, born somewhere about the beginning, or just before the beginning, of the century; not yet turned forty, and therefore, let us say, some ten years younger than Cranmer himself, he was at this moment at the height of his powers. And those powers were inspired by a burning desire to drive out the old religion. Being ready to put his capital into printing and agreeing so thoroughly with Cranmer in the common aim (which he professed much more boldly than the Archbishop would ever dare to do), he was the very man to be companion and aid to Cranmer in the work which Cromwell was forcing through.

He took as partner with himself a certain Grafton, also a man of substance and, of course, of similar views. They had printed at their charges in the town of Antwerp and brought over to England for publication a translation of the Bible based upon Tyndale's version and worked over by Rogers, who not only helped to correct the proofs but presumably to revise the text. Now with all this group, Cranmer was in active alliance, and soon in close friendship with Whitchurch himself; from which domestic intimacy it naturally followed that Mrs. Cranmer also was a friend, and we shall later see what that led to. Tyndale's Bible, with the modest " E. W." (Whitchurch's initials) on the title page and with the forged name of " Thomas Matthew " appearing boldly therein, came thus first in its entirety and with official protection into England: the year being 1537, the same year in which Jane Seymour had borne Henry an heir, little Edward, and in which she had died. In the next year Whitchurch attempted to publish Coverdale's translation of the New Testament which had been made and printed in Zurich. He had the work done in Paris, but the government of the French King discovered the character of the work and confiscated it. Then Whitchurch and Grafton, trusting rightly to the protection of Thomas Cromwell and to the now close intimacy of Thomas Cranmer, set up a printing press of their own in England, using for that purpose the recently ransacked house of the Grey Friars in London, and there it was that in the month of April, 1539, they produced, in an edition large for those days (2,500 copies) the first complete Bible to be printed in England and in the English tongue.

It was known as " The Great Bible." Its cost was far less than that of the old manuscript Bibles, which had now become so rare; it could be purchased for £10 or £12 (reckoned in our modern money), or, bound and clasped, for £15.

In the next year, 1540, a second edition appeared, for which Cranmer made so bold as to write and sign a preface of some length. He was exceedingly careful in this document to say nothing which could have aroused Henry's suspicions. The furthest he went was to say that in this Bible now being printed for everybody to read, all people whatsoever (and here he gives a list of about two dozen kinds, ending up with " artificers and husbandmen "), " may in this book learn all things

what they ought to believe." But he safeguards himself
by saying later on, "I forbid not to read but I forbid
to reason. Neither forbid I to reason so far as this is
good and Godly, but I allow not that this is done out
of season and out of measure and good order." So great
a master of prose should surely have said, "I allow
not that this *be* done"—however, let that pass. He
bids people keep in bounds and not dispute the word
of God at all adventures; in other words, he made it
clear to Henry that he was not in favour of "gospelling."
The King must understand that he was all against private
interpretation and reading with heretical exposition and
the rest of it—yet these were, of course, the very objects
for which he had worked so hard and in which, side by
side with Cromwell, he had triumphed; not only had they
put this first English printed Bible, with its special false
translation of the key words, into publication, but they
had actually got it licensed and made official by the King.

For the tricking of Henry was carried to such a pitch
as that !

Cromwell and Cranmer between them issued the thing
"By Royal authority." Henry, who was, to use his own
words, "Vicar of Christ," had been most royally bamboozled. He had been too lazy or not sharp enough to
see what was being foisted upon him; and the very thing
he had fought against was set forth under his nose for his
subjects to consume at will, and with his own special
recommendation. A copy of the Great Bible was to
be put out publicly in every church for men to read.
Bonner set up no less than six on desks in St. Paul's—and
the ball was started rolling.

The thing was done and thoroughly done, and Thomas
Cromwell still had a year to live. He was not a man
given to laughter, but he must have laughed inwardly
at his success with the dupe; and he followed it up by
continuing to Whitchurch the monopoly—which he had
given him—in the printing of the Royal Proclamations.

XI

THE SECOND PERIL

CROMWELL, with Cranmer attendant and dependent upon him, the two associated everywhere in the public mind and in the mind of the King, had managed the introduction of what was virtually Tyndale's Bible: not only its introduction but its publication, its official sanction, its dispersion throughout all the parishes of England, its being read to circles of hearers, and that often by men who would at least insinuate the new doctrines though they might not preach them openly. It was gambling with high stakes, but Cromwell had won, and it might seem that in this moment—it was the spring of 1540—he was not only secure but at the height of his power.

The last of the great monasteries was being surrendered. He had himself pocketed the great foundation of Lewes and a whole cluster of others—he had given to his favourite nephew* thirteen of the monastic estates, turning him from a pot-boy into a millionaire. So far did he feel himself immune that he was corresponding with the Protestant Princes of Germany, acting as though he need not dread too much the annoyance of a master who had no great taste for being led into that particular alliance with the religious revolutionaries abroad and with those who had defied the power of his brother sovereigns.

It was in this that Cromwell for the first time miscalculated. His very success with the new Bible had perhaps obscured his judgment; at any rate he stumbled and fell over a small thing, and with his fall, Cranmer, linked with him, was for the second time to be in extreme danger of falling also. It was to be the second great

* Great-grandfather of the famous Oliver.

195

peril in the Archbishop's uncertain path through power
—a power which he had not planned.

The little thing over which Cromwell thus stumbled
and fell was the proposal for a new marriage for his King,
a marriage into the family of one of those very Princelets
of northern Germany, his policy of alliance with whom
had been (and he knew it) distasteful to Henry.

It was the old historical tradition that the real cause
of Cromwell's sudden fall was his making Henry marry
Anne of Cleves. Therefore our modern itch for novelty
tends to reject that explanation; also our modern way
of thinking in terms of historical forces impersonally,
and underrating the effect of personal motive, makes
that mere marriage seem too insignificant to have had so
great an effect.

Nevertheless, the tradition is sound and that explanation is the true one. Had not Cromwell made this
proposal for a marriage between Henry and the German
Protestant Princes he might have remained in power as
long as Wolsey did. As it was, within a few weeks he
crashed from the height of power to ignominy, confiscation and death.

To understand why this was we must remember that
not only was Henry's caprice in play but that there were
two powerful forces at work in alliance against Cromwell.
The first was the Seymours, and notably Edward Seymour,
the brother of the woman lately dead, uncle of the
little heir. It was his strong ambition to be master
in the end—and therefore to see Cromwell ousted.
The second force opposed to Cromwell was the Howard
family, and notably its head, Thomas Howard, Duke of
Norfolk.

Edward Seymour allied himself with that small but
active party which from various motives looked forward
to driving out the old national religion. But he was very
discreet; everything must depend, with him as with
everybody else who had to manage Henry, upon not

exasperating him. A definite declaration of sympathy with revolutionary doctrine in religion would have destroyed Seymour's influence, heavy as that was through his relationship with the child, for Seymour would be the natural guardian after Henry's death of the boy who should continue the dynasty and was especially dear to his father. For Henry had looked in vain until his forty-sixth year for a male heir.

Whether there was any sincerity in Seymour's secret profession of sympathy with the new religious enthusiasts during the King's life-time and his declared leadership of them after the King's death is a thing for debate. His main motive, of course, was advancement and enrichment; he had already got hold of a lot of Church land, and after his Royal brother-in-law's death he was to pass all bounds and to have a perfect feast of spoils. Also there can be no doubt that, next after money, he loved power, though he was ill-suited to exercise it : but he may, none the less, have had some real sympathy with the Protestant cause for which his name stands in the history of the time. He can hardly have had a theological sympathy, for he was not the man to trouble much about doctrinal points, but at any rate he was probably in reaction against the official Church.

Hitherto, therefore, he had been Cromwell's ally, and especially, of course, had he been Cromwell's ally in the first steps of his career : for both men had moved in unison to destroy Anne Boleyn—Cromwell in order to enjoy undivided authority and Edward Seymour in order to make sure of his sister's being Queen. The appearance of that alliance was kept up almost to the end ; but in the last months of Cromwell's rule Seymour was (underhand) plotting against Cromwell and in alliance with the Duke of Norfolk.

The motives of the Duke of Norfolk and the Howard group for getting rid of Cromwell were simple. Those motives were not religious; they were social, political and personal: personal, because Cromwell had given offence to them as to every other class in the community, and particularly to them, because he flaunted his power —a mushroom thing of the last half-dozen years; flaunted it in the face of men who, like the Howards, had been at the head of the nobility for nearly a lifetime. Cromwell had put to death the Neville and the Percy, whose great titles went back to the heart of the Middle Ages.

There was perhaps a touch of religious feeling as well. Not that the Howards represented Catholic tradition— they had been particularly eager to take Church loot after the dissolution of the monasteries, and no one of the ancient families showed any consistent devotion to Catholic things. *That* sentiment—loyalty to the old religion—had its strength in the English people, not in the very corrupt wealthy upper class of the day. But it is true that the old families stood vaguely for tradition in general against all sudden innovation, as represented by upstart officials of the Tudor tyranny—especially when such innovations brought them in no increase of income. With this general sentiment in favour of tradition there went a vague feeling in favour of tradition in religion : but it was no more than that.

Norfolk's hatred of Cromwell was also social, because it was intolerable to all the people born into the governing rank of English society to see this combined and complete ecclesiastical and civil power put into the hands of a fellow sprung from God-knows-what-publicans in Putney—a money-lending adventurer.

It was political because the Howards also desired power, and so long as Cromwell was in the saddle none would have power but he.

What followed, during those last months of 1539 and first months of 1540 must be understood in the light of Henry's character and that of those who were intriguing against the insolent master of the State.

In the autumn of 1539 Henry had been without a wife for two years. Jane Seymour had died on the 24th of October, 1537 ; negotiations were at once begun for another marriage. In November Henry was considering the lady who later married his nephew the King of Scotland, Marie de Guise. He was personally engaged in this adventure and very much piqued when it failed. He would not allow her even to get to Scotland by way of England ; he condemned her to go round by sea.

Then there was talk of his marrying first one Princess and then another, among women of high foreign birth : a Vendôme, and afterwards the widow of the Duke of Milan. It was only when such a list had been gone through that Cromwell, through his policy of alliance with the German Princes and the Protestant movement abroad, suggested Anne, the sister of William, Duke of Cleves. Not that the Duke of Cleves was particularly zealous in the cause of anti-Catholicism, but that he was, like all the smaller German Princes, especially in the north, anxious to show his opposition to the Emperor, who stood for orthodoxy.

The young woman appeared suitable enough (she was not yet twenty-five—tall and big, which it seems was after Henry's taste for the moment), and represented by Holbein, in a portrait which was shown to the King, as a good deal better looking than she was.

Cromwell, thinking he could do anything with such a man as Henry—even to persuading him against his own senses—poured out whatever extravagance occurred to him, saying that she outshone the Duchess of Milan (whom Henry had missed) as much as the sun does the moon.

The King, of course, allowed himself to be persuaded. The story of what followed is well known and is as perfect an illustration as one could wish—both on its disgusting and its comic side—of Henry's character in these relations.

Cranmer, through his alliance with Cromwell, received Anne of Cleves upon her landing and entertained her magnificently at Canterbury on the 29th of December, 1539. Thence he sent her up to Rochester, where she was to meet the King upon the last day of the year. At Rochester Henry disguised himself in order to have a first look over her at his ease, and on that occasion was unpleasantly surprised. His unstable emotions were powerfully moved and not at all in her favour. She was coarse, she was stupid, and she could not talk a word of any language which he understood ; she could only talk German. It is a testimony to her health and, I think, to her virtue that she was very fond of her food, in quantity rather than quality ; but this unfortunately added to his disgust. Henry tried hard to escape. He gave Cromwell to understand what a shock he had received. He thrashed the matter out for some two days in his Palace at Greenwich. He ordered Cromwell to find some way out of it.

But Cromwell stood his ground, thinking himself sure of his man. The unfortunate King, after exclaiming, with what the French call " a cry from the heart," that " he felt like a man going to be hanged," yielded and submitted to the ceremony ; and it was Cranmer who married the pair at Greenwich, on the 6th of January, exactly a week after that first interview at Rochester.

But the more the marriage went on the more impossible Henry found it. *She* was placid enough, with her sewing and her large German smile, but *his* nerves— never of the best—were on edge. Men thought, a little prematurely, that, the trouble having arisen with Cromwell, Cromwell was already in danger. He was not yet so. He was given in this spring of 1540 another batch of Church lands, so that he had altogether the largest individual bundle of loot : thirty manors, thirty monastic estates—where the Duke of Norfolk himself had only been able to pouch thirteen. What was more, the King made him Earl of Essex, and he felt himself strong enough to threaten the Duke of Norfolk in private.

THE SECOND PERIL

It was during May and early June that those who were intriguing against the all-powerful minister effected their sudden conversion of Henry's uncertain mind. They had for their best lever in doing this the discovery that Cromwell had, in his negotiating with the German Protestant Princes, written much of which Henry had not been told. He had acted independently and with that contempt for Henry which so regularly appeared in those who had had to deal with him for any time.

Then came the explosion. On the 10th of June Thomas Cromwell—the spiritual Lord of England, Vicar-General for the King in all ecclesiastical affairs, correction of heresies and establishment of Godly things, Agent for the King in all things civil and temporal and, in general, chief of England—was arrested in that Council Chamber where he had so long been undisputed tyrant.

The thing had been so silently arranged and so thoroughly that it came upon him like a thunderbolt, and the organization of it was so perfect that, although the arrest took place a little before three in the afternoon, by evening the full inventory had been taken of this very wealthy man's goods—the whole to be confiscated to the King.

The blow fell with equal suddenness but perhaps even more terrifying effect upon Cranmer—for the main count against this leader and supporter of his was the count of heresy.

His second period of peril had arrived. Would he find means to survive it, as he had survived the first when his patroness the Boleyn had fallen ?

He did survive it ; and the methods by which he saved himself are a repetition of those which he had followed during the first great crisis of his life.

First, as in the case of Anne, he wrote a piteous letter to the King, marvelling that one whom Henry had so trusted and whom he himself, Cranmer, had so sincerely followed and revered should have proved a traitor.

The letter is, in tone and character, just what the preceding one had been in the matter of Anne.

Then Cranmer anxiously waited. What would follow he knew not. His patron Cromwell was kept alive for a few weeks in order to give testimony which might serve for yet another of Henry's divorces—his getting rid of the unexcited and unexciting Anne of Cleves. There was nullity to be proved, and anyone who likes to look up evidence of that kind will find it in all its nasty amplitude in the collection of Cromwell's letters. They show plainly enough, if what he relates of the King's conversations with him is true, how and why Henry was not over successful with the other sex. But what should interest the reader more is the panic into which Cromwell had fallen with the approach of death. What he writes to the King is filled with shrieks of entreaty, ending with that famous cry, " Mercy, mercy, mercy ! "

But no mercy did he obtain, and no mercy did anyone at the Court feel any wish to show him. Only the little group of those religious revolutionaries whom he had favoured for reasons wholly temporal were alarmed, rather than chagrined, by his fate. And as for those loud panic-stricken cries for life, they could only have lowered him in the eyes of those who, whether they hated or feared him, had always thought him strong. He had been condemned without trial by that peculiar method which he himself had introduced, to further his own tyranny in the service of the King—the Act of Attainder without Trial. By this method the victim forfeited life and goods and all under a statute which was demanded from the two Houses of Parliament and, of course, obsequiously granted—even in cases (unlike this) in which opinion was in favour of the human being to be sacrificed. Cromwell had devised this novel method for the destruction of Pole's mother, the aged Countess of Salisbury, but she was reserved for a later death and

Cromwell himself was the first to fall by the measure which he himself had introduced.

The Royal assent to the Bill of Attainder was given upon July the 24th; on July the 28th he was led out to die. On the scaffold he particularly begged those who heard him to remember that if he had apparently been led into error he had repented, and had returned to the Catholic Faith.

Now what was to happen to Cranmer? At first there was nothing to be done but to lie low, to interfere as little as possible in public life, not to dispute, to obliterate himself, and see whether an opportunity should arise for restoring his position with the King.

After all, he had one great thing in his favour: Henry had always been a friend and had always testified that Cranmer would serve him well. Henry would remember his past services and could hope for further services of the same kind. Complete submission in every detail to the Royal will had produced an atmosphere very different from what Henry felt in the stronger presence of Gardiner, still more different from what he felt when he was chafing against the masterful spirits of his great ministers.

But something more would be needed; he, Cranmer, had been the lesser brother, as it were, of Cromwell in all that sympathy with the reforming party which had been the ultimate cause of bringing Cromwell to the scaffold: eagerly would Cranmer now look for the means of rehabilitation.

It came, quickly enough.

Even while the work was being done to prove nullity in the matter of Henry's marriage with Anne of Cleves, another woman was being proposed for Queen. Already before Cromwell's head had fallen nullity had been pronounced by Convocation (with Cranmer at its head) and confirmed by Statute. But, weeks before that, the Duke of Norfolk and his party were proposing Catherine

Howard, the young slight daughter of the Duke of Norfolk's brother Edmund, to take the place of the huge German woman, the King's disgust with whom was increasing every day.

In the April which had seen Cromwell's elevation to the title of Essex and the apparent height of his power, the King had given the new young lady valuable grants. She had been noticed. Gardiner, the strongest character in the Prelacy and the one most determined on maintaining Catholic traditions, had entertained the King and her together in his Palace at Southwark, and on the day when Cromwell's head fell he married the two at Oatlands.

Anne of Cleves had placidly consented to all that had passed. She was to be called " The King's Sister." She was delighted to find herself with a permanent English income of £100,000 a year, and so passed into obscurity, to live on all through the next two reigns and to the very edge of Elizabeth's ascension of the throne. The condition that she should remain in the country was not irksome to her, and the splendid provision more than made up for exile—though in those days there were not many in England who could talk her beloved German.

It will surprise no one to hear that on this occasion Henry had once more been misled and kept ignorant of things he should have known. And the things he should have known were the carryings on of young Catherine Howard.

She had been brought up in a ramshackle way by her old grandmother the Dowager Duchess of Norfolk, the mother of the Duke, and her father Lord Edmund. In that slipshod household young men associated freely with the girls, and over and over again a certain Dereham —a gentleman by birth and a page in the household— had come into the bedroom where Catherine and her maids slept, bringing with him fruit and wine for their little feasts, and providing other entertainment. The old lady had heard of these affairs and had beaten her granddaughter thoroughly, but apparently to no effect.

It was from under such a roof that the girl had been foisted on to the King. But he, poor fifty-year-old dupe, suspected nothing. He went up on progress northwards through the Midlands, taking his young demure wife with him (he specially noticed and praised her bashful maidenly manner), and she—by way of additional company—still received Dereham, though whether still criminally or not is doubtful. It was known also that one Culpepper stayed in the bedroom where she and Lady Rochford were until very late hours. I say " it was known "—but not to Henry.

The King and his new young Queen were at Hampton Court for the Eve of All Saints, that is the last day of October, of the next year, 1541. After what had been for him a happy Indian summer of fifteen months, content so filled the Tudor heart that he gave orders how special public thanksgiving should be offered up for the delightful life he was now leading with his young good spouse, and on the next day, All Saints, offered up that thanksgiving was, publicly.

Henry did not know what had been happening some little time before ; indeed Henry never knew : it was the mark of his not overdignified life. But the next day, All Souls, the Day of the Dead, in the Chapel at Hampton Court, while the priest in his black vestments was singing the requiem proper to that solemn feast, and Henry devoutly attentive in his place, Cranmer appeared whispering, putting obsequiously into the King's hands a note. As Henry read it he began to cry. He had been unfortunate again.

What had happened was this. While the King was absent Cranmer had come to hear that one Lascelles could give evidence of certain things he knew about this new Royal young woman, who stood for the Catholic party. If she could be destroyed, two birds could be killed with one stone : his lingering peril would be over : the King would be grateful to the man who opened his eyes, and perhaps—who knows ?—the credit of all that went with the Howards, of Gardiner under whose roof Henry had been brought into company with his new bride, of all those who stood for what Henry himself had stood for—the firm maintenance of the national religion in spite of the schism with the Papacy—might be shaken.

Whether Cranmer were the prime mover in the thing we cannot be certain. The story seems to have come to him first. His timidity, his lack of initiative, might make one guess that others had been at work, and most probably the Seymour clan, with Edward Seymour at their head, secretly active. On the other hand, terror is a sharpener of wits and prompts even the most hesitant to action. Upon the whole, I think we should conclude that Cranmer was the author of what was done.

He took the depositions of this man Lascelles, the brother of the woman who had been companion to Catherine while she was still with her grandmother the Duchess of Norfolk as a girl, before her marriage. The gist of what Lascelles had to say was simple, even if perhaps a little exaggerated. He testified of his own knowledge that Dereham had been taken by young Catherine as her lover into her room and bed " an hundred times." That was what Cranmer had told the King, that was what the little paper so thrust into the Royal hands at Mass conveyed. And that was what had led the elderly eyes to cry, as Henry looked through his tears at the writing.

Henry ordered an inquiry. And Lascelles was interrogated ; so was his sister, who had first started the train, or at any rate who was said by Cranmer to have first started the train ; so was Dereham ; and then others. But a week passed without Catherine being told a word or suspecting anything.

On the 10th of November, the King having left the Court to avoid a painful scene but having left his orders, those orders were obeyed; and the Council came all together into the presence of the young Queen and told her what was laid to her charge. Whereupon she fell into a fit.

What followed upon this is so like what followed upon the Boleyn business, Cranmer's action is so exactly the same in both cases, that one almost feels as one reads of the one that one is reading of the other. And as Cranmer rehabilitated himself by the first manœuvre, so he rehabilitated himself by the second. He soothed the poor young woman by telling her that she could be sure of Henry's mercy and goodness. Then he left her awhile to digest that hope. The ground was prepared for getting a confession out of her.

So in that same day, but later, he returned, finding her, as he had hoped, more composed, and in that gentle wheedling way of his got her to promise that she would reply without any concealment, as she would before God, remembering the Communion she had made hardly a week past at All Saints.

In this fashion Cranmer got hold of what he wanted, enough for his purpose; she admitted the visits of Dereham, she admitted her liberties with him before marriage, she admitted that he had shown violence. Cranmer could not get her to admit more than that, but it was sufficient. He wrote it all out to the King.

On the 12th of December in the Star Chamber the Chancellor read out to the judges the deposition thus received. Rather more than a fortnight later, after further inquiries, the judges gave an answer that adultery might be presumed. Ten days later, again, Dereham and Culpepper were put to death, the old Duchess and others were committed to the Tower—but the Queen's fate was deferred.

It was not till January of the next year, 1542, that a Bill of Attainder was brought before the Lords against her; there was no denial and no evidence except a general report from those peers who had seen the Queen that she acknowledged her offence.

On the 13th of February she came forth from the Tower on to the scaffold, having with her her companion Lady Rochford (the widow of that man who had been put to death as brother of Anne Boleyn years before and herself the betrayer of Anne Boleyn), and the two were put to death.

Cranmer had rendered his service at some risk, and once again had earned the gratitude of the King. The second great peril of his uncertain career had been escaped—perhaps by his own contrivance, certainly by his own action—by faithfully serving tyranny and securing the death of that young victim.

Less than five years remained during which Henry was to grow more and more bloated, during which his disease was to make deeper and deeper ravages into his body, and during which his unstable mind was to fall into further extravagances.

During those five years Cranmer in outward things remained passive; inwardly he passed through a strain the consequences of which were to be seen in his new phase of activity and almost of power after the King's death.

He submitted to all that Henry willed, content to have escaped after the crisis of 1540-41 and to know that his unfailing service had made the King by now his permanent protector. Three times those who knew him for what he was in his inmost thoughts attempted his downfall on the charge of heresy—and each of those three times they failed. Though we need not accept the actual wording put into Henry's mouth by men writing many years later, yet they represent this much truth, that Henry did turn the tables on Cranmer's accusers and insist on retaining at the head of his Church a man in whom he could always be certain he would find complete acquiescence.

When Tyndale's anti-Catholic versions of the key words in the New Testament were attacked and suppressed Cranmer let the change go by ; when there was to be a revision of the text of the Bible by the Bishops he allowed the King to shift the matter to the young men of the decadent Universities, and then to shelve it so that no revision took place at all. He was Henry's man and only Henry's man so far as all external things were concerned. He did indeed still cautiously and privately give sympathizers with religious change to understand that he was on their side—especially sympathizers abroad ; and undoubtedly he was in a sort of secret alliance with Edward Seymour Lord Hertford, who in his ambition of ruling after the King's death (and that could not be far distant) needed Cranmer's friendship as Cranmer needed his. But neither of the men moved an inch against the King's orthodoxy. All they did do was to move him in the one matter which could be worked through love of money, the cupidity of Henry and still more of the courtiers. Shrines and sacred images which promised loot were spasmodically destroyed, not regularly nor universally. The moneys left for Masses for the dead were quarried into and the endowments of the episcopal sees were nibbled at for the benefit of the country gentry. In the matter of his archiepiscopal See of Canterbury Cranmer made a weak protest, but to no effect ; when he came to die it had lost nearly a third of its original endowment.

These were also the years (1545-47) when that conspicuous talent of his for writing shone in the composition of the Litany in English which is to-day the most familiar example of his literary power. He acquiesced, as he always had, in executions for heresy ; and he is to be held responsible, if responsibility is sought—though of course

not he alone—for the burning of Anne Askew, which
lies just as much to his charge as the burning of Frith,
the burning of Lambart, the burning of all those who
in one or more particulars did but more boldly set forth
what Cranmer in his own heart believed to be true,
who did but confess openly before men that hatred of
the sacramental system and of the ancient Church
which was also the hidden inspiration of the Archbishop himself.

He seems to have presided over the Court which, with
Anne Askew, excommunicated and handed over to the
secular arm Adlam the tailor, Otterden the priest, and
one Lascelles.* Shaxton, the Bishop of Salisbury, to
whose promotion Cromwell and Cranmer had seen in
the days when they were working together for packing
the episcopal bench with their adherents, might have
suffered with these others. He preferred to recant, and
to receive a benefice in the place of the Bishopric which
he had resigned; Latimer the same. But the others
were burnt as a matter of course because they would
not withdraw, and the deed was as much Cranmer's as
any of the others which he had officially abetted.

Anne Askew's real name was Kyme, that of a squire
whom she had married, but she was known by her
maiden name because she had left him through the
violence of her apostolic zeal, preaching new things and
powerfully affecting a whole group of the ladies of the
Court.

When Henry married again (by way of having a sort
of nurse for his last years) the widow of Lord Latimer,
Catherine Parr, it was not the Archbishop who married
them but Gardiner, nor was her case referred to the
Archbishop when not long after Henry proposed to
deal with even her as a heretic. It was Gardiner who
was given the order to draw up the case. She saved
herself by a little judicious flattery. So it went on,

* His relationship or identity with the informer is doubtful.

Cranmer doing nothing direct or effective and awaiting his release, obedient to every breath of Henry's—and expecting Henry's end.

So matters ran outwardly. But inwardly it was a very different matter. Those last years of Henry's were for Cranmer years of exasperation and of chafing which grew worse as he passed through his fifties and approached his sixtieth year.

To have had to suffer so many things and in silence, to have had to hold down unspoken so many words and to keep undone so many deeds, was, even for a man of Cranmer's servile temper, a yoke which, borne too long, might become intolerable.

He to whom the Mass had been hateful all these years had to sing it in its chiefest splendour on the great occasions of the State; he, by whom the Blessed Sacrament was loathed, had to elevate and adore it daily and publicly; he to whom the celibacy of the clergy was a corrupt Romish tyranny, had to send off his own wife secretly into exile and live alone.

He had to remain silent and in apparent acquiescence, smiling and condoning it all, while the King and his Court and the English people stood firmly in the old ways. He had himself to follow all the orthodox Catholic practices, and to be head of the Church on whose authority those practices were sanctified.

He burned inwardly, and prepared the great change, awaiting the hour when he should be able to breathe and speak and act. It would come soon. Henry was near to death.

Edward Seymour was in command; Edward Seymour his friend and ally, he with whose aid the Mass might be undone when both should be free men. Edward Seymour had destroyed the Howards: the son of the Duke of Norfolk had been put to death, the Duke of Norfolk himself lay under sentence of death. Under Edward Seymour's domination and that of his group the dying

King had made his will and nominated the guardians of the little boy who would become King after him.

On the 27th of January, 1547, in the dead of night, the summons came. The Archbishop was in his Palace at Croydon. He mounted his horse—and, strong rider that he was, pressed hard for London. He galloped up to Whitehall at the turn of the hours between the old and the new day. He dismounted; he came by that great four-post bed and knelt in that thick-carpeted room with its splendid hangings overlooking the Thames. In the corridor without Edward Seymour was plotting and whispering with Paget the secretary; for their hour was at hand.

Thomas Cranmer knelt at the bedside and took the King's hand; in the huge mass of corrupted flesh some breath of life still fluttered, and there are accounts of whispers from Henry's lips which were thought to mean this or that. By one such account he murmured the name of Our Lady of Walsingham, by another he muttered, "All is lost!" The Archbishop bade him, if he could still hear, to testify to his Faith in his Saviour; and felt (or thought he felt) some pressure of the hand in return. Then the uncertain breath ceased; and the man who had made Thomas Cranmer, who had used him as he would, whom Thomas Cranmer had served humbly and in terror and with obeisance, who had imperilled him and saved him twice, was dead.

NOTE TO CHAPTER XI

The story told by Foxe on the authority of Morice is not credible, though it is quite credible that Cranmer may have palmed off some such story on his secretary. As the tale goes, Henry was preparing to produce a communion service which should supplant the Mass; what is more the King of France was going to abet and copy him. The thing is impossible from what we know of all Henry's life and character, and all the life and character of Francis; even if it had corroborative contemporary evidence we should be justified in saying that there had been a misunderstanding or that the evidence was garbled; as it is we have no contemporary evidence at all, but only a relation at third hand—and the chief link untrustworthy.

XII

CRANMER SET FREE

WHEN " the old King that now dead is " (as one of the courtiers put it) was indeed out of the way, everything lay clear and plain for those who had put themselves in power. They, Edward Seymour and his partisans had surrounded and dominated the dying Henry in the last stages of his physical corruption and breakdown ; they had seen to it that they should be nominated in his will as the Council of Regency during the minority of his little son ; they were—the great bulk of them and all who counted—intent upon forcing through that great change which they had not dared to force upon the King even in his extreme last weakness, but which had been their purport for years. The new Council was sixteen in number, but the only names we need retain as protagonists (after Cranmer, who as Archbishop had the titular first position) are those of Paget the secretary, Wriothesley the Chancellor, and Edward Seymour himself.

We must begin by appreciating the forces that were at work to promote and to carry through that dangerous and difficult piece of work in the face of national opposition. Those forces were of two distinct kinds.

The driving power, the motive force of the whole affair, was the obvious necessity under which those who had become millionaires—and governing millionaires —through the looting of the monasteries, seizing of hospitals, parish endowments, guilds and the rest, found themselves of making their position secure. Nothing could make their position secure, nothing could guarantee them against future reaction, immediate or remote, whereby they might be compelled to disgorge, save—if it were possible—getting rid of the Faith with which the endowments they had taken were bound up. So long as the sacramental idea with its sacred priesthood, its sacred Church property, endured, they could never be completely at ease. It would certainly endure among the populace for a long time, but they could begin the process of gradually eliminating it; and it was their obvious business to substitute for the old national religion some liturgy and set of doctrines framed in that new enthusiastic spirit which, appearing in various forms upon the Continent of Europe, had acquired the name of Protestant. The key of the whole affair, the central point of their policy, was the destruction of the Mass.

To do this would be very difficult, but government being then the overwhelming thing it was, it might with the aid of time be done, by establishing officially a new state of things in which the Mass should be suppressed and forbidden, so that as the children grew up to manhood and the older people died off the new masters could gradually train opinion in the new ways, until they had produced a new England.

The head man of this body, typical and representative of them all, was Edward Seymour himself, Lord Hertford, the uncle and natural guardian of the little King, a man now about forty years of age.*

The second force at work was a different thing altogether; it consisted in that mixed attraction for the new Protestant zeal and hatred of the old sacramental idea, particularly of the Mass, which in different proportions made up the state of mind of those who now called themselves the Reformers.

Of Reformers in the other sense of the word, that is, of people who desired to be rid of the abuses within the Church, to increase its spiritual function, and to stimulate the sloth of the clergy, to see to it that vows of chastity were obeyed, to make the official Church

* We do not know exactly the date of his birth.

and its clergy worthy of strong affection and respect—
to *restore* Catholicism and revivify it as it had been
revivified over and over again in the past after periods
of corruption, hardly any were left in England who
would now have used such a term as "Reformer" applied
to themselves in this connection. For though the
desire for true Reform was as strong as ever, the battle
with an active enemy was now joined, sides had been
taken, and there was no time for ambiguity. All the
energies of Churchmen must be set to preserve the
body of doctrine and liturgy which the dead King,
in spite of his breach with the unity of the Church,
had so effectively maintained with the support of his
people.

At the head of those whose object it was to destroy
Catholicism for religious not for economic reasons,
whose hatred of the Mass was thorough—not the indirect effect of avarice—stood Cranmer. All these
years he had been suffering an increasing internal
struggle under the dreadful contradiction, by his acts
or by his silence, with what was nearest his heart. Now
he and his could be free to act.

It is important to remember exactly what this body
was; for by getting a wrong impression thereupon,
making Protestantism of greater or less strength than
it really was, misunderstanding its distribution over
English territory and among the various classes, we get
the time all wrong. Through such errors with regard
to the remote past men came in more modern times to
conceive an England divided against itself into a mere
turmoil between two conflicting bodies of equal power,
or, at the other extreme, of seeing nothing in the demand
for the destruction of Catholicism but the insolent
tyranny of a few all powerful men.

The real position was this :

So far as territorial distribution went, the movement against Catholicism had a certain strength in

those places particularly accessible to foreign influence, especially the main ports of entry from the south and east, and to some extent in the centres along the roads leading from them to London. In London itself it was strongest ; there would be groups of intensely revolutionary men outside such areas, especially in the towns, but they were not of a weight worth calculating. Of all the centres in which the new ideas had caught on, London was by far the most important, not only because it was the capital nor only because it was very much the largest centre of population (much larger than the next half-dozen towns put together), nor because it was the place where men interchanged ideas most vigorously, nor even because it was the one place in England where there was a large body of unattached men without property, insecure and ready for new things ; but most of all because it was the receptacle of foreign influence from over the North Sea. It had in its midst a great organized corporation of merchants belonging to northern Germany and the Baltic coasts, it continually received foreign travellers from the towns of the Netherlands, where Calvinism had begun to set its mark, and English travellers who had steeped themselves in the new ideas of the Low Countries, of the Rhine and of the Germanies beyond the Rhine.

Everywhere these new men were in a small minority. In London, where that minority was most considerable, they were still but a fraction of the population. So much for territorial distribution.

The great mass of Englishmen who lived in the villages and small market towns, certainly nine-tenths of the population, remained where they had been, in the religion of their habits and training. The north especially was immune from the new influences ; on the other hand, East Anglia, with its vigorous oversea trade, was of all country districts the most affected.

Now if we consider not territorial distribution but

distribution by classes, we find, as might be expected, a much larger proportion of the Reformers among the clergy than among the laity ; the reason being that the clergy were chiefly concerned with theological discussion, and though the interests of that body as a whole lay in an almost unreasoning defence of the existing order of things, yet the proportion of those who were in favour of a radical change was higher than in any other class in the population. That proportion increased as one went up in the ranks of the hierarchy, and on the bench of Bishops it was strongest of all—the reason being that under Cromwell and Cranmer's influence before 1540 every effort had been made to give promotion of men who, however discreetly they might veil their opinions for fear of Henry, were at heart for the destruction of the Mass and of Catholic tradition. Of such men, after Cranmer, one may specially note Ridleys whose position Cranmer had created and who wa, typical of the new promotions. Shaxton and Latimer had been deprived under Henry ; but it was still true that nearly half the bench of Bishops—after Cromwell's nominations—could be counted as anti-Catholic. On the other hand, as might be imagined, it was within the clerical body that the most intelligent and the most vivid resistance would be felt—and of those so resisting, the chief name was that of the man who was, upon the whole, since the death of Fisher the strongest moral influence in England, Stephen Gardiner, Bishop of Winchester.

He had been excluded from the new Council under the influence of Seymour and his set.

If the innovators were thus strong in the clerical profession and especially in its higher branches, we naturally find them strong in the Universities and particularly Cambridge. But we must be careful to remember that hitherto not one of them save those who had had the courage to face financial ruin and even death had openly declared himself—but now they were ready to act.

Lastly, in that factor which is perhaps the most important of all, intensity of conviction, mutual correspondence and support and a sort of informal organization, the Reformers were far superior to the somewhat bewildered much greater mass of conservatives, who had been confused so long by the effects of the schism and who suffered from all the defects of a defensive attempting to hold its own against a violent attack.

These two forces in combination were now free at last to set forth and attempt new things ; and in that attempt we find Cranmer following and at the orders of the lay power—that, is Edward Seymour and his partisans.

The obstacles before them when they should begin their effort were formidable indeed.

The main obstacle was the natural conservatism of the English countryside. We hear of London and much more rarely of one or two other centres of population in which there was a good deal of disturbance and dispute on the part of the intensely active small Protestant minority. But the overwhelming mass of Englishmen were not living under these town conditions : they were living as they had always lived in the English villages and small market towns ; with the regular Mass in their parish churches, with their feasts and their observances as their fathers had known them ever since England began.

Next, there was the difficulty of the King's minority. The Council or the man who should be head of the Council, might be in actual power as strong as any King, but the moral strength of the monarchy, which was the whole basis of government at that time, was lacking ; no one could believe that a little boy only just past his ninth birthday was responsible for the revolutionary orders men might be asked to obey. It would be years before Edward's reign could become a real reign or his will accepted as the origin of true personal commands ; there was a universal feeling that with only a little child to deal with, and a child wholly in their hands, the Council had barely authority to govern, and certainly not authority to impose so forcible and enormous a change upon the English people. Gardiner was the spokesman of that feeling—a feeling as inevitable as it was strong.

It might have seemed therefore a better policy for Somerset and his colleagues, and for Cranmer—Somerset's right-hand man on the ecclesiastical side—to postpone innovation until there should be a real King in the face of the people. It would be their business to see that the child was brought up in the strongest mood of opposition to Catholicism ; then, when he was old enough for people to take him seriously, his authority might be sufficient to carry through the transformation of the State and the destruction of the old national religion.

But delay would be disastrous ; if they were to let things stand as they were, with the Mass everywhere fully practised, if the new reign were to start and to continue for years with the admission that the old national religion should be respected, it might be impossible to make any change later on. Rather must they create a state of affairs in which the Royal boy should grow up with a Protestant establishment about him and the Church officially Protestant ; forming more and more the social atmosphere in which he should reign when his reign became real. Also, if the Council was to confirm its power, it was as well to challenge opposition early and get the battle over.

The first thing to be done was to perjure themselves.

All the sixteen had taken a solemn oath (with Cranmer at their head) to observe the Last Will and Testament of their late master Henry, in which it was arranged that no one should be pre-eminent in the Council, but that the whole body should act as a committee of equal members. Debate and the check afforded by discussion should delay action and give time for the new reign to develop on the old Catholic lines which Henry believed would be preserved indefinitely.

This oath they all of them broke, by allowing Seymour, soon to be Duke of Somerset, to make himself chief. He took the title of Protector. He began to use the Royal "We" and he was, in effect, King. There had been some protest in the Council, notably from Wriothesley, against this usurpation, but the reason that the mass of them supported it—and no one more thoroughly than Cranmer—was that Seymour, being the natural guardian of the little King, would be accepted easily by him as that little King grew up into his teens and could during those early years act with something of the reflected authority of the Royal person.

Edward Seymour having thus been made virtually monarch for the time, it was fairly clear by what stages the policy of introducing the new religion should be advanced.

We must remember that the object kept steadily before their eyes was the abolition of the Mass; but the Mass being the central institution of English life and rooted in centuries of habit could not be got rid of at a blow, for there was no great popular enthusiasm in any sufficient section of the people to permit that being done in England which had been done among certain of the Germanies and was to be done later in Scotland. It was necessary to insinuate, to go step by step, to substitute the totally new thing for the old thing by degrees; sudden action would certainly rouse such popular resistance as to put them all in peril.

At first, therefore, they must carry on the old religion with its full splendour; and no one lent himself more thoroughly to this preliminary than Cranmer. He it

was who sang High Mass on all the great occasions and
who saw to it that the ritual should remain as it had
been in all the first days.   But with so much to go on
with, the next step must be taken of emphasizing the
authority of government—of declaring the supreme
power of the Crown and its right to demand obedience
not by consent but from authority.

Next, one little point after another would have to be
introduced, *gradually* breaking up the Mass, as men
had known it.   It would be easy to order the destruction
of images on the ground of superstitious use, to profess
that only when there had been abuse should there be
destruction but to let the action spread wider and wider ;
for the destruction of images in connection with which
superstition could be pleaded had long been in progress
before the last King died and the wealth to be obtained
by such measures was considerable.   The shrines were
full of treasure, and there was a balance still remaining
of gold and silver, plate, jewels and stuffs which had
not yet been looted.

Next, the Communion should be made a sort of
separate thing ; still forming part of the Mass as it had
from the beginning of Church things, but given a
different dress, as it were, and set apart.   This could be
done by interrupting the Latin ceremony, introducing
exhortations in English, making as it were a sort of
secondary service attaching to the main service of the
Altar—and that secondary service a new one and a
vernacular one.

Meanwhile the pulpits should be tuned, the licences
for preaching should be severely regulated, preachers
should only be allowed to speak words which had been
put into their mouths by the authority of government—
and in the main by Cranmer himself.   Men should be
given the impression that there was much debate and
therefore confusion, that peace could only be arrived
at by some compromise and new arrangement—and

all the time it should be known that a revised version of the service was being prepared with the ostensible object of smoothing down differences and finding a common formula.

But as there was no sufficient native body outside a very few centres, of which London was the only one that really counted, to carry on this battle between the old and the new, it was necessary to call in the foreigner.

It was to this task that Cranmer particularly bent himself. Even in that first year the Italian Vermigli (who is best known as Peter Martyr, which were his two Christian names) had been pressed by Cranmer to come to England and did so, with a fellow countryman of the like Protestant feeling, Ochino. To him Cranmer gave a Prebend at Canterbury. He also got the Frenchman Alexander from Arles, giving him English benefices by way of endowment and keeping him at Lambeth. Next in order he got the famous Polish innovator, John a'Lasco ; and he did all he could to get Melanchthon to come as well.

So much for the general atmosphere. For giving the government the fullest possible power (it would need all it could get to effect such a revolution), the very first opportunity was taken, and it came of course with the Coronation.

The little boy was brought to Westminster Abbey with the greatest pomp and splendour within a month of his father's death, upon the 20th of February, Shrove Sunday. In the morning of that short winter's day the poor child, in his heavy white vestment, sat before the Choir of the Church. They had cut down the enormous ceremony for his sake to a short two hours, but even that was as much as he could bear. The Choir was crowded with Prelates in their vestments, the child, bare-headed and as yet uncrowned, facing the Altar, before which the throne awaited him ; and there, chief among the mitred figures, was the short strong form of Cranmer. Somerset, the Protector; the Earl Marshal, and the great officers of the Crown led the little boy up, his heavy train and robes supported behind him. Cranmer stepped forward towards the body of the great Church, and cried out in the silence :

"Sirs, I here present King Edward, rightful and undoubted inheritor, by the laws of God and man, to the royal dignity and crown imperial of this realm, whose consecration, inunction and coronation, is appointed by all the nobles and peers of the land to be this day. Will ye serve at this time, and give your good wills and assents to the same consecration, inunction and coronation, as by your duty of allegiance ye be bound to do ? "

The great cry arose which always arose when a King was thus to be made for the English—then and then only was the little fellow led forward to where the Blessed Sacrament stood, the Real and Corporal Presence by which he was to swear.

All this said and done, the child must yet suffer further fatigue, though already weary with the ceremony that had told upon him; for music heralded High Mass, and Cranmer sang it with magnificence from the Altar steps. Then could be seen and heard all the glory of that ritual which had taken on further and further pageant century after century since the days when first Cranmer's great predecessor St. Augustine had landed, and since first Bread had been Broken in Canterbury, nearly one thousand years before. There, at Westminster High Altar, as yet undefaced, and over the Confessor's tomb, did Cranmer intone the Gloria and the Credo, there did he whisper the Words of Consecration, bending down in outward worship, and there did he kneel before the consecrated Host and elevate It high, and in its turn kneel before and elevate the Chalice, as had been the sanctity of centuries, and as he himself had sacrificed during all the years of his priesthood, and continually in the presence of the boy's father, that King who had made him what he was, and whose devotion to the Sacrament of the Altar had been so dreadfully enforced.

But this High Mass which Cranmer sang with the blaze of candles about him and the blaze of colour in all the heraldry and robes around, the sound of the organ, the shouts of acclamation, the glory of trumpets blown from the roof above to announce the event to the town and to the world—these were not the chief historical things of that day. The chief historical thing was the new pronouncement which Cranmer made. For the congregation saw advancing down the Choir the Archbishop, with his heavy face and weak eyes, who, lifting his hand, gave them no homily but such a declaration of doctrine as Europe had not yet heard. It was not addressed to the Peers, or the people, or the Churchmen, but to the little frail figure in the dalmatic and the robes upon the throne. And this was what he said :

That no matter what promise the boy might have made, no matter what engagements made or oaths taken, his right to rule the English was from God and God alone. None could constrain him, none could question him, least of all the Church—or him whom men had held from immemorial time to be the spokesman and ruler of the Church, the Pope. No action of Edward's own or of another could separate him from that Crown which he now wore, nor could any deprive him of it. The little chap was God's Vice-Gerent upon earth and Christ's Vicar.

For the first time men had heard in England—loudly proclaimed—and in the seat of the English Kings, in Westminster Abbey—that strange new doctrine which was to be of such prodigious effect throughout the world, the DIVINE RIGHT OF KINGS : the new Protestant doctrine, fruitful of many things.

The doctrine fully born that day (it had been maturing ever since the beginning of the great revolt against Christian unity—ever since the leaders of change had pitted, each in his own State, the Prince against the universal Church) has never died.

Though the word " King " be no longer used, though the word " Divine " has fallen out of fashion, the strength of the *thing* is as vigorous as ever. The Lay State is sovereign ; it claims undivided allegiance ; it has full power over the bodies and souls of Christian men ; it admits no superior authority to represent the universality of Christendom or the Christian moral law ; it stands equal and independent with other states, its like, round about it. The Christian commonwealth of which each Christian State had been but a province and a part is wholly denied : for the Divine right has passed from the religion by which Europe once lived to governments which are but the heirs of the Kings. That Divine Right still rules. And against it the citizen has to-day no power at all.

Partly as a symbol of this new thing, partly to confirm and clinch it, a strange ceremony took place in the matter of the hierarchy. Of old the Bishops had been Bishops in the Church Universal ; their tenure was of that holy society. But now they must be reminded that they were only Bishops because they had been so created by Divine Cæsar, the King. And behold, at Cranmer's orders they must all give up their Sees, which—in the theory of the new system with its lay royal Pope, its national Church—they had had from Henry, who was dead. They were no longer in succession to the Apostles. Christ was no longer the guarantee of their corporation, but whatever Prince might be sitting upon the throne of England—to-day the little boy Edward. They must have new commissions issued to them from the throne, and only from these new commissions could they derive a new authority.

Thus was formally set the authority of government, without which what had been secretly proposed and was so carefully planned would never have been brought to its conclusion.

To that conclusion, to the rooting out of the old religion, the destruction of the hated Mass, which he had had to perform in full ceremony all these years, Cranmer devoted himself. The other great events which marked that year and the next passed him unmoved. There was an orgy of loot, in which Somerset was naturally the leader, but Cranmer took no part in it. He looked on with acquiescence while the Protector his ally, whom he followed and served, pulled down the churches and quarried them to build his Palace. He did not protest, he approved; but he did nothing to fill his own pockets. All his life, this man had been indifferent to wealth.

When Somerset exceeded all bounds what checked him was not Cranmer—not the head of the Church, whose business it might have been thought to prevent such spoiling—but the will of the people. When, among others, St. Margaret's at Westminster was threatened with spoiling and by order of the Protector the mason had put up the scaffolding to pull it down that the materials might be used for the building of his great Palace, the parishioners rioted and he gave up the attempt in fear; but not a word came from Cranmer either at this sacrilege, or at the completion of the loot of colleges, guilds, chantries, and all that was left of corporate property to be despoiled. The more thorough the destruction the better for him. It would be easier to rebuild a new spiritual thing.

And he went cautiously. Though his whole intent was to uproot the old awe before the Real Presence; yet in a catechism for the young to which he gave his name he still pretended to support it, and in all that year, though laying on all sides his preparations for the great change, he continued the outer policy of tradition. He still perpetually sang the great Masses, as that one in St. Paul's which was the requiem for the King of France.

With the next year, the second of the reign, 1548, the first cautious steps of a sort that every man would note were taken, and of these the initial one was the separation of the Communion from the Mass. The Mass went on, but the Communion was made as it were a chapter to itself ; it was prefaced by English exhortations whence the Real and Corporal Presence was carefully omitted. It was upon the 8th of March that the order went out, and the change was to be made on Easter Sunday, the 1st of April. It was the first wedge driven into the rift by which the old religion was to be cloven asunder.

And all the rest of that year there poured out from the press without restraint or censure, without protest from the all-powerful government, torrents of abuse against the Real Presence and the Mass ; and not a word could be printed in reply. While men told each other, in London at least, that something new was being got together to replace the Mass which they had known.

How that something new—a service in English, a revolution in custom, was prepared, we shall never know—so secret was the whole business. Certain of the Bishops, first in Windsor and then in Chertsey, that autumn, drew up a document which we may believe to have proceeded in the main from Cranmer's own hand. Who had approved, who had disapproved, under what machinery the thing had been so privately done, we cannot tell : all we know is that it came into being in the last months of that year, 1548, ready to be printed. It was debated in the Houses of Parliament ; the Bishops of the older tradition voted against it. Cranmer himself in the discussion openly denied the

Real Presence in the Eucharist—for months his foreign supporters and advisers had thought him lukewarm or hesitating, but he had not been so ; he was (whether under advice or of his own initiative) playing for policy. It was a calculated delay, but the time had now come to act, and with the early days of 1549 was adopted, in a Statute put forward by the authority of the State, to replace that Mass round which all the worship of England had centred since Christ was first preached in these islands, a new thing—a Prayer Book. It was ordered to be used in all Churches in the place of the Mass by the Whit-Sunday next, the 9th of June, and the critical point of the great change, the test date, was fixed.

XIII

THE RESISTANCE OF THE ENGLISH

WE are in the year 1549. It is the turning-point in the story of the religious revolution, for it is the year in which the main issue was joined and the decisive act was done—the suppression of the Mass.

That is the test; that is the boundary. For to get rid of the Mass was the soul of the whole affair. The destruction of the old religion would confirm those who had seized power; it would give security to the hundreds —or by this time thousands—of lesser men who had come to share in the progressive spoliation of the Church.

But for Cranmer, though he was a servant here as he was all his life a servant to those in power, there was a very different motive. He would get rid of the Mass because he hated it, especially because he hated its central doctrine on which it pivoted and for which it existed—the Real Presence of God upon the Altar and the daily Sacrifice for the Living and the Dead.

There was also now present that which filled him, even in this his sixtieth year, with buoyancy and zest in the work. It was this: that now (at last!) he was unbound. He could take full vengeance on that which he had hated so long and, hating, had been compelled to serve. He now, Thomas Cranmer, was about to enter into the fullness of self-expression; it was to be for him His Day.

Round about him all manner of heavy political things were passing with which he could not but mix—having by his office precedence over all others in the realm after the King, and being a permanent and most important member of the Council. But he let them go by him like a river; he took no initiative therein. Thomas Somerset had attempted to corrupt the Princess Elizabeth in the hope that the connection might ultimately lead him to the throne ; the Protector had put that brother to death without mercy because such an attempt seemed to threaten his own power ; he saw to it that the poor little boy King should sign the warrant, and Latimer preached the required official sermon to make out the one Somerset more of a villain than the other.

Somerset, during the popular risings, would try to save himself and his enormous booty and his hold over the crowned child, by showing sympathy with the rebels. His associates in the seizure of power, aggrandisement and wealth were therefore to turn upon him, depose him, set Dudley in his place, and ultimately put him to death.

It was to be a very chaos of greed, fear, plot and counter-plot, taking advantage of the royal child's minority—but all that was not Cranmer's concern. Cranmer's concern was the religious revolution in which they were all engaged, but in which he was to be not only the ostensible chief but the most active and willing agent.

Consider the various parts of the difficult task to be attempted. First, they must make sure of the King ; when he should grow up and be really master he must be of a character fully determined to maintain the newly established religion ; he must be fierce against any idea of restoring the old ; he must be a very zealot in his hatred of the Mass and of its Sacrament.

To be certain of the King as he grew up to manhood, to mould him without question to their purposes, was the primal need of those who desired to succeed in this difficult effort of imposing new ways upon a whole nation.

Next, they must replace the Mass by something other ; they must transform the service ; the rite which was the expression and the custom of the people's religion could not be merely destroyed and the churches left to ruin as the monasteries had been, nor the clergy to starve on small pensions as had the monks. A new form of public worship must be found.

There, of course, would come the shock—and it was dated for this year 1549. They had allowed more than two full years to pass in order to make the preparations complete and to allow the idea of an approaching change to become familiar. The shock would certainly be very heavy ; they must try to ride it out ; once they had done that all would be secure for the future : popular resistance defeated by arms is easy to deal with afterwards; it is dangerous only so long as it thinks it may have a chance of success by force.

But it would be impossible to effect so complete a revolution at one blow. As with the destruction of the monasteries ten to a dozen years before, so now with the much greater business of the destruction of the old national religion, it had to be done in two stages ; as first the lesser monasteries had been attacked for uselessness and decay, leaving it open for men to say that the principle of monasticism was not at stake, so now the first New Service in the place of the Mass must be of a kind that men might mistake for something like a continuance of the Mass in another form. When that pretence had done its work and the measure of popular resistance had been taken, they could proceed to the second step and produce a final service book in which no trace of the old sanctities should remain.

The third necessary requisite for the success of the attempt was the fixing of a Creed—that is, the official emission by the clerical head of the Church in England, the Archbishop, under the sanction of the clerical body and by the authority of the King—of a body of articles defining what was the new religion ordered to be believed ; and with this there must go a new code of Church laws for repressing rebellion in the matter of doctrine and liturgy, as well as for more general purposes of safeguarding morals.

These three requisites—making sure of the King—substitution of a new service for the Mass—drawing up a new Creed and a new code of Church laws—were all carried through with success. And of the last two Cranmer was the director and in the main part the author.

As to forming the little King, and moulding him into a zealous anti-Catholic, their success was not only complete but if anything too complete. Those of great fervour, who are attempting religious and political revolution, are not well-suited to humour. But posterity in a cooler mood, looking back at the English Court in the middle of the sixteenth century, finds nothing in it more comic than the intensity of poor little Edward's religion. He was not yet eleven years old when he solemnly expressed his criticisms of the book then in the making which was to replace the sacrifice of the Mass upon the Altar. The word "Godly" was ever on his lips. He would listen, in this year of 1549, by the hour together: a little fellow rapt in attention while Latimer preached in his garden denouncing all things of the ancient religion. To those who have themselves attempted to sit quiet for one hour at "preparatory school" age the mere session will seem heroic, the attention almost incredible—but so it was.

When he was only twelve years old he excitedly drew his pen through the clause presented to him which referred to the Saints: and before he was thirteen he was threatening that, if further changes in the Prayer Book were not sufficiently Protestant, he would make them himself.

Hardly, then, had he entered his teens when he was disputing theology, and he made it his business to go over carefully, correcting with his own authority, the proofs of liturgical work. When Cranmer took upon him to burn the wretched woman Butcher or Bocher for hare-brained ideas upon the Incarnation (of which more in a moment) this too precocious boy delayed her execution in the vain hope of her conversion to those transcendental truths with which he had himself been filled by his sedulous and successful captors.

At puberty the new religion and morals of Calvin's creation became a mania with him, and though he died when he was only fifteen (at the same age as his uncle Arthur had died before him), we shall find him already prepared to obey those who would supplant his own dynasty by another, because they had persuaded him that only so could he save the Gospel and safeguard his reluctant subjects from the idolatry of the Host.

And here I must admit a short digression upon that unfortunate woman Butcher or Bocher, for it was perhaps the most signal occasion upon which Cranmer acted in the ecclesiastical fashion of the day as repressor of religious dissent by fire. It is a prime example of his own attitude towards that particular form of execution.

It was in this same critical year of 1549, and in the month of May, that Cranmer condemned her on the ground of heresy.

He had known her in the past and he had sympathized with her. She was a sort of protegée of his, and he must have felt a domestic feeling in her case, perhaps almost paternal ; for when she openly spoke against the doctrines enforced by Henry VIII (which he himself so detested in his heart) he had saved her from harm. She had acted as a go-between, bringing in the Protestant books secretly and supplying them to Anne Askew— whom Cranmer also had burnt, it will be remembered. But as is too often the case with those who love to con- sider the deeper mysteries, she had gone much further afield. She was no longer content with denying the Real Presence and the things of the Mass and of Catholicism, but began to maintain a new and interesting little heresy of her own—very difficult to understand. She maintained, as her persecutors tell us, that "Christ did not take flesh of the outward man, because the outward man was conceived in sin, but by the consent of the inward man—which was undefiled." Whatever that may mean, she made it clear that she repudiated the doctrine of the Incarnation, which the newly established Church still maintained, and which remained generally believed in the Protestant world until quite recently. Probably what she was after was the old heresy, as old as the first century, that the Man Christ was not Divine, but was inspired by or filled with Divinity after his birth.

What is of more interest to us in the case of Joan Butcher or Bocher than her interpretation of the Scripture by private judgment, is the dramatic scene between her and the Archbishop when he pronounced excommunication—which meant death in the flames. He had given sentence, he had ordered her to be delivered over to the secular power, when she gave tongue and said :

" It is a goodly matter to consider your ignorance ! It was not long ago that *you* burnt Anne Askew for a piece of bread, and yet came yourself to profess the same doctrine for which you burnt her ; and now, forsooth, you must needs burn me for a piece of flesh ! "

Young Edward insisted (it was the first act of initiative in his life) that she should be kept in storage as it were, in order that every effort should be made to convert her. He would not sign the warrant—this boy rising thirteen— because he said that to burn a lady still in theological error was tantamount to making himself responsible for her damnation.

It was a nice point, and Cranmer had to work hard to convince him—for *he* was determined to have the woman burnt unless she would recant. It would never do to have his religious revolution imperilled by chance vagaries. But recant Joan would not, though Cranmer himself and his creature Ridley disputed with her again. It remained to get the warrant signed by little Edward. Cranmer did the trick at last by using the Bible, pointing out that Moses (who was certainly orthodox) had blasphemers stoned, " Yea, with their blasphemies still on them." So young Edward, crying bitterly and still most reluctant, consented to the signing of the warrant by the Council, and Joan Butcher or Bocher was burned.

She died game ; and to the preacher who had been put up to give the usual official sermon at her execution she bawled that he lied like a rogue—and had better go home and study the Scriptures.

It was in May, 1550, that the tragedy was completed, and though this was the most striking it was not the last of the burnings under Cranmer's authority ; for the next year a former surgeon living in London, a Fleming by nationality, George Van Paris by name, having been excommunicated by his own Calvinist conventicle for denying the Divinity of Our Lord, was brought up before Cranmer and Ridley. Coverdale interpreted for him ; he refused to abjure ; Cranmer pronounced the judgment, and he was therefore burnt in his turn.

But to return to the successive stages of the great attempt. The next step, having made sure of the King, was to carry out the change in the Liturgy. We saw in the last chapter how the new book was secretly prepared, and how, to his permanent fame as a writer, we must ascribe not only the spirit of it but the most exquisite of its phrasing to Cranmer himself. It seems to have proceeded mainly from the hands of certain Bishops, six in number : Cranmer himself the seventh. They had also six helpers drawn from lower ecclesiastical ranks (Deans for the most part), and it would also seem from his presence among that number that Cranmer's own man Ridley—whom he had protected and advanced from the early days under Henry VIII, when he had shown strong anti-Catholic feeling—was here again his right-hand man. He was at the moment Bishop of Rochester; he was later to be promoted to the Bishopric of London in the place of the Catholic Bonner.*

The new book was passed by Convocation, it was submitted to the Council, and laid on the table of the House of Lords to be given Parliamentary sanction under Statute upon the date December the 9th, 1548. It had passed Parliament by the 21st of January of the next year, 1549, and the Statute further ordered that it should come into force on the Whit-Sunday following, the date of which would be June the 9th, but might be used earlier where copies could be obtained.

It was so used earlier in London—as early as Easter—as an exception : but not in St. Paul's till the required date. That Whit-Sunday, then, was to be the critical day. Then and in the succeeding weeks would come the effort to impose in the thousands of parish churches all up and down agricultural England, upon the still solidly established peasantry and all the old peace of the country-sides, the new expression of a new religion.

Now what was this book of Cranmer's, commonly called " The First Prayer Book of Edward VI " or " The Prayer Book of 1549 " ?

It is not familiar to the modern general reader, even within its own communion, for the English Prayer Book now in use,† the chief expression of the established religion of England for nearly four hundred years, is not the first Prayer Book of Edward but the later one of 1552—which was quite a different affair. The key point by which it can be judged is its fifth section—the Communion Service—and this was essentially what contemporary Germans called an " interim," which

---

* It was as Bishop of London that Ridley abandoned the large income of that see to the spoilers. They suppressed the new Bishopric of Westminster and endowed him with part of its revenue.

† Allowing for the revision of 1662 and one or two other minor changes.

is Latin for "meanwhile"; that is—a temporary arrangement intended to lead up to a final one later on; a half-way house. For in this first Prayer Book of Edward VI, the Prayer Book of 1549, the Communion Service is so framed that many—it might be hoped—would say that it was still in essence the Mass after all. The word "Mass" is used on the title page ambiguously, but still in evidence, for the section is there called, "The Supper of the Lord and Holy Communion, commonly called The Mass."

The order of the service is the same as that of the Mass, that is—the Collect, the Epistle, the Gospel, the Creed, the Preface, the Consecration of the Elements, the Our Father, the *Agnus Dei* and the Communion. Moreover, many of the main Latin phrases in the Mass are retained in their original place, and translated into that fine English proper to the master-pen of Cranmer. But there were widely different things in which innovation was manifest : the first, of course—the outstanding one in the appreciation of any ordinary man—was the change in the language; the other was the change—by implication—in the doctrine.

The change in the language would obviously be the challenge thrown down to the mass of Englishmen and the point upon which there would necessarily be conflict. The men in power could have no doubt of that. There would be resistance in some form, and probably resistance by force; the sanctity of the Mass was associated in the popular mind with the Latin language, just as it was associated with vestments and all the rest of the ceremonial, and even though the new service had been the Mass literally translated from beginning to end without a word changed, the surprise and shock of a vernacular form would have been enough to provoke violence.

There had been all over Europe plenty of demand for this particular change from Latin to the local language among those who were contemplating great changes in general. The appeal to the obvious had been made, and had had its effect with a minority—especially in towns—" Surely worship should be in a language which all men understand ? "

But that was not the way in which the mass of men, who are always traditional, looked at it ; least of all the unvocal masses of the countrysides. Latin not only represented a mysterious sanctity but it stood for the universality of the Mass, common everywhere throughout the West. And though not one word of the whole Sacrifice were uttered, though it had all been in dumb show, no more than a series of acts, it would still have been for the bulk of Englishmen the central religious mystery which they had attended all their lives and their fathers before them from generation to generation, from what may be called the beginning of English time ; for the Mass is not a set of prayers : it is a drama.

But, for those who were intent upon the political and religious revolution they had taken in hand the use of the vernacular was essential. It helped to destroy the sense of mystery and by it the power of the clergy ; it made the new religion national ; it broke down that general unity of religion throughout the West on which was founded the hieratic authority of the universal Church with the Pope at its head, and to destroy that unity the destruction of the Mass was essential.

The doctrinal changes in the new service were of more direct and definite spiritual importance, though to the average man they meant nothing and could indeed in this first Prayer Book hardly have been noticed. Cranmer had already in that new separate English Communion of his omitted those words which specially emphasized the Real Presence.

Now, in this new vernacular service, he not only omitted whatever would emphasize the Real Presence but also the Sacrificial quality of the Mass. This was called, in the English of the day, its "satisfactory" character— by which word was meant the doctrine that the Mass was offered up to God in satisfaction, a perpetually renewed sacrifice of Calvary, having effect for the living and the dead. For the Mass was and is in the eyes of Catholics that by which the Crucifixion is extended throughout time, and the consecration in the Mass is also the vehicle whereby Jesus Christ remains perpetually and corporally present among men, not through their imagination and opinions but in the Sacrament Itself, whether men be present to worship It or not.

It was all this that Cranmer must uproot. Therefore from the new service were omitted the offertory prayers, alluding to the sacrifice and the prayers for the dead ; and therefore was inserted with reiteration the phrase that the sacrifice of Calvary had been made once and for all.

The Epistles and Gospels for the day were taken from that new English translation of the Bible, based upon Tyndale, of which we have already said so much ; and as an example of its effect when its words first thus fell publicly Sunday after Sunday upon the then horrified ears of country congregations, I will give a critical example.

A central figure in the old worship, as everyone knows, was that of Our Lady, the Mother of God ; everyone knows equally well that the destruction of this devotion, which was regarded as superstitious and conflicting with the original spirit of the Church, was a main object of the Reformers. The Gospel for the second Sunday after Epiphany is taken from St. John, chapter ii, verse 4. It is the miracle of the water and the wine at the marriage of Cana. In the original Greek Our Lady is represented as pointing out to the notice of Our Lord that their host had no wine left to give his guests. Our Lord then replies as follows :

" Τὶ ἔμοι καὶ σοὶ, γύναι ? " The first of these five words means " what " ; the second means " to me " ; the third means " and " ; the fourth means " thee " ; and the fifth means " woman " or " lady " according to the context. It is the common Greek form of address to one of Our Lady's sex, used quite as much with respect as in a general sense, so that now it may mean " Madam," now " Lady," now even plain " Woman." The words were sometimes used as an idiomatic way of saying " Mind your own business." They were also used, of course, in their plain meaning. That they are so used here is evident from all that is recorded of the grave utterances of Christ and from the context, " Lady, should we act ? I have not yet manifested Myself." Further, He accepted her suggestion, she saw His decision and gave orders accordingly. But the opportunity of indulging his hatred was too much for Tyndale. It was the object of Tyndale to make out the reply of Our Lord to be particularly derogatory to Our Lady, so that the sentence read in Tyndale's translation, " Woman, what have I to do with thee ? " —which is as fine a body-blow at Mariolatry as you could wish. The old English vernacular (usually mistaken for Wyclif's translation) of Tyndale had no excuse for this falsehood. But Cranmer's Bible deliberately adopted the mistranslation, and the new false phrase was the one kept to strike and shock the ears of English country congregations.

There was a third quality in this new liturgy of Cranmer's ; a quality of literary beauty, of excellence in English prose, unsurpassed in anything before or since his time. For Thomas Cranmer, as anyone who will read the mere outstanding facts of his life can see, was many things that many men have been—a hypocrite, a time-server, a coward, a great scholar, timid and suave in manner, courteous also, usually averse from cruelty, a splendid horseman, a gentleman, in his modest fashion an intriguer, and a quite successful layer of traps for the unfortunate—such as the woman who made him and whom he betrayed. Yes, he was all this : but he was something more. He was a master of the Word, he possessed the secret of magic. He had been granted power in that which is perhaps the highest medium we know of expression among men, English at its highest.

Such high genius excused not his character or morals and could not be accepted as a plea on the Day of Judgment—but for such as it is, there it is. Cranmer was of that small band, standing out as isolated figures far separated down the ages, who have the gift of speech, and who are not workers in this or that, not ploughmen nor carpenters nor followers for gain of any craft, but who serve the Muses and the leader of their choir, the God of the Silver Bow.

The marvellous achievement fell upon his contemporaries without effect ; in the succeeding forms of the Liturgy long after the book of 1549 had been given up, the main passages in which this piercing beauty shines were retained, but it was long indeed before the effect of that one unique quality was apparent. We know it now ; and from at least the middle of the seventeenth century, the restoration of the Stuarts, that is for nearly three hundred years or even longer, men have realized what a treasure of prose they possessed in the English Prayer Book.

It is by *that* quality that Cranmer has impressed himself upon history. Thereby, through the Litany which is from his hand, through the collects, through the prefaces, through the admirable music of the special prayers, mainly due to his invention, he gave a strength to the newly established religion which it could never have drawn from any other source. He provided a substitute for the noble Latin rhythms on which the soul of Europe had been formed for more than a thousand years, and he gave to the Church of England

245

a treasure by the æsthetic effect of which more than by anything else her spirit has remained alive and she has attached to herself the hearts of men.

Of such moment is that despised unlucrative art the trade of the children of Apollo, who are not herdsmen nor carpenters nor practisers of any sort of craft but serve the Muses and the God of the Silver Bow.

In making this act, the imposition of the vernacular the sudden oversetting of the ancient popular liturgy and the substituting for it of something utterly unusual those in power expected, as I have said, to meet the decisive shock; for they were challenging the humble masses of the English people. They would have to put their attempt to the ordeal of battle; nor were they disappointed at the result.

The populace were everywhere in a ferment, the Englishman of the fields and of the plough, that is the main body of the nation, was in a state of bitter discontent. The new lords had begun to seize the common lands—and remember that in those days the average Englishman owned the house in which he lived and the little farm by which he lived, though subject to dues, for his land was still his—not his squire's.

Had there been a King in England (said he to himself) all this evil would not have happened! It was a gang without right who were at work, and all things were being changed—even Holy Church herself and the religion by which his fathers had lived and in which he himself desired to live and to die. And things were being changed without authority; not by an impartial Monarch who might plead to be acting in the name of the community and for its good, but by a greedy gang in whose hands lay the nominal monarch, still but a little child.

The hatred of the common people everywhere for this new tyranny and moral confusion had muttered and half moved already in more than one place, but the new service, a revolution in habits, was what set fire to the train of powder.

The people rose everywhere, save in the north; for though in the north the old religion had a firmer hold than anywhere else in England, the great rising of the whole people in its favour there was only just over a dozen years ago, and the dreadful massacres which had followed upon its repression were not forgotten. The north had then been put under martial law, there had been hangings in every village, and a general butchery by the Royal troops before the regular executions began. The north therefore still crouched cowed, and the one small movement which took place in Yorkshire was easily put down. The north had not the heart to move again till twenty years later; the generation which had seen Cromwell's butcheries was dead. When the north did then move it was to provide the last and most tragic rising of the English people, killed almost as it was born by the government of the Cecils in 1569, when the Percy and the Neville themselves were done to death.

But now in 1549 elsewhere than in the north, save within striking distance of the government in London, the explosions were universal. The populace rose in Sussex as in Somerset; in the Midlands, Leicestershire, Worcestershire, Rutlandshire, Warwickshire; in Suffolk as in Surrey, in Hampshire and Berkshire, even in Hertfordshire within a day's ride of London, even in Essex where they were so near to the power of the government.

They were unorganized, they had no leaders, for the gentry were united against them—being now the possessors of the Church loot and the authors of the new thefts of commons and guild property and the rest. In Buckinghamshire they became formidable; in Oxfordshire they were very nearly successful; but the most important centres were those in which they did manage to get someone who could organize them. The men of Devon and Cornwall got Humphrey Arundel, the Governor of St. Michael's Mount, to lead them, after their first rising upon the Monday following the introduction of the new service, the 10th of June. They gathered an army of ten thousand men and attempted to take Exeter ; while the men of Norfolk, beginning to rise at the same time, got a prominent man—not a gentleman, but a rich man called Ket, lord of three manors—to be their leader ; and he with twenty thousand men made a camp which overawed Norwich.

Happily for the government and for Cranmer's religious revolution, the populace had no decisive armament. They had no guns, no sufficient stores of powder ; but, even so, the universality of the rising and its appearing in so many places (in which it had the advantage over the old Pilgrimage of Grace) would have made it exceedingly formidable, had not an accident most fortunate for the Council, the Archbishop and their partisans turned the tide.

This accident was the presence on English soil of well-trained foreign mercenaries, Italian and German, taking government pay and willing to obey any orders for the cutting down of English men and women, to whose lives they were naturally indifferent. It was with the aid of these, and of its artillery, that the government at last obtained the victory. All over the place the insurgents were ultimately defeated. In Oxfordshire Russell, one of the principal members of the governing side, and of course one of the men most enormously enriched by the looting of Church wealth, went about killing at large, and in particular hanging priests to their own steeples by the score. The men of Devon and Cornwall were destroyed by the use of the guns, and the foreign troops whom Russell also had brought up with him at last—a little late but just in time and before Exeter could be taken. Something like half of all those who had risen were destroyed. In Norfolk, where the task was most formidable, and where the rising was more concerned with economic grievances, Dudley (who had now taken the title of Warwick) used the same methods successfully. But only at the second trial; for the first effort to put down the rebels here had failed. His German troops particularly distinguished themselves—and with that success the Council and their newly established religion were once more in the saddle.

The test had been applied, the shock had been joined. It had proved more violent, perhaps, than they had expected—but all was well and even better than before; for a rising that fails must always confirm the power of those against whom it was made.

Parliament met that autumn, and the most severe repression was ordered at once by that committee of the landed classes. It was made a felony to call meetings, or even to speak of changing the laws. The gentry passed further Acts giving them the right to enclose all the land they wished, and attaching the heaviest penalties to any resistance against such thefts from the general patrimony of the people. It was even a felony for men to gather with the object of restoring the old customary dues in the place of the new rack-rents; it was made treason to act against any individual member of the Council—as though they had been Kings.

From such a success (which was followed by the rise of Warwick in the place of Somerset) the next step in the religious revolution was to be taken, after an interval of two years. The completion of the new Liturgy by the setting forth of a final Prayer Book—from which all tincture of the Mass should have disappeared. It was preceded by vigorous propaganda, in which the foreign preachers and writers played their part just as the foreign mercenaries had played their part in the field.

To a'Lasco the Pole, Emmanuel Tremelius the Italian Jew (at Cambridge), to Peter Martyr from Florence (who had been made Regius Professor at Oxford and was especially active in suggesting further changes in the Liturgy) was added a host of others. Though Fagius of the Rhine died in the year of the first Prayer Book, it was not before he had been made Hebrew reader at Cambridge. Bucer came, Driander from Spain, and perhaps the most amusing of them was the Frenchman Jean Veron, who had not minced his words when he caused to appear in English the year before his " Five Abominable Blasphemies contained in the Mass."

The influence of such men supported the enthusiastic English innovators, men like Hooper—who reluctantly accepted the Bishopric of Worcester—hesitating whether he could wear the idolatrous vesture of a Bishop and openly desiring that all priests might be drowned in the sea. Under the influence of such men the second definitive Prayer Book was thrashed out. It is in substance that which is used in the Church of England to-day. The Communion Service in it was a wholly new thing wherein nothing of the Mass was recognizable. It began with the Ten Commandments, it suppressed the Introit, and there followed nothing of the old service but only newly invented English prayers, perhaps the most of them from Cranmer's own pen; the Epistle and Gospel, the Collects and the Prefaces remained. The Gloria was taken out, even the Our Father was taken out and put back at the end of the Service, and—most important of all—the formula for the administration of the Communion was changed to that definitely non-Sacramental form, that overt denial of the Real Presence, which was the moral driving force of the whole affair. " Take and eat this in remembrance that Christ died for thee, and feed on Him in thy heart by faith, with thanksgiving."

So was the second step undertaken, and after the great repression there could be no question of further risings. Whether, however, this second Prayer Book, the Prayer Book of 1552, had time to be universally imposed may be doubted.

It was all during the year 1551 that the Royal Commission was remaking the Liturgy and giving it its final fully Protestant form. It was finally scheduled on to a new Act of Uniformity on April the 6th, 1552, but was not to come into force until All Saints, the first of November of that year. Now as young Edward died in the early summer of the next year it is probable enough that many English parishes, especially in the remote parts, never used the new Book. But the bulk of England received it, and with it new customs altogether. The Altars were pulled down, the stones of them sometimes put contemptuously in the porch so that they might be trodden underfoot ; in their place plain Communion tables were substituted and these in the midst of the Church, and, what is more, the minister (though still technically called priest) did not stand before it but at the end, as might a host at a meal.

There remained the third and conclusive step : the framing of a definite Creed for the newly established worship, and also a new code of Church laws.

The Creed was constructed in the shape of forty-two Articles of Religion, for which Cranmer again was responsible. He laid them before Convocation in the January of 1552, in May the Privy Council dealt with them, in September they were returned to Cranmer to be put into their final order and for titles to be given to them ; and nothing more was done until the new Liturgy had come into force on All Saints Day. Four months later, on the 2nd of March, 1553, they were finally passed by Convocation and formed—as it was hoped for ever and in fact for the remaining four months of the reign—the official Creed of England. Give them time to work, let them be rigorously imposed for a long life-time, and they would become, from what they now were—the mere commands of a detested clique in power—the accepted doctrines of the whole nation.

It has sometimes been said that Cranmer, in framing

amous forty-two Articles, based himself upon that Confession of Augsburg which the Lutheran movement in Germany had presented to the Emperor more than twenty years before, and which had set down, in what was thought to be the most acceptable form, the tenets of the Lutheran leaders.

But anyone who will compare the two documents* will see that Cranmer's work is very different. The Convention of Augsburg was deliberately vague, and framed with the object of a reconciliation; it was to prevent the Emperor acting against the Reformers. The forty-two Articles are dogmatic, definitely Calvinist and definitely anti-Sacramental. And the key point in them is the Article in which the Real Presence is definitely and clearly denied. The forty-two Articles, became law as late as May, 1553, and had actual force therefore, not for all time, but for about a month. Nevertheless, they are a clear and strong indication of Cranmer's intention in his moulding of the new Church of England.†

To these Articles were added the new code of clerical law, which again was Cranmer's work. It was called *Reformatio Legum Ecclesiasticarum*, and whereas the forty-two Articles had been drawn up both in Latin and English, this draft of the new laws was a wholly Latin document. It contained many innovations contradictory of the old Canon Law universal to civilized Europe. For instance, it did not allow marriages to be marriages unless they were performed according to the new Book of Common Prayer; it proposed to imprison or transport

* The Latin original of the Convention of Augsburg is lost, but we have the translations.

† It should be remarked that these forty-two Articles never formed part of any Act of Parliament, because Parliament was not sitting at the time, but undoubtedly it was intended to order Parliament to register them, which it would have done if the King had lived on into the autumn. And therefore on the printed title (not fraudulently but in anticipation) the document is said to have been thus ratified.

for life anyone who was convicted of adultery, and, if the culprit were a husband, to hand over half his fortune to the wife whom he had injured—unless, indeed, he were a clergyman, in which case he had to lose the whole. Divorce was made easy. You could obtain it for disease or desertion or long absence, or even for incompatibility of temper. But in the last case you might not marry again, which sounds unreasonable. Married women might not leave property by will—in which they were likened to children, heretics, libellers, prostitutes, convicts and slaves—although there were no slaves, by law, at the time. There was an especially strong announcement of the value and dreadful consequences of excommunication by the authorities of the newly established Church—Cranmer assures the faithful that they are cut off by it from the favour of God and from future happiness in Heaven and doomed to everlasting Hell and the tyranny of the Devil.

But again, the key point is the declaration of punishment for the affirmation of distinctively Catholic doctrines. Anyone who affirms the supremacy of the Pope (which would be treasonable, anyway, under the new laws) is of course heretical; but, what is more significant and novel, anyone who affirms Transubstantiation must suffer death by fire as a heretic.

This last point is exceedingly important, for it gives us a full light upon Cranmer's mind. He would use his freedom to banish idolatry by force from a reluctant England.*

---

* Putting to death for heresy meant then in Cranmer's mind—as normally in all others of that day—death by fire. He uses the word " Puniendum." That word of his, " Puniendum," used in that connection, both referring to punishment for maintaining the Pope and punishment for maintaining the Sacrament of the Altar, could and did only mean that one thing—the stake—the faggot—the flames.

XIV

THE THIRD PERIL

IT must have occurred to the leaders, as it certainly occurred to their contemporaries, that the attempt to impose a new religious system upon the mass of Englishmen involved a very heavy risk.

It had been done as cautiously as was possible under the circumstances; there had been a delay of one year before the Mass was even slightly tampered with by the segregation of the separate Communion, and the English exhortations preceding it, omitting the doctrine of the Real Presence. There had been a delay of two and a half years before the Mass was openly transformed by being changed in doctrine as well as in language, given a new name and translated into English. After that, and when the heavy fighting which the popular risings against the change, and against other arbitrary acts proceeding from the same source, had been suppressed by the use of foreign mercenaries and artillery, there had again been a long delay of more than three years before the next great step—the destruction of all savour of the Mass in the Communion service—was effected, and the second Prayer Book imposed. It was not till after this had been done that the new Articles of Religion were authorized and the new legal code in religion, including death for supporting Transubstantiation, drawn up.

But, even so, the thing had gone far too quickly for a change of such violence and such magnitude. It had in support of it many enthusiasts in London, as we have seen, though these were still, of course, a minority of that town. They were in a larger proportion among the wealthier classes, both because these were the owners of Church loot and because any new intellectual movement always has a larger proportion of adherents *at first* among the better educated. In the same way, in modern times some thirty years ago, there was a much larger proportion of Socialists among the highbrows, when Socialism was an intellectual fad, than among the English working men.

But allowing for all that, even if we were to give one sixth of London numerically to the religious revolution, and more for the very wealthiest landed classes, the basis on which the proposed new structure reposed was dangerously insufficient. We know this not only from common sense, which assures one that a new religion cannot be imposed by force in a few years, but also from the best contemporary evidence on the proportion of supporters which Cranmer's establishment had among the English people as a whole, rich and poor, town and country. This estimate was made by William Paget.

Now William Paget was, of all the governing set, the coolest and the most rational; he was also the most indifferent to the religious quarrel and the most determined upon orderly government coupled with the advancement of his own fortunes. His evidence is highly valuable, because he was just the kind of man who, especially in a private letter not intended for any effect of propaganda, sets down a conclusion at which he has arrived. He knew the country thoroughly well, he had travelled all over it, he had been an experienced and industrious official under Henry VIII ; it was due to him as Secretary that Somerset had been able to be named Protector. It was all to his advantage to make out the prospects for the future as rosy for the new rulers as possible. Yet when he gives his deliberate estimate of the situation he tells us that of a dozen Englishmen under the nominal rule of Edward VI, *one* at the most could be said to welcome the religious revolution.

Time, however, coupled with the ruthless despotism of a sixteenth-century government, would confirm what had been done—*if* the monarch upon whom all depended (when he or she was an adult) were zealous on the side of the change and holding the old national religion in genuine abhorence. The mass of Englishmen had had so much tossing to and fro, what with schisms, new services, debates and wrangles of all kinds, that, seeing the way in which their spirits had been broken through the recent repressions of rebellion, a strongly anti-Catholic King might well, with a whole generation before him in which to work, secure the permanence of the new Protestant establishment and gradually impose it not only on the surface of society but on the mind of England.

That, no doubt, had been the idea when Edward was still a little child. He was to be trained in the hatred of Catholicism, and then, when he became a man, his royal authority would see the Religious Revolution through. But he grew up not very strong. His health had always been bad ; he had, for instance, fainted in the first days of his reign during the long ceremony during which he had to give their titles to the members of the Council, who had assigned to themselves new wealth out of the Royal fortune and new Peerages. And earlier than that, before his father died, when he was a little boy of eight to ten years of age, anxious care had been taken to get him out of the town as much as possible and into the pure air.

Still, a delicate boyhood does not necessarily mean an early death ; but when the critical years of puberty came he seemed worse. He had a bout of weakness and illness during the disturbances of 1549 before and after his twelfth birthday, and when Dudley (Warwick) had overset the power of Somerset and withdrawn the boy from the custody of that uncle. Even so, the situation was not alarming. But it began to get alarming in 1552, when he was in his fifteenth year. The adventurers, the authors and beneficiaries of the great religious attempt were, by then, beginning to feel frightened, and of all of them Cranmer—with his secretive soul and close observation—must have appreciated the position best.

He had most to lose if the little Protestant King were succeeded, as the existing law demanded, by his Catholic sister Mary.

Why, then, was nothing definite done till the next year, the last of the King's life ?

The Statute governing the succession was that which gave Henry VIII's will the force of law, and Henry VIII's will laid it down plainly that if his son Edward died without heirs Mary should come next in succession and should be Queen. Mary was a woman who knew her own mind and was steadfast in it ; she was mature, being thirty-seven years old ; she stood for all that the new man had attacked ; she was the daughter and heiress of the legitimate Queen whom Cranmer had divorced ; she had fought tenaciously to have the Mass in her house and had succeeded, because the Council feared the anger of the Emperor ; her name had always been beloved by the people, whose religious tradition she so strongly upheld. Should she succeed to the throne when Edward died—and his death was now fast approaching—then their effort would be ruined. Many of them would be in danger of their lives, some might attempt to fly ; and probably, in the long run, the restoration of the Church spoils upon which they had all battened would be demanded. For, after all, it was only seventeen years since the beginning of the loot, and the process was still in full swing.

Why, then, was there so much delay ? Why was not everything prepared in ample time to assure an anti-Catholic succession ?

The best answer to that question is to say that men do not take very dangerous decisions at long range— they only take them when they are urgent. But there are secondary considerations as well in this case. It was not too easy to fix upon the Protestant successor who should supplant Mary. There must be some kind of support by some body appreciable in numbers and in wealth before the Tudor dynasty could be thrust aside. Then there was the getting of the unfortunate little King to act, for without his authority nothing could be prepared. Then there was the intrigue and counter-intrigue, jealousy, plotting and secret treasons which honeycombed the whole Council, each man seeking his own advantage at the expense of all the others—though all in common would find a supreme advantage in preventing Mary's accession.

For all these reasons, I say, but principally for the first, because men do not take terribly dangerous decisions until they are spurred to do so by urgent necessity, the action came very late, only a few weeks before the boy King died.

Dudley (Warwick), who had now given himself the title "Duke of Northumberland," had such complete control of the little King and was a man of such energy that he was for the moment the master of the Council, and therefore of the realm. He pretended to be filled with strong anti-Catholic sentiments which certainly he did not feel ; he was therefore well suited for the rôle of deciding and causing the King to decide. Now, upon whom should he pitch, he and those who were working with him ? Who should be the successor to the throne in the place of Edward's half-sister Mary ? After Mary and Elizabeth, the two remaining children of Henry VIII, there came next in succession under Henry's will the descendants of his younger sister Mary. Mary Tudor had married Charles Brandon, Duke of Suffolk ; her surviving child Frances, the heiress of her claims, had married Grey, to whom had been given on account of his wife's descent and because her brothers were dead the title of Duke of Suffolk in his turn. This Duke of

Suffolk and his wife the Lady Frances had three daughters, the eldest of whom—and the others in succession—would inherit the claims of the Lady Frances. The eldest was a learned girl of sixteen called Jane; and as Lady Jane Grey rather than by her later married name has she gone down to history.

The Duke of Suffolk and his wife were both strongly anti-Catholic. The whole household was high Calvinist in tone, and the children had been brought up in the strongest atmosphere of the new religion.

If Mary was to be set aside there must be some ostensible plea for so drastic an action, contradicting a Statute of the realm, the expressed wish of the late King and the expectation of the whole people. The only plea to hand was the fact that her mother's marriage with her father having been declared null, Mary had been made illegitimate by a special law. But if Mary was illegitimate, so was her half-sister Elizabeth, Anne Boleyn's daughter; for the marriage with Anne Boleyn had also been declared null. Cranmer himself had been the author of both declarations. There remained of legitimate claimants only the Grey blood; the eldest of these, and apparently the natural heiress of the throne if the Grey blood was to be favoured, was the Lady Frances. And of her strong Protestantism there could be no doubt.

But the Lady Frances did not fulfil all the requirements of the plotters. They not only needed the succession of someone who should be Protestant: they needed the succession of someone who should be in their hands as Edward had been, that they might mould the new reign after their own fashion, without any serious chance of interference. Therefore (to her great disgust!) the Lady Frances, Duchess of Suffolk, was told to stand aside, and on her little daughter Jane the choice of the plotters was fixed; and chief among them was Northumberland. More than one marriage had been proposed for Jane in the past, but now—quite late in 1553, well on into the spring of that year, perhaps as late as May—it was decided that she should be Queen upon the death of her sickly little cousin. Therefore did Northumberland suddenly determine that his second son, Lord Guildford Dudley, a lad in his twentieth year, should be hurriedly married to this girl of sixteen.

The perilous decision must not be put down too much to Northumberland's ambition or individual will, though that played a very great part in what was done. There must also be admitted the factor of convenience. To have Northumberland's son married to Lady Jane Grey " fitted in," just as to have Somerset Protector at the beginning of the reign " fitted in." It suited the general plan of the conspirators, that is of the Council, who were working thus desperately, though late, to save the situation; for the strength and authority of Northumberland would be behind them ; it would be to his personal interest to support the thrusting of this young girl on to the throne as usurper.

Oddly enough, we do not know the exact date of the marriage between Jane Grey and Guildford Dudley. It may have been towards the end of April, it may not have been till May, 1553. It was at any rate not more than seven weeks and perhaps not more than six weeks before death came to the rapidly failing little King ; and when it was solemnized it would be in the eyes of all only a question of a few days or weeks before the succession should be open to the plan for making Jane Grey Queen, and this plan could be driven through with all the weight of those in actual power behind it, the men of the Council. Cranmer, the chief in precedence ; Northumberland, chief in power ; Paget ; Arundel, who alone represented the old nobility ; and Fitzalan, Norman in descent, and of very high and ancient place in the pre-Reformation peerage ; Herbert, that very wealthy ubiquitous hard-working man, the most industrious of them all. It remained to get a Royal document upon which they could act, and Edward's signature to the same. Northumberland obtained it. It is known to history as " The Devise." Through it, if it could be made effective, they would be saved ; and Cranmer, who stood in greater peril than any—Cranmer, upon whom Mary would necessarily concentrate all the griefs of her mother's dishonour and her own persecuted life—would breathe again.

The Devise was presumably suggested by Northumberland. But the suggestion was not made in opposition to the King. Far from it. The chief conspirator acted more subtly. The Devise expressed that mood into which Northumberland latterly, and before him Seymour, had trained the boy. For the motive which determined the little King's consent was hatred of the Catholic Church, the uprooting of idolatry, the securing in England of pure religion, to which was added a certain smack of glory—for by so acting Edward would have lasting fame on earth and would, of course, attain Heaven. Of his two half-sisters, he knew well enough what to think of Mary—*she* was desperately attached to the Whore of Babylon. Should she become Queen upon his death the whole realm would fall back into the abominations to which eleven-twelfths of that realm were still so strongly attached, and the Crown itself and all the future of the English State would go down into the moral abyss. Edward, in spite of his debility, managed to draft the document. In this first draft he left the Crown to the *heirs male* of the Lady Frances, and next to the heirs male of the Lady Jane ; next after these to the heirs male of her sisters ; he excluded Mary and Elizabeth.

In this action of young King Edward's, made though it was on the suggestion of Northumberland, the boy had followed his own leanings. Perhaps he did not know how near death he was—he certainly expected that he would live to see the Parliament in the autumn—there was no reason (he thought) why he should not even live on to see some boy born who should inherit the claim of the Greys.

But Northumberland knew better and so did those who were working with him : all of them, Cranmer with the rest.

Edward was not going to live, and the document as it stood would not have provided for the succession at all were he to have died—as he did die—in a few weeks ; for there were no *heirs male* to the Greys. The anomaly must have been pointed out to the young fellow, and therefore a certain change was made which completely transformed the draft. The original phrase had run, " To the Lady Frances' heirs male . . . to the Lady Jane's heirs male." The " s " at the end of " Jane's " was scratched out with a stroke of the pen and after the name were added the words, " and her," so that the phrase now read, " to the Lady Jane and her heirs male." Jane thus became first in the succession. The document was re-copied in that form, and young King Edward put his name before and below and on either side.

All this was done in the first days of June, just after the marriage between Northumberland's son and the Lady Jane Grey. But there was one very bad obstacle ahead. The Devise had not the force of a Statute. No doubt your sixteenth-century man regarded the King as a God on earth, and in general terms would have said that his will was law. Still, technicalities are technicalities and decisions are decisions, and men combating the monstrous proposal to change the dynasty from Tudor to Dudley might grasp at a technicality, and say that, as the Devise was not a Statute of the Realm, it was not of full force, as Henry VIII's devise of the Crown had been.

Moreover, it was essential to make responsible as many leaders as possible, so that all should be in the same boat and that it should be the more difficult—should Mary succeed after all—to punish for treason any one man. Above all it was essential to get hold of the chief lawyers who had a prescriptive right to say how, by tradition and enactment, the succession should stand.

Therefore, on the 11th of June the Chief Justice and another Judge, the lawyer who was Chancellor of the Court of Augmentations, and the two Crown lawyers —the Attorney- and Solicitor-General—were summoned to the Palace at Greenwich, where they found Edward very ill, lying on a couch with the nobles about him. On the following day they were shown into the presence of the King, who told them what his determination had been and how his motive was the salvation of true religion. The lawyers were not allowed to speak at any length ; they were sent off to look up their precedents.

On the 14th of June they returned, this time not before the King but to the Council where it sat in Ely Place in Holborn, saying that to agree with the Devise— being against the Statute of Henry which had arranged the succession—would make them guilty of treason. Montague, the Lord Chief Justice, used these words : " In God's name, my Lords, think what you do. It would be treason in us all to have had a hand in it."

At which pronouncement Northumberland, who had suddenly come into the Council Chamber, flew into a passion and offered to fight any of them. They were ordered to return the next day.

They began to waver ; they said that if an Act of Parliament would support the action they might consider signing. They were told that it should be ratified by Parliament all right later on ; and they gave way.

When the lawyers, who were the most important people to be got hold of, had thus yielded, everything could be rapidly pushed forward. The signatures of all the Council, as well as of the two judges who had been called and of the law officers, were appended to the document, which was finally set down on parchment on the 21st of June. Other signatures were got in later, but the essential had been done. Little more than a fortnight later poor Edward breathed out the last breath of his life.

It was in Whitehall that he died, under the same roof as his father had died. Men talked of poison, procured by Northumberland, and it is true that the lad had been left in the hands of an incompetent woman who professed magical powers; but there is no need to imagine so much: he was dying quite certainly anyhow. An hour before his passing Doctor Owen, his physician, who had been recalled to his bedside in spite of the intruding woman, heard him muttering and bent over him. "We heard you speak to yourself, but what you said we know not"; to which the dying boy answered: "I was praying to God." And then a little while later he muttered: "Lord, have mercy upon me and take my spirit." And that was his end.

The common people began to talk wildly among themselves of portents; all England was at stake; there was no King and who should be King? Some said that the elephantine ghost of Henry had appeared upon the battlements of Windsor; others thought it had shaken the roofs of Hampton Court—and, indeed, in that hour in which young Edward died a fearful storm had terrified the city with thunder and lightning and hail.

The first and most necessary thing for the conspirators to effect was the capture of the Lady Mary. They must hold her securely.

She had been sent for under the pretence that her dying brother required her at Court; she was on her way and at Hoddesdon on the North Road, not more than an hour's fast riding from London. Edward had died on the evening of that Thursday, the 6th of July—by the Friday Mary would have found herself a prisoner.

But there were two forces present in the Council—two forces that are always present when a gang of evil-doers set to work.

There was a centripetal force, the force that kept them together, which was their common evil deed and therefore their common danger. Cranmer, their titular head as Archbishop, the man whose name always comes first on the orders of the Council and their official pronouncements; Northumberland—the real political head, with his immense wealth, military prestige and organization; the industrious Herbert, who knew and remarked all and whom Northumberland had made a peer under the title of Pembroke; Arundel, Paget, and, most important as an outside figure, Ridley—Cranmer's man, who, through the Archbishop, had become Bishop of London—all these and the rest of the conspirators were bound together by their common bond. They had all joined, with Cranmer very prominent among them, in supporting the conspiracy against the blood royal, and if they failed the lives of all of them were forfeit.

The other force was centrifugal—a force which would drive each apart from the rest and make each prepare to betray all or any of his colleagues; and this force was the desire of each to safeguard himself from the wrath to come should the plot fail. There was further—and it was perhaps of most effect—the rancour which so many of them felt against Northumberland. He had been the head foreman of the gang. When he had deposed Somerset and put that rival to death he had made the others understand that he would be master. He had deprived this one of honours, fined that other; he had humiliated Paget and for a moment had debased and frightened Arundel. He had not got rid of such colleagues, but he had given them all reasons for revenge —all; except Cranmer. For Cranmer did not tempt him by wealth nor threaten him by ambition, and

Cranmer's permanent office and readiness to serve secured him from aggression.

To this last element in the Council Mary owed her safety. The Council sat continuously after the King's death far on into the night; they did not break up until the early hours of the next morning; they all seemed unanimous. The same trick was to be played that had been played when Henry had died six years before. The death of poor Edward was to be kept a dead secret while they were making all their dispositions for changing the dynasty and putting Lady Jane Grey on the throne. But one among them—probably Arundel —betrayed.

That very night Mary, at Hoddesdon, was told by a secret messenger that her brother was dead. So, while Cranmer and the rest under Northumberland thought themselves in those hours of darkness secure of the Crown, taking it for granted that Mary would be in their hands by the next morning—she, with the energy and courage of those days, was already on her horse, riding hard through the night eastward and northward, finding relays and pressing on.

It was an astonishing ride; all the next day she rode, the 7th; and on the next, the 8th. By the evening, when she had covered eighty miles, she dismounted at Kenning Hall, in safety.

The very next morning, Sunday, the 9th of July, she launched her defiance, heading it "Mary, the Queen," claiming she was their sovereign and bidding them obey. That proud message reached the Council on Tuesday the 11th; and it was due to her initiative alone.

Her cousin, the Emperor, upon whose power and counsel she continuously relied, did not think it possible that she could succeed against the organized strength of the existing government. It had command of the ships of war; it had the stores of powder and the treasure; it had the capital. It had also what was but a moral force, yet a very great one, the intriguing, the bribing, the perpetual industry of the French Ambassador Noailles. By so much as Mary stood for the Hapsburg, for the Spanish and the German connection, from whose blood she had come—by so much as she was the cousin of the Emperor Charles V and his close dependent and friend—by so much was it urgent for the King of France, Henry II, to prevent her reaching the throne. And the power of the French House was behind all that conspiracy, as it was to be behind the later abortive plots against Mary Tudor. Indeed, the Council had been allowed to arrange for a force of French mercenaries to land and support them. In these they might find salvation, as they had found salvation during the popular rising in their mercenary troops from Germany and Italy.

While Mary's proud proclamation was on its way, posting from Norfolk to London, the news of Edward's death had at last been " released." It had been kept a dead secret four whole days, communicated only to the authorities of the City, whose support Northumberland and the rest needed. It was not till Monday the 10th that the death of Edward was announced to the populace and Queen Jane proclaimed in the streets of the City.

Then came the first sign of danger. It was bad enough that Mary should have got away, but what if the popular mood in her favour should prove too formidable? Even here in London and under the very eyes of the government, with armaments and the power of repression by awful punishment on every side—even here in London where, if anywhere in England, you might find a plenty of zealots for the new religion, there seemed to be no comprehension of the new dynastic claim. There were no cheers. The proclamation of Jane was heard in silence—save apparently for one lad whose feelings got the better of him and who had, as a consequence, his ears nailed to the pillory. The Tudors London, like the rest of England, knew —but what was all this about the Greys? The populace does not follow genealogical tables. It thinks in very broad terms, and for it a Tudor was a Tudor. Only the very oldest men could remember how, as very little children, they had heard the news of Bosworth and the advent of the Tudor Crown. Everyone else had lived and grown up under the Tudor name. Moreover, Mary had been the accepted heiress in all men's minds ; even that small minority which detested the old religion took it for granted that she would come to the throne, and hoped that, between her loyalty to what the bulk of the nation would desire to have restored, the Mass, and their own repugnance for the same, some compromise might be found ; at least only the most active enthusiasts felt otherwise. This new little Queen Jane, of whom they had never heard, meant nothing to them. She was no more to them than the daughter of the Duke of Suffolk, and who was he but a Grey of Groby? A subject like anyone else !

The ebb tide made in the early afternoon, and on that stream little Jane Grey—small in stature, a child in face—was borne down the stream from Sion House, where she had been staying up river above London, down to the Royal apartments in the Tower where monarchs always stayed before their crowning. She reached the turrets of that Palace and Prison in the midst of that summer afternoon, and made a splendid entry, with her own mother bearing up her Royal train.

On the next day, the Tuesday, the 11th, Mary's proud letter arrived and was presented to the Council. I could wish to have seen the faces of those twenty-one men when its terms were read to them : twenty of them at least wondering which of the others had betrayed

—whether one or more. Particularly I could wish to have seen Cranmer's heavy suave mask of a face, mildly glancing with short-sighted eyes at one face and another to left and right. Who had done it ? Whoever had done it had darkly increased the Archbishop's peril !

But they still seemed unanimous, upon the surface at least ; and Cranmer—for all his knowledge of men, acquired by so many years of watchful submission and repeated following of change in power—might doubtfully believe himself secure.

For on the next day, the Wednesday, the 12th, Cranmer and the rest drafted their reply in which they very boldly and strongly put Mary Tudor in her place and reaffirmed : " Our Sovereign Lady Queen Jane, invested and possessed with just and right title in the Imperial Crown of this Realm, not only by good orders of old ancient laws of this Realm but also by our late Sovereign Lord's letters Patent, signed by his own hand and sealed with the Great Seal of England." They reminded Mary that she was illegitimate and therefore, " uninheritable of the Crown Imperial of this Realm and the Rules and Dominions and Possessions of the Same." (How turgid and magniloquent were all the documents of those days !) They told her to cease " by any pretence to vex and molest Our Sovereign Lady Queen Jane and any of her subjects from their true faith and allegiance " ; they told her that if she would " show yourself quiet and obedient as you ought " —well and good—but if not, she would find herself " grievous " unto them. And they significantly added that she would find herself " grievous also unto herself." With that they bade her heartily farewell, and every individual of the twenty-one signed his name to that document : Cranmer at the head of the list and Cecil in the midst, with Northumberland, Arundel and Pembroke.

But worse news was coming in. Gatherings were

beginning in favour of Mary, gatherings of the common people in the countrysides ; even certain of the gentry were joining in the movement. It was necessary for the Council to take arms.

Who should ride out in command ? It was a dangerous honour, for if the conspiracy failed whoever rode at the head of the government troops had openly taken arms against one who might be Sovereign after all. Therefore was there some generous competition, one man urging another to accept the great post. To Northumberland it seemed only natural that he should remain in Town, while Jane's own father, the Duke of Suffolk, should lead the troops. But secretly every one of them, save perhaps Cranmer and possibly Cecil —all the great Lords at least—desired that it should be Northumberland. After all, it was his quarrel ! And Suffolk was in no mood for martyrdom, if martyrdom had to come. True, should success follow (which, after all, seemed most probable), should Northumberland come back completely victorious, Suffolk would be the father of the Queen. But he was taking no risks. And as for the others, by manœuvring they got their way, and on Thursday, July the 13th, exactly a week after poor Edward's death, Northumberland rode out for Cambridge, where he would be at the head of eight thousand men, all trained, and one quarter of them well mounted and well furnished cavalry.

Some have thought that had he struck at once and had his heart not failed him he might, with a force so superior in character, have overcome the growing resistance ; but he was depressed by the lack of all popular backing, and he mournfully remarked as he rode out of the City that none cheered him. Before he reached Cambridge (where he ordered the Vice-Chancellor to preach a sermon against Mary's claims), she with consistent energy had moved again towards the sea coast to be in communication with the Emperor, and meanwhile the common people were rising in her favour upon every side.

Never had there been before, never has there been since, such an explosion of popular feeling in despite of power. The release of England had come ; the heiress to whom all had looked forward for so long would be Queen at last ; the tyrannously imposed new-fangled things (as they seemed to the conservative mass of the villages) were to be swept out and their churches and their old familiar Mass were to return and the country was to be itself again. And all these enclosers of common land, oppressors of the people, robbers and looters of holy things, the captors of the poor little diseased King, now dead, the heretic Bishops, the kill-joys and spoil-sports, the incomprehensible rabid zealots —they were all to be swept away as well. The sailors who had been detached to watch the eastern coast and prevent Mary's escape mutinied and declared for her : the squires were beginning to come in as well as the mass of the yeomen, and sundry even of the great nobles were moving. Before the end of that week the Tudor woman had about her some thirty thousand men.

Perhaps even that force might have been met, rapidly growing though it was, by the excellent trained body of troops which Northumberland had in hand and which could come up to striking distance through the eastern counties in a day or two ; but yet another menace to Northumberland and the Council appeared and to the plans of the French Ambassador : the Midlands were moving—Oxfordshire in particular, where men re-membered the butcheries of Russell and the priests hanging from their own churches—and with the Midlands coming down from behind him, Northumberland's communications with London might be broken. He wavered—by the time he got to Bury he yielded.

In London itself Ridley, the Bishop, Cranmer's man, did all that the Word could do and still used an active eloquence in favour of the now uncertain cause. He preached at Paul's Cross, violently, against Mary Tudor, Papist and Idolatress and Bastard ; but all about him in the streets of the city, in the confusion of warring cries, the cheers for Queen Mary were rising—and that night some lit bonfires as though her victory had already been assured, while in St. Bartholomew's another preacher bade the congregation kneel down and thank God that Mary's triumph was at hand. Away off in the east Northumberland was retiring, and on the same Sunday, the 16th, a vast turbulent body of ten thousand men—not without gentlemen among them—had gathered round Paget's house (though Paget was with the others in the Tower, apparently still adhering to Queen Jane). They had occupied the Palace at Westminster and seized arms and ammunition, wherewith to defend Mary's title. Two days more, Tuesday, the 18th, and Cranmer himself must have known that the game was up. He and Suffolk, her own father who was commanding in the Tower, alone could be trusted by those few who still demanded Queen Jane.

But the word "trusted" is ambiguous ; certainly Jane's cause still remained Cranmer's, for it was now too late for yet another conversion to be made by the man who had followed power regularly for now twenty years. The new power that was coming would not receive him. The whole story of the last six years, in which he had triumphantly imposed the new religion, could not be wiped out. Others could change, under the necessity of saving their skins—but who should save Cranmer ?

It must have seemed to him in his heart that this his third great peril would prove fatal.

That Tuesday afternoon, still, in spite of sixty-four years, a strong and good horseman, he mounted again and rode off for Lambeth and for Croydon—where he might hope perhaps for some few days of doubtful repose. But on the morrow the principal men of the Council in the Tower approached Suffolk for leave to go out. They said they desired to confer with the French Ambassador in that matter of the foreign French mercenaries who were to come over and help them; and whether Suffolk believed them or no he could not prevent their departure. So Arundel and Pembroke and the rest went off, but they had no intention of meeting the Ambassador nor any belief that there would be yet time for the Frenchmen to land.

There stood in those days on the same site where now stands St. Paul's Station a large square castle with high turrets, its southern walls washed by the Thames. Its ruins long remained—even to the beginning of the last century. It was called Baynard's Castle. Thither did they repair, thither did they summon the Lord Mayor of the City, his Recorder and a group of his Aldermen. Arundel declaimed against Northumberland; Pembroke drew his sword and cried: " If the arguments of my Lord Arundel do not persuade you this sword shall make Mary Queen or I will die in her quarrel "—and all those in that company then signed the proclamation which called the daughter of the Tudors Queen. They went out to Cheapside and there proclaimed her title with four trumpeters and two heralds in splendid colour ; it was about half-past five in the summer evening.

They went on to St. Paul's and sang the Te Deum, while Paget and Cecil and Arundel were off to pay their homage to Queen Mary. The populace of London, now wholly relieved, went mad with joy ; the bells were ringing in all the steeples, the bonfires were alight everywhere as darkness closed. And Pembroke and the others went about fanning the enthusiasm and throwing money to the crowd ; and one that was present and that heard and saw has written that in all his time, " I never saw the like ; nor by the report of others was the like ever seen; what with the shouting and crying of the people and the ringing of the bells no man could hear what another said, and there was dancing and banqueting in the streets all that night."

But Cranmer, the Apostle of the Lord, he who more than any other had moved the Calvinist enthusiasm of the unfortunate girl in the Tower—he was away safe for the moment in his Palace.

Within the Tower Jane Grey was miserably ill and trembling. Suffolk, rushing into his daughter's room, found her all alone in the Council Chamber—forlorn, deserted—under the great canopy of State which over-shadowed what had been her Royal chair. He told her to come down, for all was over; and she, unfortunate little girl, came down and clung to him and said: " Can I go home ? "

She never went home. When Mary had ridden in triumphantly with Elizabeth at her side through the streets of London the child was kept as a sort of hostage, not arrested, but not allowed to leave. Vengeance was taken only on the armed leaders of the conspiracy; even Cranmer was allowed some liberty, though he was to regard himself, save when he went out for public occasions, as a prisoner in his own Palace of Lambeth. What would come to him he did not know.

*   *   *   *   *   *

Cranmer was in his Palace at Lambeth. There to maintain himself confined until it should be decided what should be done with him. Ridley had ridden out to attempt to make peace with Mary and had failed. He had ridden to meet her hastily in Norfolk, to assure her that he had repented of all his ways and to beg her to wash out the memory of all that he had done, but she would not believe him. She could not forget how he had come and molested her only a year before, coming from her oppressors to try to force her hand and telling her not to refuse God's Word—to whom she had answered, " You durst not have avouched for God's Word in my Father's day what you do now." She spurned his suddenly converted homage, and sent him back a prisoner to the Tower.

Northumberland had been tried and put to death. He had, under the shadow of death, strongly proclaimed his return to the religion which—likely enough—in his heart he had always maintained, though in the feverish time of power and acquisition, in the chaos of the little King's nominal reign, he had acted all the part of the briefly imposed new creed. Upon the 22nd of August, three weeks after the Queen's triumphant entry, he was led out to die.

On the scaffold he had leant over the eastern rail to speak to the people and had proclaimed his ancient Faith, while the lame executioner in his white leather apron stood by, leaning on the axe. The doomed man appealed to the sincere and generous Heath, that Catholic Bishop whom later Queen Mary made her Chancellor, whether his protestation of faith were not sincere, and Heath gave testimony to that truth : then Northumberland told the people that all the evils which had come upon the realm were due to the day, now nearly twenty years gone by, when the religious trouble had begun in England. After that he knelt down, made the sign of the Cross in the sawdust beside the block, and, offering his head to the axe, he died.

* * * * * *

In that same month of August, 1553, Cranmer, in his Palace at Lambeth, was bidden keep within doors. He knew not what was to come, as he sat there a prisoner at the goodwill of the new power, waiting.

All his work had crumbled. He heard the news that came from the City, how, though as yet there had been no declaration of change, many priests had begun to say Mass again, how their number was increasing and the Mass becoming common—universal; how not a few men filled with such zeal as he himself secretly nourished had had the courage to protest, some with violence. That Mass which he had himself sung with so much pomp year after year as Henry's man, which he had maintained, he and his master Somerset, with careful art during the first years of the reign of little Edward—that the new religion with which he was filled might be the more carefully and gradually imposed in due time: that Mass which he hated so profoundly—which he hated the more because he had been constrained to it during all his best years bitterly against his heart—that Mass had returned. So he sat in his Palace at Lambeth with these memories burning in him.

Even as he so sat in those late summer days (and the garden from his window lay drowsing in the heat) there came rumours of things that were said of him. It was told that he had himself returned to the Mass; "Cranmer also" (men repeated) "had said Mass as those other priests were saying it. He had asked the Queen whether he might not sing the Requiem for the dead Boy King, her brother. He had asked whether he might not sing it in her presence in St. Paul's, and so make his peace with her. He had set the Mass up again in his own Cathedral at Canterbury. It was due to him that Mass had been said again in the place where once had stood, before its destruction, the Altar of St. Thomas." All these things were being said about him—and they were lies.

He would bear it no more in silence; those smouldering embers in him broke into flame; and he who was such a master of the pen sat down to write. He would do a brave deed at last—he would enlarge his soul.

" As the Devil, Christ's ancient adversary, a Liar and the Father of Lying, now goeth about to overthrow the Lord's Holy Supper again and to restore his Latin satisfactoryness "—(he means the Holy Sacrifice of the Mass offered up in satisfaction for the living and the dead)—" a thing of his own invention and device . . . therefore I must speak." (He must—he could not keep silence.)

"I have borne all things quietly, but when untrue reports and lies tend to the hindrance of God's truth they are in nowise to be suffered ; therefore this is to signify to the world that it was not I that did set up the Mass in Canterbury, but it was a false, flattering and lying monk. . . . If the Queen's grace will give me leave I shall, by the might of God, be ready to prove to all that the Mass has no foundation in Christ's Apostles but is manifestly contrary to the same and contains horrible abuses."

He went on and on, writing from the fullness of his heart and the hatred therein.

Nor did he destroy the paper. His timidity seized him again. He dared not have the thing printed as a proclamation, though friends said later that he had intended to make it public in some way ; but he did make one copy, and gave it to one man whom he thought he could trust.

That man was so moved by it that he must needs show it to others. On the 5th of the next month, September, men were reading further copies of it aloud in Cheapside ; and by the morrow the thing was being copied and re-copied so continuously that the Emperor's Ambassador compared this flood of manuscripts to pamphlets issuing from the press. The copies written out by hand were appearing as fast, almost, as though they had been printed.

Therefore, within the week, the Council sent for Cranmer, and his long ordeal had begun.

XV

THE ORDEAL

ALL the Council had been guilty of conspiracy and treason. They had all signed the document in which it was proposed to keep the rightful Queen from the throne and to crown little Jane Grey in her stead. Legally the position was simple: Mary had the right to have them all condemned as traitors, lock, stock and barrel—from the prime movers, Cranmer and Northumberland, downwards.

They had, of course, all of them to make what excuses they could. Northumberland, having not a leg to stand on, had begged very pitifully for life, acknowledging his errors. Arundel could plead that he had repented of his evil ways and that but for him Mary might not have been alive. Pembroke could remind her of how he had drawn his sword in her favour and acclaimed her. Others more particularly guilty could pretend, after the event, that they had hesitated, that they were reluctant, that they had only acted under pressure.

This in particular had been the cue of the astute William Cecil. He had had to sign, said he, because he was secretary, and it is only fair to admit that this exceedingly intelligent man had appreciated the danger more than most. He really had tried to get out of it by hedging—pretending to feel suddenly faint at the Council table. And indeed he had acted the part so well that all were deceived—and one sent him a receipt for a cordial to cure him: a cordial made by boiling a hedgehog (quaintly called a porcupine) in various spices.

Even Cranmer, who was deeper in the thing than anyone else, who was still with Jane Grey when all save her father had thrown up the sponge, and to whom the prevention of Mary's accession was a more obvious necessity than to anyone else, even *he* had come forward with a very transparent piece of pleading. He assured Mary that he had been at heart against the whole affair ; that he had begged Edward not to draw up the Devise ; that he had only reluctantly signed after heavy pressure and upon dread of disobeying his Sovereign.

Nevertheless, all save Northumberland had been spared —even Cranmer : even Ridley, who had preached the famous sermon on Mary's bastardy, and then, when he saw that his side had lost, had abjectly thrown himself at her feet, begging to do homage and assuring her of his change of heart.

There were two certain reasons for this attitude on the part of Mary, and perhaps a third. The third may have been her own hesitation to do anything decisive after she had come to the throne. She had been kept in the main secluded ; she was frightened of the world ; she knew—but did not understand—the vile motives of public men.

But the two certain reasons were, *first*, that the Emperor, on whose advice she had for years been dependent, was all for compromise; *second*, that she could not—it was physically impossible—strike down wholesale all those who had planned to deprive her.

As to the first of these reasons, the Emperor's counsel, it weighed strongly with her, and he was most insistent. He even begged her to let the Church establishment of Edward stand—so little did he understand the English and the situation in England. In the same year, it will be remembered, he had advised her to fly, having no comprehension of the overwhelming popular feeling in her favour. But his advice continued to impress her, and she knew that in this matter of clemency there was good ground for it.

For the second point, the impossibility of dismissing all who had plotted against her, conditions were conclusive. Though she had the mass of the populace at her back she had no organized party. She might have created one had she possessed that sort of talent, but even so it would have taken time. You cannot govern without men having some habit of government ; and of those who had, for now so many years, conducted the affairs of England there was, among the few of any talent, only one really serviceable to her—Gardiner the Bishop of Winchester, whom she had released from the Tower. He was and always had been strongly Catholic in feeling, though he had as strongly served Henry in the matter of the divorce. He was the most typical national figure of his time, and he was sincerely loyal. She made him her Chancellor—this is, Prime Minister —but for the rest she had to rely largely upon the men who had betrayed her but had subsequently rallied to her.

But among those whom she had been forced to spare, was she forced to spare Cranmer ?

Not in the sense in which she had been forced to spare Arundel or Pembroke ; yet it was plain policy at first, both for her and for the old members of the Council whom she had retained, to give Cranmer an opportunity for neutrality. They could not allow him to leave the country, as they had allowed so many others who were violent opponents of Mary and her religion ; but they could keep him in honourable seclusion until some sort of compromise should be arranged with him. He might be forced to resign. He might even return to his old Catholic position under Henry. The publishing of his angry letter had put an end to all this, and now he found himself with Latimer and Ridley in the Tower.

The life they were allowed there, these three Chiefs of the anti-Catholic experiment, was tolerable enough ; it was just what they themselves (or rather Cranmer) had imposed upon their opponents when they were in power. They could talk and read and write together as much as they liked; and, like other political prisoners, were kept there not as a punishment, but to prevent their escape—to make sure of them when or if they should come to trial. For we must remember that the idea of prison as a regular substitute for other punishments, corporal and monetary, is a modern idea. Though prison existed as a punishment, it was not the essential or common form of punishment; and with political prisoners it was the prevention of their action against the government, not their suffering, that counted.

Two months passed before the forms of the law were called upon. On the 13th of November, Cranmer was brought up to the Guildhall together with Lady Jane Grey and her husband. He behaved characteristically enough, crying out, "Not guilty," in a loud voice; and then, when the jury had brought in their verdict of treason—on which there could be no doubt—he turned round and admitted his guilt. The sentence of hanging was pronounced, but it was known to be nominal only, and they all went back to ward.

But then followed Wyatt's rebellion, and everything changed.

Wyatt's rebellion came very near success. The proposed Spanish marriage of the Queen had against it a far wider body of public feeling than that small kernel of genuinely anti-Catholic zealots whose intensity of conviction and courage had hitherto been the only danger to the throne.

Wyatt's rebellion had two effects. It brought poor little Jane Grey to the block with her husband, and it lay at the root of the Council's increasing determination to repress rebellion by violent means. What they and the Queen feared was revolution, though the Emperor still strongly counselled another attitude and though Philip of Spain after his marriage with Mary certainly shared the views of his father; but the Council, and with them the Queen, believed that the peril of revolution

—especially after the Queen's life had been threatened in fanatical Calvinist sermons—could best be met by prosecutions for heresy rather than by prosecutions for treason.   Hence the burnings which began in the next year and continued until Mary's death—nearly three hundred in number.

But Cranmer, a prisoner, only heard distantly of these things ; he could not mix with the public life which would have fully informed him ; he was not a spectator. The long interval between his condemnation for treason and his death on another account—an interval longer than two years—was a time for him completely cut off from the world save for such visitors as were allowed to see him, and save for the hours in which he was engaged in public disputation—or for those last days when he was given that curious interval of comparative freedom under the roof of the Dean of Christ Church.

There was in those days a passion for a long and particular debate upon foregone conclusions ; it was the sort of ceremonial which then satisfied men's souls, particularly in matters theological. When any great issue was toward involving religion people on both sides would not be content with action ; they must have the ceremony of particular and close debate in public, with trial of dialectic and still more of learning ; with excerpts and quotations from the Scriptures and the Fathers, interpretations and wranglings over individual words. One famous example out of dozens is the immensely long debate in public held some years before, when Cranmer was in power, between Cranmer himself and Gardiner, his then victim. But it was not the victim nor the victor in these affairs who took the initiative ; both delighted in the practice. These debates have proved a very useful thing to history, for they exhibit to us in detail the reading, and sometimes the minds, of the men engaged. Thus in the former great bout between Gardiner and Cranmer you have one of the best illustrations of that age-long discussion upon the meaning of the famous words in Tertullian upon the Real Presence—which discussion has, I think, by this time been fairly laid to rest.

So it was to be with the prisoners in the Tower. Although they knew and their opponents knew and the whole world knew that the thing was empty and could have no effect upon their fate, yet they and their opponents and all their contemporaries took a most vivid, keen interest in the affair, as a sort of game.

On the 8th of March, 1554, came the order to the Governor of the Tower to hand Latimer, Ridley and Cranmer over to Williams, who was to take them to Oxford. The order was carried out in April, and the date fixed for the disputation was the 14th of that month. They were put for custody into the Town prison, which had come to be called by a name that went with its University surroundings, the figure in logic, "Bocardo," because "it was difficult to get out of it." It was one small building on the first floor overlooking the north Gate of the city, forming as it were part of the city wall and coming against St. Michael's Church—the old Tower of which, standing in the Corn Market, is one of the few really old things remaining in Oxford. For the place has very little left which goes back to the true Middle Ages.*

There were three questions, the first two turning upon the central point of the Real Presence, and the third upon the Sacrifice of the Mass.

First, in the University Church of St. Mary's the Mass of the Holy Ghost was sung, then, following the University custom, a procession was formed which left and returned to the Church. There, seated in order

---

* The Tower and the Cloister of New College, the fine stretch of wall in the gardens of the same, and perhaps half a dozen other fragments. The rest of pre-Tudor Oxford, of which there is not much, is all of the later Middle Ages, after the corruption had begun in the great change and the Black Death.

before the Altar, facing the Nave, those commissioned for the debate sat, and when they had sent for him to the Mayor—who had official custody of the prisoners —Cranmer was brought in before them, between armed men—his guard. He stood, refusing the seat that was offered him—a figure venerable enough with the long white beard which he had worn ever since Henry's death, more than seven years past, leaning upon his staff and facing them, ready for argument, in which he delighted.

Weston was Prolocutor. He read out all the official matter, the articles and the nominal object of the game, namely, to bring the disputant back to orthodoxy ; and Cranmer gave the ritual reply—that on all three points he presented a denial. He denied the Real Presence under the Species of Bread and Wine ; he denied that the substance of Bread and Wine were no longer present after consecration ; he denied that the Mass could be a propitiatory Sacrifice for the sins of the Living and the Dead.

At this stage it is very important for us to understand the exact point at issue, for our judgment of Cranmer's fate turns on it.

It has been confused by strong partisanship and also by the disappearance from the modern world of the forms and procedure involved.

When heresy was the subject in question, no matter who might be the trier and who the tried, nor what the definition of heresy might be, the essential for condemnation or acquittal was not evidence of what the accused had said or done, let alone thought, but *his continued affirmation of the same.* For instance, Cranmer had had Anne Askew burnt as a heretic not because she had denied the Real Presence but because she *remained constant* in denying it.

Did the accused before the conclusion of the trial admit in a form of words that he or she would for the future abandon the heretical position ? Then condemnation for heresy could not follow. Further—and this is of especial importance in the case of Cranmer—even after condemnation it was taken for granted that a belated recantation should save the condemned man or woman from the extreme penalty, and commonly would allow them to go free. Some have thought it worth while to debate pedantically whether this was strict English Civil Law or not ; it could not be Canon Law because the Church was technically unconnected with the execution of the sentence by the Civil power. Technically it was the Civil power and not the Church which executed the condemned heretic.

Now it was not laid down so far as I know in any Civil Code of Law, nor was it laid down in so many words in the English law of custom, precedent and statute, that recantation *after* an ecclesiastical condemnation for heresy should save the condemned prisoner's life. The point is that the practice was taken for granted and was universal. There have been quoted one or two very doubtful precedents in which it is thought possible that a man who had recanted after condemnation was burnt all the same ; but even these doubtful and fragmentary records are inconclusive : for it may well have been, as often happened, that the unfortunate victim plucked up courage again and went back on his own recantation. What is certain is that all over Christendom recantation, even *after* sentence, saved the condemned from the fire. All men knew it would do so, and that when they recanted after sentence the accused recanted with that intent.

A distant parallel to the very important moral point here involved is afforded by the modern practice of reprieve. You might find a doubtful precedent for a reprieved man being hanged after the reprieve, but without doubt it would be an outrage. We have to bear this in mind when we consider the ordeal of Thomas

Cranmer, because the sequence of events—which is perfectly clear—will, in the light of such principles, enable us to judge the morality of what was done.

1. Cranmer steadfastly maintained under examination those opinions for supporting which he had been arraigned; he then was tried and necessarily condemned as a heretic. He did *not* recant before sentence.

2. Having been sentenced, not to death but to stand condemned by the Church as an obstinate heretic who had refused to give up his heresy, he was handed over to the Civil Arm, that is, the authorities of the State. It was for them to put him to death in due course by the method assigned in those days to such a case, which was the stake.

But after his sentence Cranmer recanted. He recanted, in form after form, each more drastic than the last; he made a true, complete and abject recantation. Yet, immediately afterwards, in spite of the recantation, he was burnt.

To burn him at the end of such a sequence was to break an implied contract, and was therefore inexcusable in morals.

This public disputation which Cranmer held and showed such zeal in holding (it had been as it were his trade all his life and he excelled in it), did not form part of the proceedings proper. It was a sort of preliminary stage in the affair. It " fixed " his declarations in his own mind and in those of his accusers; and when he there, leaning on his staff, with his armed guard on either side, and facing the Commissioners above him in the Choir seats of St. Mary's, denied the two allied doctrines of the Real Presence and the Sacrifice of the Mass, he was clinching his position.

The first formalities of that Saturday the 14th of April, 1554, ended. He was taken back to Bocardo, there to write out his thesis and send it round to Lincoln College, where Weston was staying. He did that all the Sunday. On Monday the 16th he appeared in the Divinity Schools just under the North Wall, and in the hall thereof, at 8 o'clock in the morning, argued pro and con eagerly, without taking bite or sup, till all were exhausted—till long after noon, till 2 o'clock. He carried on for six hours, "learnedly and boldly".; or rather, he and his opponents alternately did so.

Then, on the Thursday following, the 19th of the month, he was brought out again that they might hear him debate on a side issue, but in the same matter. Harpsfield was disputing to get his degree and Cranmer was chosen to take the opposing part, and in that Thursday's discussion he touched the real core of the business.

The orthodox party in power maintained, of course, that the interpretation of the plain words of Scripture, what are called "The Words of Institution" spoken by Our Lord at the Last Supper, were to be taken as meaning what they said, because the Church so interpreted them.

But he, Cranmer, would not have that. Not the Church was the authority but Scripture as interpreted by each reader, and he would maintain that the allusions to the Sacrament later in the New Testament were patent of his interpretation, not of the Church's. He then pressed on with the usual arguments which had been worn threadbare through more than a century of argument throughout Christendom.

The whole thing was a warfare of exact texts, definitions and deductions from them—a duel in logic and citation.

But the trial itself was to follow. It was the next day, Friday the 20th, that Cranmer, with Latimer and Ridley (who had also held their separate disputations, and also maintained their original Protestant attitude intact), was brought up before Weston and refused to retreat. Cranmer replied first; Latimer and Ridley followed. We probably have the words in which the Archbishop maintained his ground. As for Weston's contention that Cranmer had been defeated in argument, the prisoner answered : " All that was false, for he was not suffered to oppose as he would or unless he would have brawled with them, and ever four or five interrupting him." Latimer and Ridley followed suit, and all three were found to be constant in heresy.

But before the sentence of heresy was finally read out they were asked if they would turn. The three bade their judges read on in the name of God, for they were not minded to turn. When the sentence of excommunication had been pronounced against them as obstinate heretics Cranmer spoke again. " From this your judgment and sentence I appeal to the Last Judgment of Our Lord; trusting to be with Him in Heaven, for whose presence in the Altar I am thus condemned."

Then they took him back to Bocardo, but Ridley and Latimer did not go with him to the prison in which they had first been held all three together. Ridley was put in custody with the Sheriff, Latimer with the Bailiff of the town.

Execution did not follow. More than a year passed.

Here, again, has arisen a point on which much modern writing has gone wrong. It has been imagined that the delay was due to the insufficiency of the law as it then stood : that the revival of all the laws against heresy had not yet been made and that therefore they could not be put to death. It is not so. Cranmer himself had had the woman Butcher and the man Paris burnt for heresy under the law standing just as it stood when he himself so firmly maintained the position which the present Court judged heretical. The delay was due to a desire that nothing should be done save under the full authority of the Pope. It was only after this had been restored by Statute and after the famous scene of reconciliation, when the Commons had unanimously acclaimed reunion with Rome, that the last act was played out.*

Cranmer filled the interval with persistent and multitudinous writing; but it was not writing undertaken to abjure the fixed doctrines to which he had testified, and to which his whole life since the release of his conscience by the death of Henry bore witness. He laboured there in Bocardo as he had laboured all his life, with his short-sighted eyes close to the paper, writing protests against the nature of the trial—a demand for his being purged, with the rest, of the treason for which he had first been condemned in the Guildhall, and arguments against the fashion in which his trial had been conducted.

He wrote boldly to Mary herself, disputing at immense length her right to submit the realm to the Papacy again, and arguing at least for the old position of Henry; without question of Sacrament or doctrine surely the Monarch of England should be monarch of England Imperial and admit no jurisdiction without the Realm?

She did not answer him.

He wrote also, day after day, carefully his answer to Gardiner. Gardiner had defended the Real Presence in the quaint fashion of the time under the signature Marcus Constantius. Cranmer, not to be outdone, wrote his equally detailed reply with gusto under a Latin title of his own.

And Ridley and Latimer were at the same employment, writing away busily. Ridley fenced also with Gardiner and touched him (he said) like a fencer in eighteen points: Latimer, answering the Catholic Tunstall, gave *his* effort a very uncompromising title, calling it the " Abominations of the See of Rome and the Roman Pontiffs."

The union with Rome having been accomplished and

---

* There was one objector in the Commons, but he changed his mind after his first objection.

the Papal power restored, to Rome was application made for the last formalities. They were duly performed, empty, as all legal formalities are.

There was a formal citation for the Archbishop to appear before the Papal Court within eighty days, a formal condemnation for contumacy, then the appointment of Legates to deal with him in his own place. But all the while, even on these forms, Cranmer was protesting vigorously. Why talk of contumacy, when manifestly he, being a prisoner, could not travel? And by what right should the Pope pretend to extend his jurisdiction into the realm of England?

From the Papal Court, therefore, came technically the final action, consonantly with this recently passed reconciliation. Three Bishops, having powers from Rome, went once more through the form of trial with Latimer and Ridley. And sentence was pronounced upon the 1st of October, 1555—eighteen months after their first condemnation. On the 16th these two were led out to die.

The place where the stake was set up, in the dry ditch of the town (now filled up), was but 150 yards or so outside the North Gate of the city, to the right or east thereof, in front of the south face of Balliol College, which stood opposite the town wall, beyond a broad uneven way.

When they were bound to the stake, Ridley said, in order to console Latimer (thinks the contemporary anonymous writer): "It will not be long before we are together in the same place." Then fire was set to the faggots. The wind blew the fire and smoke towards Latimer, thereby exploding the bags of gunpowder tied to him, so that—calling on the Heavenly Father —he died. But on account of this same wind Ridley was only touched by the summit of the flames and cried out miserably in the fire. His brother, pitying him, piled up the faggots, which only damped the fire; but at last it reached him and the powder, and he too suddenly fell. The crowd said: "Would that they had been burnt earlier, for then we should have had better crops."

From the low roof of the prison above the North Gate* Cranmer himself watched the burning of his colleagues. He heard old Latimer's famous exhortation, he heard Ridley's cries in the fire as it burnt ill; he heard the explosions of the gunpowder which mercifully ended Ridley's life—Ridley, whom he, Cranmer, had so fostered and cherished, giving him London the better to cast out the Mass.

*   *   *   *   *   *

But did there not appear in the airs, between the eyes of the old man who looked towards the stake and the figure of Latimer on which he gazed; did there not float between them a vision which concerned them both? Might there not be seen in the smoke as it began to rise and whirl under the wind a cradle of chains suspended over a slow fire, and therein the agonized writhing form of Forrest, the Confessor of Queen Catherine, sent to such death in this awful fashion by Cranmer's own act, and amid Latimer's jeers?

It was fifteen years ago—but had they forgotten such a scene? Cranmer, who had so willingly condemned that martyr for holding unswervingly what all men had held; Latimer, who had preached by the hour at the execution and had boasted of his gusto and joy therein, and how he had "played the Merry-Andrew" at the roasting of the Friar.

*   *   *   *   *   *

Many such a scene had Cranmer witnessed; they were familiar to the time and to him; but to-day he

---

* Or was it from the squat tower of St. Michael's adjoining and forming one building with Bocardo? The "Recantations" has "Turris."

knew that he might himself be soon playing the part not of judge but of victim. The sight meant a very different thing to him now from what it had meant all those past years since first he had worked for the government under his old master Henry, twenty years ago. He had been then in the vigour of his maturity, a man still under fifty, and the Primate of the Realm, and going strongly with the tide. Now he was old; vigorous still indeed in mind as in body but nearer seventy than sixty, in his sixty-seventh year.

Was he shaken by that sight? It may be. We cannot tell. If he were it may account for what followed.

* * * * * *

It was long after Ridley and Latimer had suffered that the formal document condemning Cranmer was signed at Rome, upon the 14th of December, 1555. And therein were appointed (obviously through the action of the government in England) two men to proceed to the degradation of the Archbishop, prior to the carrying out of the sentence.

These two men were strangely chosen—one was Bonner, against whom he had acted with special violence, thrusting him out of the See of London in order to give it to his creature Ridley, and now restored to his place. But the other was Thirlby, whom Cranmer had cherished almost as much as he had cherished Ridley, and who was now Bishop of Ely. These were the men who were appointed to act in the scene that was played out before the Altar of Christ Church in the Cathedral, in Wolsey's great College.

There Cranmer, now with shaven head, dressed up in grotesque canvas vestments, imposed one on the other —as of a deacon—a priest—a Bishop—with the Pall upon his shoulders, a Mitre on his head and a Crozier in his hand, had piece after piece stripped off him.

One piece of canvas after another went off; but

when they came to his Pall he cried out : "Which of you can take my Pall ? Which of you has a Pall ? " meaning that he was an Archbishop and no Bishop had the power to degrade him. Then, with a sudden change of mood, he said that they might take what they would, for he had done with all such stuff long ago. Yet he clung to his Crozier, and it had to be dragged away from him by force and after a struggle.

He pulled out of his sleeve a document he had prepared, an appeal to the next General Council—one part of his voluminous literary labours in the prison. So the full ceremony of degradation was accomplished as the ancient rules ordained; and they scraped in ritual fashion the tips of those fingers which had been blessed and anointed for the Holy Sacrifice so many years ago and with which he had held the Host aloft in the thousand Masses he had sung ; but now he might never touch it more.

XVI

THE FIRE

CRANMER was with the Dean of Christ Church, enlarged.

He was leading an easier life than he had led in Bocardo; with a garden at his disposal, good food, and ample quarters.

Why he had been so treated we do not know, nor do we know one other thing which, if we knew it, would explain one way or another the next four weeks of history. Had any hint been given him that through recantation he would be saved? And if such a hint had been dropped, by whom had it been dropped? Or was he left in such surroundings in order that they might move him to a better mind—their comfort persuading him how well it would be to have such ease continued?

Of two things we are certain. First, that no authoritative word was given him promising reprieve if he should fully recant—for to the very last, to within half an hour of his death, he knew not which way his fate would fall. But the other thing we know is that some violent commotion had overset his mind; for this is what followed.

While he was being approached by those who hoped and believed he would recant, of whom the most persistent was the learned Spanish Dominican, Garcina, he upon his side engaged his subtle mind upon the discovery of some formula which would not too much stultify him nor too much deny the whole vehement increasing work which he had done since first he had been taken out from his obscurity, as being the Boleyns' man, to do the work of Anne Boleyn for the lover whom she had ensnared.

The method upon which he hit was ingenious, but it was insufficient. It occurred to him that his great stand-by during all these years, the one principle (and the only one) on which he had not eaten his own words and broken his own oaths and solemn promises, was the supremacy of the Crown in spiritual affairs. What if he were to say : " Very well, as I accept the complete right of the English Crown to decide what should be believed in spiritual matters, and as it has now decided for reunion with Rome and the supremacy of the Pope, I will do the same " ? In two such documents he wrote down this principle and hoped it would be accepted as recantation, and therefore enough to save him.

He put the matter first thus :

> Since the King and Queen, with the Counsel of Parliament, have admitted the Pope's authority in this Realm, I am willing to subject myself to their laws in this matter, and to admit the Pope to be the supreme head of this Church in England ; so far as the laws of God and the laws of this Realm allow it.

Later he put the matter again thus :

> I, Thomas Cranmer, Doctor of Theology, submit myself to the Catholic Church of Christ and to the Pope as Supreme Head of that Church, and to their Majesties the King and Queen and to all their laws and orders.

This last was stronger, and ought surely to be accepted ? But it was not. For it was not a complete submission ; it was not a plain, unconditional admission of error and recantation in full form. It brought in the King and Queen, who had nothing to do with it ; for either a man does or does not accept the propositions of any body of doctrine such as the Catholic, which is a thing to be decided in the point of such doctrine alone, and not through any mention of other things. Therefore the process must continue.

He began to admit that his opinion might be but his own ; that one man might be saved by one opinion and one by another ; and to one last most searching question he yielded. He said that " by such probing they had him by the beard " ; and a little after he wrote with his own hand for the Bishop of London—Bonner who had degraded him—these words, dated the 16th of February, 1556 :

" I am willing to submit myself to the majesty of the King and Queen and their laws and orders, as much though they regard the Primacy of the Pope as others ; and I will as much as lies in me cause others to do the same." And he said further that " as for what he had written he was willing to submit it to the Catholic Church and to the next General Council that might be called." But being told that this last phrase was unpleasant, he added : " Let it be noted by these presents that I, Thomas Cranmer, Doctor of Theology and once Archbishop of Canterbury, formally and consistently believe all the articles of the Catholic Faith such as the Catholic Church has believed from the beginning. Moreover, as to the Sacraments of the Church, I believe formally in all points whatsoever the Catholic Church believes and has believed from the beginning. And in token thereof I subscribe my hand."

Messengers came to Oxford to say that he was set down for execution on the 7th of March. But delay was granted, and Cranmer, who wished to make reprieve as certain as possible, insisted on writing down for Garcina a further recantation ; it was to this effect :

" I, Cranmer, anathematize each heresy of Luther and Zwingli and all teaching against the same doctrine " (i.e. against the Catholic doctrine of the Blessed Sacrament of the Altar). He goes on to say that there is only one Holy and Catholic Church, visible, and that he acknowledges that the chief of it is the Pope, Bishop of Rome and Christ's Vicar ; and as to the Sacrament : " I believe and worship in it the true Body and Blood of Christ under the species of Bread and Wine, without any metaphor, converted and transubstantiated, the Bread into the Body and the Wine into the Blood of Our Saviour by Divine power." He adds that he believes in the other six Sacraments ; that he believes in nothing but that which the Catholic and Roman Church may hold ; that he repents of having ever held anything else and begs God to forgive him and all the faithful to pray for him for what he may have done against the Church, and especially those whom he had led away by his example into schism.

He ends by subjecting himself to the Supreme Head of Christ's Church, as well as to his Sovereign, and calls all to witness before the all-good and powerful God that he is doing this " from no sense of panic or fear but freely and from his soul " ; " that I may do good both to myself and others."

This he signs ; and the witnesses are Sidall, a Canon of Christ Church, and Garcina.

To men who came near him after this (it must have been while he was in Christ Church) he rejoiced that he was once more with the body of Catholics and in the fold ; and he began praising Thomas More and calling him to mind. He begged to have Masses said for him, and went to confession and took Communion with outward joy. And when he was asked whether he now believed that Jesus Christ the Son of God were present in the Bread and Wine in Body and Blood he agreed, and said most certainly he believed it. " And you forgo all that you have said about this most Holy Eucharist ? " " I renounce it altogether," said he, " and the things that I have said about the same I repent of them." And when he was asked to adore Jesus Christ, God and

Man, so present (that is in the Sacrament), " I adore,"
replied he, " God and Man here present " ; and in
continuation of this he repeated it on his own account
when he was in his rooms, and made a whole speech
about it. Next, when he was told that his life might
not be spared, he said he never feared death, but the
intolerable weight of his sins.

But he was sleeping badly and affected with dreams ;
seeing, as he thought, Christ and Henry when he slept,
and Christ refusing him the Gates of Paradise and
Henry turning his back upon him. Then waking, he
wrote his fullest and most famous recantation.

" I, Thomas Cranmer, formerly Archbishop of Canterbury, confess and mourn from my heart that I have
grievously offended against Heaven and against the
Realm of England, nay, against the Universal Church
of Christ, which I have persecuted more cruelly than
did once Paul, who also was a blasphemous and con-
tumelious persecutor. Moreover, may I, who have
surpassed Saul in my malice and wickedness, be able to
make good as Paul did that only which I detracted from
Christ and the use of the Church. Indeed the great
Faith of the Gospel consoles my mind.

. . . . . .

" I, who have ill-used my office and authority, and
have taken away from Christ His honour and from this
realm its Faith in its religion ; none the less now at
last having turned me to the great goodness of God I
acknowledge myself the greatest of all sinners, and desire
to give what due reparation I can, first to God, next to
the Church and the Supreme Head thereof and to my
Sovereign ; and lastly to the whole realm of England.
For just as that unhappy robber, though he could not
return the money and wealth which he had stolen
(for neither his feet nor his hands, being fastened to the
Cross, could do their office), yet by heart and tongue,

which were not bound, gave witness that his other members would have given satisfaction had they enjoyed the liberty of his tongue, and with that tongue confessed Christ to be innocent and reproved the insolence of his mate and abjured the life that he had led before and begged forgiveness of his sins, and so as with a key opened for himself the gates of Paradise; upon his example I firmly confess that I may have hope through the mercy of Jesus Christ, that He will pardon my sins.

" I lack hands and feet whereby to set up again that which I have cast down, all that is left of me is my lips about my teeth; and may He that is merciful beyond all belief receive the offering of those lips. In such a hope here I offer as a victim at the very least my body and my life. I confess in the first place my most grievous ingratitude towards the most good God, I confess myself utterly unworthy of any benefice or kindness, but most worthy not only of human and temporal but of divine and eternal punishment, because I sinned grievously against King Henry VIII and especially against his wife Catherine the Queen when I made myself the cause and author of that divorce which since was the root of all the calamities which have come upon this Kingdom. Hence the death of so many, hence schism in the whole kingdom, hence heresies, hence the destruction of so many bodies and souls as hardly could I set down the tale. Not only did I open myself to this grave beginning of woes but I make confession that I opened wide the door to all heresies in which I was myself the chief teacher and leader. But what chiefly tortures my mind is that I should have proffered against the most Blessed Sacrament of the Eucharist so many blasphemies and insults, denying the Body and Blood of Christ to be truly and really contained under the species of Bread and Wine. Even bringing forth books attacking the Truth, wherein I fell lower not only than Saul and the thief on the Cross, but indeed lower than anything the earth has ever held of most criminal.

"Lord, I have sinned before Heaven and before Thee; before Heaven, because I have denied this great and Heavenly gift, and have sinned towards the earth also, which has so long been without this Sacrament, and against the men whom I called back from this super-substantial food. I was often a murderer of men in this . . . and I have defrauded the souls of the dead from the benefit of the most exalted sacrifice, and it is known to all how I have, after opposing Christ, stood opposed to His Vicar and in manifest writing denied his power, wherefore most urgently do I beg the Supreme Pontiff that he should forgive me through the clemency of Christ all that I have done against him and against his Apostolic See; and I humbly pray the Serene Sovereigns of England and Spain, Philip and Mary, that with Royal clemency they also will forgive me, and I beseech and pray also the whole kingdom, nay, the Universal Church, to have mercy on my miserable soul —I to whom nothing now is left save my tongue whereby to undo the evil and the damage I have proffered. But principally because before Thee alone have I sinned, Oh, Most Merciful Father, who lovest all those who come to Thee however sinful, receive me, even as Thou didst forgive Magdalen and Peter, or that Thief—who, looking upon Thee from the Cross, by Thy Greatness and Glory was found worthy of the promise of his trembling, anxious heart, and was consoled. So do Thou turn upon me those eyes of Thine whose property it is and custom to show mercy and speak to me also, saying: 'I am thy Salvation'; and in the day of my death say to me, 'To-day shalt thou be with Me in Paradise.' Written in the Year of Our Lord, 1555, on the 9th day of March*, by me, Thomas Cranmer."

* * * * * *

* Such is the date in the original Latin of the "Recantations," "*Die Nonâ.*"

Cranmer was back in Bocardo, awaiting that date —the 21st of March—when he should appear publicly and solemnly, under sentence of death, to learn at last whether or no (for almost to the last he was left in doubt) he should be given to the fire or saved. It was fixed for the day after the morrow, and he, on the 19th of March, we believe, wrote out in full that final document confessing and repenting of his errors, which he was to read publicly in St. Mary's when he should appear.

In it he declared again, with definite and emphatic language, his acceptance of that which he had lived all the last twenty years to combat and deny, the Real Presence of Jesus Christ in the Host. Such was his last penning, the seventh of that strange series.

The dawn of the 21st of March broke on the windows of Cranmer's prison room. The rain was falling. Garcina entered. He brought no promise of reprieve, nor any announcement of doom ; but a paper briefly summing up the attitude which Cranmer had taken, made public and affirmed with so much vehemence. It was a memorandum of what should be read out when he came before them all in the last hours to meet whatever fate was before him. In it came an appeal imploring those who heard him to pray for him ; a prayer on his own account, begging of them to live well as he had not lived ; a declaration of Queen Mary's right to be Queen indeed of England, and at the end of all, a full confession of the Faith.

Thomas Cranmer wrote that paper out and signed it, and kept it upon him for what was to come.

Immediately after, under the rain, a procession formed in great solemnity.

On these high occasions it was customary for the sermon, always preached, to be delivered from a platform in the open air, as it had been when Anne Askew suffered and when Jane Bocher suffered, who so boldly replied to the preacher. But as the rain still fell steadily on this March morning the arrangements were changed : the sermon was to be preached in St. Mary's Church. There was Cranmer to hear the last exhortation, and, as he now safely hoped, to be told that he, by recantation, had touched the hearts of those in power, or their policy, and would escape the fire after all.

Opposite the pulpit whence Cole, the Provost of Eton, was to preach was a sort of stage whereon Cranmer himself was set ; and all about him was that congregation of the University and the priests from without, and of the public as well. The rain beat upon the windows, and all men watching Cranmer saw him deep in dejection with the tears upon his face and, as it seemed, repentant of all that in him which they so much abhorred and of which he had so openly and vehemently repented, manifestly, before all men.

Then Cole, that Provost of Eton, began. First he made a recital of all Cranmer's enormous misdeeds : how he stood at the root of all the alteration in this realm of England—the turmoil, the chaos and dispute ; how he had permitted himself to be judge in the matter of the divorce (but this, it was admitted, was not of malice but of weakness) ; how he had then become a great setter-forth of heresy, written upon it, continued it, yea—even to these last weeks till grace had touched him.

So much for the preliminaries ; the denunciations which were to be expected showering down on that aged, shorn, humbled—self-humbled—head.

But there came something more which struck like a shaft into the heart of that bowed old man who sat listening. For Cole continued by saying this : that never had evils so enormous been excused, never had a man continuing so long in them been pardoned, *and for the sake of example pardon could not now be granted : the Queen and the Council had taken their decision and Cranmer was to die.*

What Cole had to say further mattered no more to Cranmer, though what he had to say further was long enough : how fall from such a height to such depths should be an example to all—how the man now condemned should meet his end—how he should remember as he himself had said in his famous published torrent of regret and penitence, that the penitent thief had been told by Christ Himself : " This day shalt thou be with Me in Paradise," and how he might thus brave himself against the terrors of the fire. And Cranmer heard from those lips before the sermon ended how he had glorified God by doing penance at last and by confessing, how God, in His mercy, had reclaimed him and called him home. So Cole ended on that note of praise, but added that in every Church of Oxford he should be prayed for, and Masses said for his soul and Dirges sung ; and every priest that heard was exhorted to say such Masses for Cranmer's soul.

Then, the sermon being ended, Cole begged all that great assembly in the Church of St. Mary's to pray in unison for the man that was to die.

Cranmer knelt down with the rest, forming one of that great company at prayer, and a man of the day speaking of what he saw with his own eyes, wrote : " I think there were never such a number so earnestly praying together ; for they that hated him before now loved him for his conversion and hope of continuance."

When this praying was over Cranmer rose all in tears. He had wept often enough while Cole was speaking ; he did not cease to weep now that he was standing up to answer for himself.

" Good people," he began, " I had intended, indeed, to desire you to pray for me, which, because Mr. Doctor hath desired and you already done, I thank you most heartily for it. And now I will pray for myself as I can best devise for my own comfort, and say the prayer word for word as I have here written it." Whereat he pulled from his sleeve that document he had written in the hours before, early in the morning. He read it, still standing up.

" Oh, Father of Heaven, oh, Son of God, Redeemer of the World, oh, Holy Ghost, proceeding from Them both and Master of the World, have mercy upon me most wretched catiff and miserable sinner; I, who have offended more grievously than any can express. Whither should I flee for succour ? To Heaven I may be unable to lift up mine eyes; and in earth I find no refuge. . . . Oh, Lord God, my sins be great, yet have mercy upon me for Thy great mercy. Oh, God the Son, Thou wast not made Man for few nor small offences. . . . Although my sins be great, yet Thy Mercy is greater. I crave nothing, oh, Lord, for mine own merits, but for Thy Name's sake, that it may be glorified thereby, and for Thy Dear Son Jesus Christ's sake. And now, therefore, Our Father which art in Heaven . . ."

Then, falling upon his knees, he recited the " Our Father "; but it was noted by some that he added not, as was customary, the Angelic Salutation to Our Lady, and that the " Hail Mary " did not follow from his lips.

Then he rose again, and told them how everyone at the approach of death desires to say something whereby he might be remembered, and implored the Grace of God that by what he was about to say at his departing, God also might be glorified. Next he begged them not to yield in anything for reasons of this world. Next, that they should obey the King and Queen gladly, and that they should love each other, and that the rich should give to the poor. He begged all the rich that might hear him to ponder that, saying that the poor were now so many and food and drink so dear : " For though," he said, " I have been long in prison, yet I have heard of the great penury of the poor. Consider that that which is given to the poor is given to God, whom we have not otherwise present corporally with us but in the poor."

Now having said so much, he did not add the words in the draft prepared and written out by him early in the morning when it was doubtful whether he should live or die—that Queen Mary was Queen of right, and had just title by the Blood Royal. But he went on: " I see before mine eyes presently either Heaven ready to receive me, or Hell ready to swallow me up. I shall, therefore, to-day show you my very faith ; for now is no time to dissemble, whatsoever I have written in times past." And when he had declared his belief in God the Father Almighty, Monarch of Heaven and Earth, and His Articulate Word made manifest to us by Our Saviour Jesus Christ, and His Apostles and Prophets in the Old Testament and the New, he came to something which had not been written in the manner they expected.

There was one more thing, he told them, which troubled his conscience more than any other thing he ever did or said in his life—the setting abroad of writings contrary to the truth which he thought in his heart. What writings ? Not those of the life he had abjured —but these late writings, in which he had abjured it : his Recantations. " They were written contrary to the truth which I thought in my heart, and written for fear of death, to save my life if it might be. . . . All such bills which I have written or signed with mine own hand since my degradation, wherein I have written many things untrue. And forasmuch as I have written many things contrary to what I believe in my heart, my hand shall first be punished ; for if I may come to the fire it shall be first burned. And as for the Pope, I refuse him, for Christ's enemy and anti-Christ, with all his false doctrine."

So they would burn him, would they ? Then he would speak at last. And he had spoken.

There arose a tumult and hubbub, with men crying

out against him and all moving as though they would seize him.

But Cranmer ran out from that Church, over the waste ground northward, past the few houses and past Brasenose College Gate and down narrow Brasenose Lane at full speed—this old, short man still so vigorous ; and after him all the crowd of them, keeping pace as best they could under the driving rain : and so on and on under the wall to the North Gate, under the floor above which his old prison was, and so to the stake before him where the hundreds of furze faggots were piled, and the wooden faggots above them.

Even as he went one or two, panting, still begged him to remember and save himself, and to witness to the truth. But he paid no heed to them all.

He put off his outer robe quickly, standing before them in the long shirt which came down to his feet ; he was bound to the stake by that iron girdle which is still kept as a relic of that long past day.

There stood by one Edge of Brasenose College, earnest in the Faith, who implored him to bear witness to it before he died. But Cranmer paid no heed, until he answered at last : " But as for that recantation, I repent it right sore because I knew it was against the truth." And as he would still be speaking, Lord Williams of Thame, the Royal Officer who had charge, cried out : " Make short ! Make short ! " Then did Cranmer take one or two about him by the hand, and Edge left him, still calling on him to repent. But he answered : " This is the hand that wrote it, and therefore it shall suffer first punishment." And men saw and bore witness to this, that he held his hand out steadfastly into the flame.

Also, as the fire rose about him, he made no cry or complaint, which was a marvel, but still held out his hand till flame and smoke hid all.

This is the way in which Cranmer died.

INDEX

A

ACT of Attainder without Trial, 202–203

Adlam, excommunicated and executed, 210

Alasco, John, 224, 249

Alcock, John, Bishop of Ely, activities of, 22–23; erects Jesus College, Cambridge, 23–24

Alexander VI, Pope (Borgia), appoints new preachers, 26

Alexander of Arles, 224

Ampthill, Catherine at, 102–103

Annates, threatened confiscation by the Crown, 88; continued payment to Rome, 94

Anne of Cleves, marriage to Henry, 196, 200; Holbein's portrait of, 199; Henry's unfavourable opinion of, 200; the marriage annulled, 203; income settled on, 204

Anti-Catholic movement of fifteenth century, object of, 81, 172 *et seq.*

Architecture, English, 9

Arthur, Prince (brother of Henry VIII), marriage and death of, 51

Articles of Religion, Cranmer's, 251–252 (*see also* Creed)

Arundel, Humphrey, rising of, 247

Arundel, Lord, conspires against Mary, 268; declaims against Northumberland, 276, 283

Askew, Anne, burnt at the stake, 210, 289

Aslacton (birthplace of Cranmer), 3

Augsburg, Confession of, object of, 252

B

BARNES, Robert, leader of "Little Germany," 156; and the new theology, 43; sermon preached by, and reaction against, 44 *et seq.*

Barton, Elizabeth (Holy Maid of Kent), how she was entrapped by Cranmer, 114, 125; Cromwell and, 123 *et seq.*; put to death at Tyburn, 128

Baynard's Castle, 276

Beaufort, Margaret (*see* Richmond, Countess of)

Benedictine convent, converted into a Cambridge college, 21 *et seq.*

Bible, Tyndale's, 30, 180; an English translation published "by authority," 160, 192; compilation of the, 164 *et seq.*; translations of, 169–170; a development following translation, 170 *et seq.*; unauthorized translations with commentaries, 175; use of to destroy Catholicism, repressed by the Church, 176, 178

Bill of Attainder against Elizabeth Barton, 127

Bishops, whence drawn, 17; how doctrine of Divine Right of Kings affected, 227

"Bishops' Book," the, Cranmer and, 153–155

Black Death, the, 10, 171

"Black Joan," Cranmer's marriage to, and her death, 34

Boleyn, Anne, power over Henry, 52, 55, 58, 65, 68, 75, 86, 107, 109, 134, 135; and Gardiner, 89; officially admitted as consort of Henry, 90; secretly married to Henry, 91; legitimacy of marriage proclaimed, 105–106; coronation of, 108; birth of a daughter (Elizabeth), 115, 119; public detestation of, 120; and the Princess Mary, 122, 123; declared Queen by Bill of Succession, 126; utter dependence of Cranmer on, 134;

INDEX

Boleyn, Anne—(*continued*)
friction with Henry, 137; her ejaculation on death of Catherine, 138; was she accomplice to death of Catherine? 140; accused of adultery, is executed, 143 *et seq.*

Boleyn, Thomas (Lord Wiltshire), 29, 70, 110; ordered to house Cranmer, 65; Henry's ambassador to the Pope and to the Emperor, 67; instances of his stolidity, 68–69

Bologna, coronation of Charles V at, 67

Bologna, University of, 71

Bonner, Edmund (Bishop of London), and the Papal Nuncio, 92; degrades Cranmer, 297; and Cranmer's recantation, 303

Bosworth Field, battle of, 7

Brandon, Charles (Duke of Suffolk), marries Mary Tudor, 261

Bucer, Martin, 250

Butcher (or Bocher), Joan, condemned and executed for heresy, 236–239; her retort to Cranmer, 238

C

CALAIS, held by England, 8

Calvin, John, reformer, 47

Cambridge University, 17; Jesus College and its history, 21 *et seq.*

Campeggio, Cardinal, co-legate with Wolsey in matter of Henry's divorce, 56; a secret Decretal Bull and instructions, 56–57; adjourns the Court, 58

Canterbury, endowments of despoiled, 150

Capitalist system, revolt against, 46 *et seq.*

Casale, letter *re* Boleyn's embassy to Rome, 67 (note)

Catherine, Queen, ground on which Henry claimed divorce, 51; her popularity, 52, 75, 120; refuses to admit authority of a Legatine Court, 58; her case considered by Convocation, 99; asserts her right to title of Queen, 103; summoned to appear at divorce

Catherine, Queen—(*continued*)
trial, refuses to plead, 103–104; illness and death, 136–137; poison suspected as cause of death, 138 *et seq.*

Catholic Church, fifteenth century reaction against, 172 *et seq.*

Catholicism, movement against after Henry's death, 215 *et seq.*

Cecil, William, goes to pay homage to Mary, 276; his excuse for signing the Devise, 283

Chapuys (ambassador in London of Charles V), and Cranmer's recall, 90; learns of appointment of Cranmer as Archbishop, 91; and the divorce trial, 104; remonstrates with Henry, 107; and the dying Catherine, 136; suspects poison as cause of her death, 138–140

Charles V, Emperor, 269, 270; coronation of, 67; embassy from Henry to, 68, 69, 76, 79 *et seq.*; and the Netherlands trade, 80, 86; negotiates with anti-Catholic Princes, 82; visits Italy, 87; desires summoning of a General Council, 93; advises Mary to compromise, 284

"Christian Brethren," the, 110

Christian Church, the, founded, 164

Chubbs, first Master of Cranmer, 31

Church courts and their function, 13

Church of England, influence of Cranmer's writing on, 31

Clement VII, Pope, attitude to policy of divorce, 53, 54; appoints Court to try the case, 55, 56; Campeggio's instructions from, 56–57; recalls case to Rome, 58; orders Henry to take back his wife, 67–68; brief bidding University members to pronounce freely on legality of marriage with a deceased brother's wife, 70 (and note); creates Cranmer Penitentiary for England, 72; recognized by Henry as head of Church Universal, 74; grants Bulls for consecration of Cranmer, 92–93; truce with Henry, 94; receives news of divorce result, 108; his policy of delay, 115;

INDEX

Clement VII. Pope—*(continued)*
annuls Cranmer's decisions and issues brief of censure, 115; forbids publication of decision of Consistory Court, 127

Cleves, Duke of, 199

Cole, Provost of Eton, sermon preached at burning of Cranmer, 309–311

Communion service, separated from the Mass, 229

Communists, ideals of, 46–48

Convocation, admits Henry's title to supremacy over Church of England, 73; cowed by Cromwell, 87; sits to determine questions of fact and law *re* Henry's marriage to Catherine, 99; declares non-jurisdiction of the Pope, 131; pronounces nullity of marriage of Anne of Cleves, 203

Coverdale, breach with Tyndale, 179, 189; revises Tyndale's Bible, 189; acts as interpreter for Van Paris, 239

Cranmer, Thomas, date and place of birth, 3; boyhood days, 4, 5; learns rudiments of Latin, 5; as horseman, 6, 87, 275; sent to Cambridge University, 18; enters Jesus College, 24; chosen a Fellow, 27; as linguist, 28, 31; talent as prose writer, 29–31, 209; his Masters at Cambridge, 31; an entanglement and marriage, 33–34; lectures on theology as means of support, 34; re-elected Fellow after death of wife, 34; takes M.A. degree, 34; takes holy orders, 44; private views on the Real Presence, 44, 50, 112–114, 132, 153 (and *passim*); first meeting with Cromwell, 56; sent for by Henry and ordered to further his divorce, 63 *et seq.*; ordered to Cambridge to influence votes on divorce affair, 66; embassy to Italy, 67, 69; challenges Doctors of Divinity in Rome to debate, 71; illness in Rome, 72; made Penitentiary for England, 72; and Anne Boleyn, 72–73; rewarded for his services,

Cranmer, Thomas—*(continued)*
73; reports against publication of a private pamphlet drawn up by Pole, 74–76; instructed to act as Orator to Cæsar, 76; subservience of, 79, 109, 144, 145, 149, 151, 187, 201, 203, 204, 209 (and *passim*); failure of his mission to the Germanies, 80; clandestine marriage of, 83–85; brings his wife secretly to England, 86; her remarriage after death of Cranmer, 86; recalled from the Germanies, becomes Archbishop, 90 *et seq.*; a perjured oath of Allegiance, 95; remarkable letter to Henry, 100–101; opens Court *re* Henry's divorce, 103; declares Henry's marriage with Catherine null and void, 104; a "Godly Letter" to Henry, 105; decision that Boleyn marriage was valid, 105–106; crowns Anne, 108; examines and condemns Frith, 110–111; and Elizabeth Barton, 114, 125; "Anti-Christ" sermon of, 131; and Cromwell, 133; and fall of Anne, 144 *et seq.*; pronounces invalidity of Anne's marriage, 145–146; motives actuating servility of, 152–153; and Nicholson-Lambart, 156–157; and Six Articles Act, 159; growing distaste for Catholicism, 179, 211 (and *passim*); aids introduction of Tyndale Bible into England, 186 *et seq.*; his preface to second edition, 191–192; solemnizes marriage of Henry to Anne of Cleves, 200; at bedside of dying Henry, 212; on Council of Regency, 215 *et seq.*; and coronation of Edward, 225–226; proclaims doctrine of the divine right of Kings, 226; his responsibility for changes in the Liturgy, 239 *et seq.*; for the 42 Articles, 251–252; for new code of clerical law, 252; supports conspiracy against Mary, 268 *et seq.*; his excuse for signing the Devise, 284; prisoner in Lambeth Palace, 277–278; angry letter against the Mass, 279–280, 285;

INDEX

Cranmer, Thomas—(*continued*)
condemned for treason, 286 ; taken
to Oxford and confined in Bocardo,
288 ; in public disputation denies
doctrines of Real Presence and the
Mass, 289 *et seq.* ; condemned for
heresy, and recants, 291, 303–308 ;
degraded as Archbishop, 297–298 ;
retracts his recantation and is
burned at the stake, 312–313

Creed, a new, and a new code of
Church laws drawn up, 236, 251–
252 ; authorized, 257

Cressy, Cranmer as tutor to sons of, 59

Croft, Richard, marries Mrs. Whitchurch, formerly wife of Cranmer,
86

Croke, and University of Ferrara, 71 ;
and University of Padua, 71

Cromwell, Thomas, Cranmer's letter
to, 29 ; Cranmer's first meeting
with, 55–56 ; as manager of Henry's
political affairs, 73 ; cows the
Church, 87 ; threatens confiscation
of the Annates, 88 ; determined
policy of, 119, 121, 123 *et seq.*,
151–152 ; and Chapuys, 122 ; uses
Cranmer as agent for destruction
of Elizabeth Barton, 124 *et seq.* ;
becomes King's Vicar-General, 133,
152 ; ambitious of full power over
the Church, 138 ; intrigues against
Anne, 140 *et seq.* ; restores Cranmer
to favour, 150 ; how he smuggled
Tyndale's Bible into England, 185–
192 ; policy of alliance with German
Princes, 196, 199 ; cause of his
fall, 196, 201 ; two forces at work
in alliance against, 196–198 ; monastic spoils, 134, 200 (and *passim*) ;
made Earl of Essex, 200 ; arrest,
condemnation and execution, 201–
203

Culpepper, and Catherine Howard,
205 ; put to death, 207

D

Decretal Bull, a secret, 56–57
De Lasco (Catherine's doctor), 136,
138

Dereham, an affair with Catherine
Howard, 204 *et seq.* ; put to death,
207

" Devise, The," and its object, 264
et seq.

Diplomacy, the essence of, 82

Divine Right of Kings, doctrine
proclaimed, 226

" Dolphin " the (inn at Cambridge),
location of, 33

Driander, and the new Prayer Book,
250

Dudley, Lord Guildford, marries
Lady Jane Grey, 263 ; executed,
286

Dunstable, Henry's divorce trial heard
at, 103

Durham House, Cranmer at, 65–66

E

Eccleston, John, of Jesus College, 30
Edge, of Brasenose College, and
Cranmer, 313

Edward VI, policy of Council of
Regency towards upbringing of,
221 ; coronation of, 224–226 ;
compelled to sign death warrant of
the Protector's brother, 234 ; how
moulded into a zealous anti-
Catholic, 236, 264 ; early death of,
237, 251 ; tricked into signing
death-warrant of Joan Butcher,
239 ; his delicate boyhood, 259 ;
and the succession, 260 *et seq.*, 264
et seq.

Elizabeth, Princess (afterwards Queen),
birth of, 115, 119 ; Cranmer as
godfather, 122 ; declared heiress and
successor, 126 ; shown by her
father to the Court, 137 ; rides with
Mary through London, 277

England, before the Reformation, 8
et seq. ; a completely Catholic
country, 16 *et seq.*

Erasmus, appointed Lady Margaret
lecturer at Cambridge, 26–27, 32 ;
his " New Instrument," 27, 34,
39–41 (*cf.* New Testament of
Erasmus) ; leaves England, 27 ; and
Warham, 27, 88

318

INDEX

INDEX

Henry VIII, birth, 6; orthodoxy of, 42, 51, 80, 81, 185; questions validity of his marriage with Catherine, 51-52; appeal to universities on question suggested to, 54; irresolution in matters of policy, 55, 60, 63; moves to Waltham to escape outbreak of the Plague, 58; sends for Cranmer *re* divorce of Catherine, 63 *et seq.*; and dispatches him to Italy, 67 *et seq.*; as supreme head of Church of England, 73-74; his book attacking Luther by name, 80; strong views against marriage of priests, 84; takes Anne on a royal progress to France, 91; demands Catherine's jewels, 91; secret marriage to Anne, 91; sum advanced to Archbishop-Elect, 92; backs up Papal foreign policy, 92; truce with Rome, 94; corrects a remarkable letter from Cranmer, 102; changed feeling towards Anne, 115, 135; threatens the Pope with an appeal to the General Council, 115, 121; vacillating nature of, 119; undiplomatic action by, 121-122; prevented by Anne from meeting his daughter Mary, 123; an unknown liaison of, 135; suspected as accomplice to death of Catherine, 140; his " Godly and Pious Institution of the Christian Man," 154; presides at trial of Lambart, 157-158; and Six Articles Act, 158-159; birth of an heir (Edward), 185, 191; hoodwinked by Cromwell and Cranmer, 190-192; negotiations for remarriage after death of Jane Seymour, 199; marries Catherine Howard, 204; charges against her communicated to, 205, 206; marries Catherine Parr, 210; death, 212; and the succession, 260-261

Heresy, definition of, 170; how punished, 253 (and note); an essential for condemnation or acquittal for, 289

Hewitt, Andrew, martyrdom of, 110

Holy Maid of Kent (*see* Barton, Elizabeth)

Hooper, Bishop, and Second Prayer Book, 250

Hosmer (or Hosemann or Heligman) (*see* Osiander)

Howard, Catherine, marriage to Henry, 205; charges against communicated to the King, 205, 206; Cranmer's examination of, 207; execution of, 208

Howards, the, and Cromwell, 197-198

I

INCARNATION, doctrine of, repudiated by Joan Butcher, 237-238

Industrial Capitalism, revolt against, 46, 47; definition of, 48

Israel (*see* Jews)

Italian Universities consulted on divorce question, 70

J

JESUS COLLEGE, Cambridge, founded, 23-24

Jews, sacred books of, translated into Greek, 164

K

KING'S COLLEGE CHAPEL, Cambridge, Henry VII and Countess of Richmond at, 26

Ket's rebellion, 248

Kingship, pre-Reformation idea of, 14-15

Kingston (Commander of the Tower), receives Anne as prisoner, 144

Kyme, Anne (real name of Anne Askew, *q.v.*)

L

LAMBART (or Lambert), John (*see* Nicholson)

Lascelles, evidence against Catherine, 206, 207

Lascelles (probably different man from preceding), excommunicated and executed, 210

INDEX

INDEX

Rome, sacked by Emperor's troops, 53 ; decision of Consistory Court *re* Henry's first marriage, 127 ; reunion with, 294

Rotherham, Provost of Cambridge, 25

S

St. Paul's Cross, Lutheran books burned at, 42

St. Margaret's, Westminster, threatened spoliation of, and a riot, 228

Scottish universities, present-day, 18

Seymour, Edward (Lord Hertford), plots against Cromwell, 196–197 ; and Cranmer, 209 ; and the dying Henry, 211–212 ; appointed guardian of Henry's son Edward, 212, 216 ; takes title of Protector, 222 ; becomes Duke of Somerset, 225 ; spoliation of churches, 228

Seymour, Jane, Henry and, 141 ; dies in childbirth, 191, 199

Shaxton, Nicholas, Bishop of Salisbury, 219 ; resigns bishopric, 210

Sidall, Henry, as witness of Cranmer's recantation, 304

Six Articles Act (1539), 159

Skelton, Lady, appointed guardian of Princess Mary, 122

Skip, John, Bishop of Hereford, chaplain to Anne Boleyn, 43

Smeton, Mark, arrest of, 143

Somerset, Thomas, to save himself and his booty, feigns sympathy with rebels, 234 ; put to death, 234

Stokesley, John, nominated as Bishop of London, 70 ; bamboozles Henry, 71

Stone castles, ancient, 11

T

Taunton, Cromwell M.P. for, 73

Taylor (afterwards Bishop of Lincoln), and Lambart, 156

Ten Articles (1536), 158

Thirlby, Bishop, degrades Cranmer, 297

Tremelius, Emmanuel, 249

Tudors, usurpation of, 6–8

Tunstall, Bishop, Latimer and, 294

Turkish menace to civilization, 82

Tyndale, William, 178 ; as master of prose, 29, 30 ; sets up his printing press, 179 ; New Testament of, 179 ; this suppressed, 179 ; opposes Henry's divorce, 179, 186 ; Bible, 180 ; put to death, 180 ; his Bible, under a new name, smuggled into England, 185 *et seq*

U

Universities, the, clerical body and, 17 *et seq.* ; a monk's suggested appeal on question of Henry's divorce to, 54 ; Cranmer's repetition of this suggestion, 60, 63 *et seq.;* Papal brief bidding members to speak on lawfulness or unlawfulness of marriage with a deceased brother's wife, 70

V

Van Paris, George, burnt for heresy, 239

Vaughan, meets Cranmer at Lyons, 91

Venice, Croke and Cranmer work for Henry's divorce at, 71

Veron, Jules, 250

Villages, and their government, 12

W

Walled towns and inhabitants, 11

Waltham, Henry VIII and his Court at, 58

Warham, Archbishop, and Erasmus, 27 ; and validity of the King's marriage, 52 ; and the headship of the Church, 74 ; unfavourable to annulment of marriage of Catherine by an English Court, 88–89 ; death of, 90

Wars of the Roses, 23

Warwick (Duke of Northumberland), succeeds Somerset, 249, 259 ; his control of the boy King, 261

Weston, Hugh, and Cranmer's trial in St. Mary's, Oxford, 289, 292

INDEX

Whitchurch, Edward, marries Cranmer's widow, 86; printer of Bible based on Tyndale's version, 190; Cranmer's intimacy with, 190–191; attempts publication of Coverdale's New Testament which is confiscated, 191; produces first complete English Bible, 191; monopoly of printing of Royal Proclamations continued, 192

Whitehall Palace, marriage of Henry and Anne in, 91; death of Edward VI at, 267

White Horse Inn, Cambridge, debates on new movement at, 42

Williams of Thame, Lord, 313

Wolsey, Cardinal, Gardiner becomes secretary to, 33; the red hat conferred on, 40; orders burning of Lutheran books, 42; favours divorce of Catherine, 52; appointed on Legatine Court to try the case, 56; cause of his fall, 58

Wriothesley, Sir Thomas, 215, 222

Wyatt's rebellion, 286

Y

YORK HOUSE, taken from Wolsey before his fall, 91

Z

ZWINGLI, and the Eucharist, 111